STUDY

Your Eternity Depends On IT!

George Nelson

authorHOUSE®

AuthorHouse™
1663 Liberty Drive
Bloomington, IN 47403
www.authorhouse.com
Phone: 1 (800) 839-8640

Published by AuthorHouse 08/31/2018

ISBN: 978-1-5462-5780-6 (sc)
ISBN: 978-1-5462-5782-0 (hc)
ISBN: 978-1-5462-5781-3 (e)

Library of Congress Control Number: 2018910299

Print information available on the last page.

TABLE OF TOPICS

ACKNOWLEDGEMENT

With her help on the computer, phone calls and especially the editing, I want to thank my wife, Bonnie. She was the rock that kept this project going. Her endless hours of work and encouraging me in my time of frustration, is the reason why we have a finished book. My partner, my closest friend, my wife.

Thank you!

This just may be one of the best writings about truth:

There is no magic word but there is *direction*.

There is no real *direction* without *learning*.

There is very little *learning* without *study*.

There is no true *study* without an open mind to the *truth*.

There is *truth* without scripture. You won't have it, but the truth will still be there. Whether you accept it or not; it doesn't start or stop the truth.

The truth is still truth, so study to find the truth!

IF

you don't want to read the TRUTH, then don't buy this book!

IF

the truth is what you seek, then read and understand what the point is!

IF

you want to know what the point is, you will find out, It's YESHUA!

IF

you don't know and want to find out who Yeshua is then read!

IF

you seek truth, without religious brainwashing, then keep going!

IF

you're looking for a book with all the answers, this isn't the book! That book was already written, it's called The Bible. We hope you might find answers to some of your questions. What we hope is, this book might get you into the truth of the word through your own studying.

THIS BOOK HAS NO CHAPTERS, JUST HEADINGS

We say this book is in the form of headings, not in chapters, and not following the Bible from Genesis to the book of the Revelation. What this book consists of is a number of writings that may have been brought to life from people asking us questions and then us using a huge amount of study about what scripture says or doesn't say about that topic. We also discuss what is right and wrong with the interpretations of some denominations. We want to help you identify what to follow, and what's leading you away from truth. You might say we study who the Messiah is and why most wouldn't recognize Him if He was standing right in front of them.

Does this book have things that people won't agree with? YES! Does that make you wrong and us right? NO! Does that make us wrong and you right? NO! But whether you agree or not, maybe, just maybe, it should get you to study to prove yourself right or to prove us wrong.

Here is one bit of advice we have found through experience: don't study with your mind already made up by a teacher, preacher, church, denomination, rabbi, or us. You need to study with an open mind to truth without being dead set on going to Hell because you believe what someone else tells you. If you're brainwashed, you have already aligned yourself with an individual, philosophy, book, or direction. Wouldn't it be smarter to study to find truth? Maybe you will find that you have always believed the right way. Maybe with studying you might find a change is needed in order to find the right path. Either way, it would give you peace, but peace with brainwashing is only temporary peace at best!

STUDY

Take each of our writings and use it to get you started in an in depth study. Use your intelligence without any brainwashing from preachers, teachers, denominations, and YES without any brainwashing from us. In reality, that statement is so easy to say but it is one of the hardest avenues you will ever try.

Now study. Study to find the real truth. Hope your time is constructive and enjoyable. Use each of these writings to get you motivated to find what you're looking for. We don't care if you agree with us or not. We hope you study with an open mind, use your intellect, get a true philosophy, and grasp what the original writers really said, not what anyone else wants to lead you to believe.

When we first started to hunt for the truth in scripture, we found our original ideas were correct in theory. But the big question to us was this: Is our theory based on denominational leading or were the answers going to come from the Bible only? What we found was that the truth is in the scriptures, but the interpretations of denominations to fit their philosophies were leading people away from that truth. We don't blame them for trying to lead individuals into their way of thinking because, with a certain amount of twisting, they sound and look correct. We believe some organizations brainwash people to think, "If I believe like them and I feel good about what they write or believe, well then it must be truth." Although that notion is totally incorrect, we believe if an organization can brainwash individuals then their job is over 90% accomplished.

If you feel good, get goose bumps, cry, or run around a church praising your Lord, that doesn't necessarily mean you are experiencing truth! It isn't enough to feel good when you study if your eyes are closed to truth. We believe that means you're just reading words and that you have already been told what they mean so, again, they fit your philosophy. By the time you do any study whatsoever, your study fits your way of life because you study what and how they want you to.

If you're determined to follow your denomination, church, pastor, or teacher no matter what the scriptures really say, then Satan loves you more each day!

NOT TEACHERS OR PREACHERS

We will state a number of times in this book that we are not preachers or teachers. That alone makes our findings interesting. When you study for a long period of time, you may see that you start to grasp one direction on any topic. But then something catches your eye and that word, sentence, verse, or chapter seems to jump off the page with new meaning. You may like or dislike this newfound understanding. If that does happen, you've just started a great self-evaluation of your beliefs, your life, your death, and your existence here on Earth and in Heaven.

After reading the contents of this book, go back over every topic word-for-word, then use these topics to help guide you into your own study.

Let us tell you up front: most preachers, teachers, rabbis, churches, or denominations won't agree with these findings. But we're not trying to fill a building or collect a tithe for existence.

We will say, before we die, it would be interesting to receive feedback from people. Of course, we expect to get the usual bashing from the leaders of certain denominations. That's a given. But to get information from the people who use the topics as a jump start for an open minded study to find truth would make the 30 years of our own study worth putting down on paper.

DO YOU REALLY KNOW THIS MAN WE CALL THE MESSIAH?

This is an informative writing about who the Messiah is according to what we have found in scripture.

We are not trying to persuade anyone to any religion or denomination. We don't even want them to be a Jew or Christian. That choice is up to the individual, not us. One thing we will address is this: if you read this book, see things that aren't just right, and you don't change your ways, we believe you're in trouble.

My wife and I are Christians saved by the blood of a Jewish Messiah. He always was, and always will be a Hebrew. We are not Preachers or Teachers, just ordinary people who believe we have a message. That fact will be stated a number of times, just so people don't get the idea we are trying to get anyone leaning toward any religion.

As you read you will find the writings are from the scriptures, which are inspired by God. You will find a lot of people who disagree because they feel threatened. They will not accept and will try to discredit this book by using their religion's philosophy. But this book contains what we found as the truth. Most people don't really like truth unless it lines up with their way of thinking. The Prophet Jeremiah (Yirmeyahu in Hebrew) told the truth and most of his own Jewish people didn't like what he said. As a matter of fact, they had him put in jail and even tried to get him killed. Now that doesn't sound like a very credible person to follow does it? What most people would say is something like, "If it's really God leading me, everything will be just perfect." I guess Jeremiah would have loved that concept. We have the feeling that there are a lot of people everywhere and in every church and synagogue that need a change. We hope this book helps you to learn something or unlearn something and guides you to a place that is correct in understanding the Bible as one book, both the Old and the New Testaments. You may call it the Old Testament (TANAKH in Hebrew) and the New Testament (B'rit Hadashah, the Hebrew for New Covenant) as you look at it as a Christian or Jew. Either way, it's still God's Word. You can't change that.

We feel there are far too many people who are not saved and they fill Churches and Synagogues every week. The worship of the Messiah is the most important activity anyone can do, but in most places, the name they use is a free pass to Heaven. But is it? We believe how much or how many times you use a name doesn't get you one step closer to or give you a guarantee of Heaven.

THE NAME

When the Messiah walked the earth he had a Hebrew name and it was Yeshua. We know that the Hebrew children are given their name at their circumcision. The name Yeshua is the masculine form of Yesh'ah and that name means Salvation in the Hebrew language.

After a great amount of study, we believe that neither the Romans nor the Greeks liked the Jewish Nation. As a matter of fact, when the Greeks translated the scriptures they wanted to distance their readings and belief away from the Jewishness of the New Covenant.

In the Greek translation of the Word of God, the Jewish Messiah was called "Iesous." But the Greek word for Save is "Soter" and the name Iesous has nothing to do with that word or any other word that pertains to Salvation. The name "Iesous" has nothing to do with someone being drawn to the Savior. WE CAN'T STRESS THAT ENOUGH! Now the English word "Jesus" came from the Greek word "Iesous."

We Gentiles, as a society of believers, have used the name Jesus for so long that we believe it must be the real name that is above all names. That's the name we sing to. That's *the* name the worshiped King James Version used so it has to be true. We see people who believe they are saved by that name. People prophecy in that name. Some say they have seen miracles performed in that name. Is it important what name we use when we pray? Does God, the Father of the Universe, have many sons with many names that can save? We have these other religions that claim their Savior, by a different name. They even kill in the name of their Savior. Is that wrong for them, or are they just using a different name for the true Messiah?

STUDY

Matthew 1:21 (CJB) - *She will give birth to a son, and you are to name him, Yeshua, because he will save his people from their sins.*

Joseph and Mary were told they would have a Son and they were to give him a certain Name, because he would save his people from their sins. Let's look at this again, if Joseph and Mary were to deliver salvation for the Hebrew nation through the birth of this child, then this child's name should mean Salvation. Joseph would not have given him any other name but the one that means Salvation! We're talking to Christians, Jews, and Messianic Jews.

People say they worship the Jewish Messiah. Well then, let's start. We believe that once this point of view is understood there would be such a Holy Arising of people wanting to worship The True Messiah by his Name that the scriptures would explode. The world would change and God's Word will be exalted. But now, don't get too excited! You have to read and understand that Christians are not the center of the religious universe. We may be grafted in, but the center is still the Jews and the Jewish Messiah. Scripture doesn't say that the Messiah will come to the United States and set up his Kingdom. As a matter of fact, our choice of leadership lately seems to have an anti-Semitic theology that avoids backing Israel.

We believe the scriptures tell it plainly that most religions don't see the truth because their church or religious doctrines get in the way. That sounds like a false statement but it's true. There are things in every denomination that look good and seem right if you look through the eyes of that religion and read a certain verse in the eyes of their understanding. We have religions and denominations that seem to focus on one main topic and the rest of scripture seems to just follow along. Here is just a very short list of what we have seen: the necessity to speak in tongues, the worship and deification of Mary, once saved always saved, the handling of snakes, only the old songs are godly, the King James translation is the only true error-free version of scripture.

That was just naming a few, but there are many more. People seem to turn their backs on so many points that it divides religions and taints what the Word is really saying. The NAME is the NAME, no other name will do.

My first lesson on this was way back in 1968 when I was in the Army. I was at my first duty station, Fort Bragg, North Carolina. This other private and I came to the company on the same day. I, being from the very small town of Potosi, Wisconsin, and trying to be friendly, asked him his name.

He stated his name was Rodolfo Dolovos Cesena (I can't be sure that is the right spelling, but hopefully it's close). Looking at him with total confusion, my comment was "I'll never remember all that, nor would I ever be able to pronounce it, is it alright with you if I just call you 'Junior'?"

He smiled and said sure. However after a few months Rodolfo came up to me and said "George, would you not call me junior no more." Being a nice guy I said "Sure, but why the change?" He said, he didn't mind me calling him "Junior" but now everybody was calling him "Junior." Not Rodolfo, not Cencena, but Junior.

See, in the military, since your last name is on your shirt, most people are called by their last name. That was the first taste I ever had of calling someone by a name that wasn't their real name and it changed everything for that person. It's been almost fifty years since I was in the Army and it took until I started studying and believing in what God is showing us, to remember that part of my history.

Words do change things. Names do change people. Names are Important. The true name of each person is not only important, but also necessary for results. That concept has not been altered through history but it will not change the course of events that God has set in place. At the right time, the right area, through the right people, His plan will be fulfilled! Many are called, but few will answer. There are two roads to take and the direction is clear. The ending will come. If you call out a name, we hope it's not going to be "Junior" or some other made up name. As far as we are concerned, it better be the true name of our one and only Savior! Our Lord! The Jewish Messiah! The Name that is Hebrew, The Man who is God!

THE NAME IS YESHUA!

DEATH

1. Philippians 1:20b-21, 23 (NIV) - *Christ will be exalted in my body, whether by life or by death. For to me, to live is Christ and to die is gain... I am torn between the two: I desire to depart and be with Christ, which is better by far.*

2. John 14:3, 6 (NIV) - *If I go and prepare a place for you, I will come back and take you to be with me that you also may be where I am... I am the way, and the truth and the life. No one comes to the Father except through me.*

3. John 11:24-25 (NIV) - *Martha answered, "I know he will rise again in the resurrection at the last day."* (The Messiah said:) *"I am the resurrection and the life. The one who believes in me will live, even though he dies."*

4. 1 Corinthians 15:36b, 48 (NIV) - *What you sow does not come to life unless it dies.* (The Natural body, or Spiritual body, what you sow does not come to life unless it dies. Like the seed.)... *As was the earthly man, so are those who are of the earth; and as is the Heavenly man, so also are those who are of Heaven.* (In the twinkling of an eye, at the last trumpet, the dead will be raised imperishable and be changed.)

5. Philippians 3:21 (NIV) - *Who by the power that enables him to bring everything under his control, will transform our lowly bodies, so that they will be like his glorious body.*

6. 2 Timothy 4:8 (KJV) - *Henceforth there is laid up for me a crown of righteousness, which the Lord, the righteous judge, shall give me at that day, and not to me only, but unto all them also that love his appearing.*

7. 1 Thessalonians 4:16-17 (NIV) (The living will not precede those who have fallen asleep) - *For the Lord himself will come down from*

Heaven, with a loud command, with the voice of the archangel and with the trumpet call of God, and the dead in Christ will rise first. After that, we who are still alive and are left will be caught up together with them in the clouds to meet the Lord in the air. And so we will be with the Lord forever.

Study each of these and really read what it says. Concentrate on these thoughts: twinkling of an eye, dead raised first, last trumpet, the dead are raised imperishable, award me on that last day, and not only me but all who longed for his appearing. When Paul wrote about the last day when he will be rewarded like everyone who believes he does not refer to the day he died, but the day when the Lord returns. When everyone else is rewarded, Paul will be rewarded at the same time, not at the time of Paul's death.

Let's look at a few writings in the Old Testament about death and afterwards:

1. Isaiah 26:19 (NIV) - *But your dead will live, Lord; their bodies will rise. Let those who dwell in the dust wake up and shout for joy. Your dew is like the dew of the morning, the earth will give birth to her dead.*
2. Job 19:26 (NIV) - *And after my skin has been destroyed, yet in my flesh I will see God!*
3. Psalm 16:10 (NIV) - *because you will not abandon me to the realm of the dead, nor will you let your faithful one see decay.*
4. Daniel 12:2 (NIV) - *Multitudes who sleep in the dust of the earth will awake; some to everlasting life, others to shame and everlasting contempt.*
5. Daniel 12:13 (NIV) - *As for you, go your way till the end. You will rest, and then at the end of the days you will rise to receive your allotted inheritance.*

Also examine these verses from the New Testament:

Revelation 20:12-15 (NIV) - *and I saw the dead, great and small, standing before the throne, and books were opened. Another book was opened, which is the book of life. The dead were judged according to what they had done as recorded in the books. The sea gave up the dead that were in it, and death and Hades gave up the dead that were in them, and each person was judged according to what they had done. Then death and Hades were thrown into the lake of fire. The lake of fire is the second death. Anyone whose name was not found written in the book of life was thrown into the lake of fire.*

1 Corinthians 15:22-23 (NIV) - *For as in Adam all die, so in Christ all will be made alive. But each in turn: Christ, the firstfruits; then, when he comes, those who belong to him. (The last enemy to be destroyed is death.)*

1 Corinthians 15:52 (NIV) - *In a flash, in the twinkling of an eye, at the last trumpet. For the trumpet will sound, the dead will be raised imperishable and we will be changed.*

Matthew 16:27 (NIV) - *For the son of man is going to come in His Fathers Glory with His Angels and then he will reward each person according to what they have done.*

2 Corinthians 5:7-8 (NIV) - *For we live by faith, not by sight. We are confident, I say, and would prefer to be away from the body and at home with the Lord.*

Philippians 1:23 (NIV) - *I am torn between the two: I desire to depart and be with Christ, which is better by far.*

Romans 8:23 (NIV) - *Not only so, but we ourselves, who have the firstfruits of the spirit, groan inwardly as we wait eagerly for our adoption to sonship, the redemption of our bodies.*

If a person has a sound sleep at night, it seems as if only seconds passed between closing his or her eyes and the alarm going off in the morning. Consider these passages:

2 Peter 3:8 (NIV) - *but do not forget this one thing, dear friends: With the Lord a day is like a thousand years, and a thousand years are like a day.*

STUDY

Psalm 90:4 (NIV) - *A thousand years in your sight are like a day that has just gone by, or like a watch in the night.*

If death is truly a rest, like the sleep at night, time would pass like seconds rather than thousands of years. When Christ judges everybody, it's really the first judgment after your death. We have no reason to fear death, because it's a peaceful rest until judgment. It wouldn't matter if Christ comes back today or a thousand years from now, it would seem like a sound sleep at night.

If you look at the verses above, they point to the books being opened. All are judged by what is in the books. Therefore, if you were already in Heaven, you would still have to stand trial again, just like the ones who are in Hell and the ones who are alive. Instead, we believe you do not get judged and go to your eternal place until Christ comes back. Then, no matter when you died or what you have done, the books are opened for the final judgment.

The scriptures state that books—not one, but many—are opened. If you look at the Bible with a closed mind to truth and believe what someone else tells you, then you are putting your wants and desires (and maybe your peace of mind) ahead of what the word is really saying. Some say peace of mind is really important. It may be, but only if it is aligned with truth.

If you want a glorious body, as it states in Philippians, and you believe the dead in Christ will rise first and be with the Lord forever, as it states in 1 Thessalonians, you must consider the order in which things will happen. If we are dead and in Heaven, aren't we already there forever? Daniel said sleep in the dust of the earth, some to everlasting life, and others to everlasting contemp. He also said go your way till the end, you will rest, and then at the last days you will rise to receive your allotted inheritance.

Our point isn't whether you should believe your pastor or teachers. They only tell you what they have been taught. We want to encourage you to open the Bible yourself and STUDY to find truth. We can see where people get a lot of their teachings. Many of these teachings allow individuals to feel good about the person who has died.

STUDY

We often hear statements like, "They are in a better place now." Or, "At least they aren't suffering any longer." Another popular saying is, "He is looking down on me." While that may be a nice thought, consider the fact that if he really was looking down on you, he also would see every time you messed up. For those sentiments to be true, you would have to be judged more than once. We contend that scripture does not support such a notion. If you examine the scripture we cited, and the ones around them, you will find that you are lifted up from the grave at the time of the Lord's return, not before!

We know that statement doesn't fit a lot of sermons these days, and it might make a lot of people uncomfortable. However, as you read you must learn what the Word says. It is not important what I say, or what beliefs a denomination wants you to follow.

THE TWELVE TRIBES SCATTERED

I read a section of a book a few years ago, urging people reading the book of James to remember that the Twelve Tribes were scattered among the nations. It claimed the people James was addressing were actually Gentiles who had been mixed in with the Jews in that area of the world. This book stated this "cousin of the Lord" was not writing to the Hebrews at all, but to the Christians who had the misfortune of having worshiped with the Jews.

We have no idea how many preachers have made statements similar to that one. We are less concerned about the factual errors—such as whether James was the Lord's brother, or to whom the letter was addressed—and more concerned with how many people are being convinced to believe a lie to make a particular religion, church, denomination, or individual grow in number or stature.

The lie doesn't send you to Hell. The problem is that the lies just keep accumulating, getting larger, and eventually becoming a slippery slope, a hill, and finally a mountain. It is difficult, if not impossible, to see past that mountain of lies. You must tell that mountain be removed and cast it into the sea.

You will always be stuck behind the mountain unless you cast it into the sea. Believe me, it's not that easy to move a mountain. You may have to do it one rock at a time.

Many people only read one version of the Bible. That means those people are only receiving what the writer of that particular version points to. They are only seeing what the writer wants them to see. If you believe the version you prefer is the only true version, without any mistakes, we believe Satan has you right where he wants you. He really doesn't need to do one more thing unless your eyes are opened.

We are not swayed by any version. We don't confess what the NIV, KJV, or what any other version says as truth, by themselves only. The Catholics believe you aren't reading the true word of God unless you read the Catholic Bible. Some Evangelicals believe unless you are reading the King James, you're not reading the Bible. According to them, there are no mistakes. It is perfect. (If that is true, then we guess the person you call Jesus was here a number of times. See, in the KJV a person has to read Acts 7:45.)

Let's take a look at a few of the verses in James:

> James 1:12 (CJB) - *How blessed is the man who perseveres through temptation! For after he has passed the test, he will receive as his crown the life which God, has promised to those who love him.*

> James 1:13 (NIV) - *When tempted, no one should say, God is tempting me. For God cannot be tempted by evil, nor does He tempt anyone!*

> James 1:13 (KJV) - *Let no man say when he is tempted, I am tempted of God; for God cannot be tempted with evil, neither tempteth He any man.*

We went to the KJV. In it, everyone sees what is said so plain and clear, right? Now let's go to Genesis:

> Genesis 22:1 (KJV) - *And it came to pass after these things, that God did tempt Abraham, and said unto him, Abraham and he said, Behold, here I am.*

So who in scripture can you state was tempted? Job, Abraham, Christ. I guess you would have to say that Job was tested. Abraham was tested with

Isaac, his son, in Genesis 22. However, the KJV says tempted, while the NIV says tested. I'm not saying the NIV is the one to read. You have to study yourself and make the choice for you, not for me.

While studying this, we noticed that the Complete Jewish Bible (CJB) says tested and in Genesis 22:1 it says God tested Abraham.

> James 1:14 (NIV) - *but each person is tempted when they are dragged away, by their own evil desire and enticed.*

Did you catch that? "By your own desire." You just might say your desire gets roots and grows. When your desire grows, it has a chance to give birth to sin. The Bible says when sin is fully grown, it gives birth to death.

What does that mean to you?

When your sin is so prevalent in your life, it has you. You most likely won't even notice it anymore. It becomes a way of your life. You can't hide it any longer. You are consumed by it, and then Sin has you!

In this last part, we didn't try to confuse anyone by using three different versions, or point to one over the other. We wanted everyone to see you can use the version you like best, but it is very helpful to study with more than one version to really dig for the truth, in our opinion.

Why would God, The King of the Universe, have to tempt you?

Is he tempting you to live a Holy Life? No, that's His Command! His laws—His commands—are before us. He doesn't dangle them in front of us, to take or accept them or not. IT'S OUR RESPONSIBILTY, NOT HIS!

We will state this many times, "No matter what, the Word doesn't change, we may, but the Word doesn't!" Most people are not looking for truth. They want to feel good, and they may pretend that it must be truth, if they feel good. If that's how you feel, then look out! Satan loves anyone who just feels good and stops, without trying to find out why.

STUDY

We need to study with an open mind, an open Bible, and hopefully more than one version. Then you just might find truth, instead of a denominational theory, doctrine, or the way they want you to believe.

We can't stress this enough, don't base your belief on what we say or on what the person who leads your church says. Base your belief on what the Bible says. The only way to find that is through a good study. It may take a long time to grasp what the people are trying to say, or it may jump off the page at you. Who knows, you may find the truth every time you open your Bible.

To us, these are three interesting facts about the twelve tribes of Israel:

(1) Judah is put in the position of having our Lord come from this line. Yet Reuben was the firstborn. Because Reuben was the firstborn he would receive a double inheritance.

(2) Levi is mentioned to be the descendants who would come from Aaron, Moses brother, and the priest line would come from him. They would not have any land given them in the land of Israel, because they would devote themselves to the duties of the temple. Yet in Genesis 49:5 it says that Simeon and Levi were warriors and used weapons of violence, and Levi became the line of the Priest.

(3) Joseph had two sons on the list, Manasseh and Ephraim. One was to take Joseph's spot of land, and one was to get Levis spot of land. Joseph was dead and Levi didn't get a plot.

TOO MANY THINGS TO DO!

In our society today, we have an overabundance of both Mary and Martha.

There are people who want and expect everyone else to do the work, because they are doing their thing. You know people like that. Sometimes it's the preacher, the teacher, the song leader, etc.

Then there are people who are more concerned about the running of the church, working for the board, doing for the pastor. They want to serve, but they seem to neglect the more important aspect of God and His leading.

Everyone should have a balance of both. The Martha concept is of work. We believe if one is too focused on this idea, you are so busy doing things for the church that you don't spend or have quality time with the Messiah.

There are people we know who say things like, every minute they work for the running of the church, helping the congregation, doing for the pastor, or doing the stuff the board should be doing, is their quality time with the Lord. It may be quality time with the Martha outline of religion. Your denomination or philosophy may make it look like it's totally needed. Our question to you is, at what cost to your spiritual health?

People listen to gospel singers. They may have a group that may help them feel good. The music may tickle their memories, their past, or even their religious desire. The songs sound great, maybe even bring a tear to their eye. No matter when you visit them they have Christian music playing. What could be more spiritual than that? Even if they are doing paper work (and we assume they must concentrate on their work), they play music. Even if you're talking with them, they play their Christian music.

You'll often find your friend saying in the middle of a conversation, "Isn't this a really good song? Does this song or group minister to you?"

It might sound like they want confirmation that you like the singer or group. But what it is really saying is, the topic you're talking about, doesn't keep my attention. Whatever you're saying isn't important enough to keep my attention.

We believe that is what the Martha complex is. After all, isn't that what Martha said to the Messiah? She had her eyes on the building and the work, instead of on the One they should have been on. He is the One they should be following without distraction.

There are people who need to be needed. Some feel that if they didn't stay distracted, then everything would decline. They believe it's up to them to keep the world from falling apart. In their minds, without them, the God of the Universe wouldn't get anything done in their church. Maybe God's not in control and He would be lost without them in control.

It would seem that when the person with the Martha complex dies, the church is doomed. The Pastor won't get anything done and the board will be in mass confusion. The doors might have to be locked!

It becomes far too easy in that situation to make it all about you. You need to have your name and face in front of everybody. They should know that you represent the church, pastor, and board. Everything goes through you. You are the beginning and the end.

The church needs you to look after the music, the lights, the doors being unlocked and locked. That job may even belong to someone else, but you take it upon yourself to make sure all of it gets done. After all, that place couldn't function without you!

STUDY

Although you're the type of person who would like to know what scripture says, you don't have or won't take the time to study. Maybe the greeters won't show up, then what would happen to the church? You sit in church, while the message is being said, but your mind is on three other things because you have to be in control of it.

MARTHA! MARTHA! MARTHA!

You need to have a blend, of Mary and Martha. One person can't do it all and still have a smooth running church. The Mary concept is better. It points to and leads to the Messiah!

We don't believe The Messiah instructed us to make sure we're concerned about the building, the running of it, or what time to open the doors. He doesn't say to make sure everyone else gets fed.

You need to see that, babysitting the pastor or anyone else won't get you one inch closer to the Father. We believe the Messiah said: "I am the way, the truth and the light, no one goes to the Father except through me!"

Mary wanted what the Lord had to give her, not what had to be done outside of Him.

Believe me, that's not you!

PRAYER

When we pray, do we pray for all the things we want, need, and desire? Or is prayer to speak to the Father? Is your prayer a want list, like a child at Christmas time? Are you saying a lot of words in the hope God will notice your prayer because of the amount of time you take doing it?

Do you ever just want to talk to the Father? Do you ever start out saying Hello and praising the Father for who He is? When Christ showed us the way we should pray, he stated Our Father, where he resides (who are in Heaven), praised the Father's name (hallowed be Your name), asked for the Father's kingdom to be brought to earth, stated not our will, but His will be done. Then He says, the way He runs Heaven, do it on the earth also. Then He asked the Father for our daily substance. Then the Messiah says forgive us Father, the way we forgive others (very important). Then He asked the hard testing be kept from us. Then He says keep us safe from Satan's attacks (the evil one). That sums up, what we call the Lord's Prayer.

Do we ever sit down and think what is being said? Or do we just state words because that's what we were taught for years? How many of us sit down without any preconceived ideas and put deep thought into what the Messiah was trying to get us to realize with these words? Christ was trying to get us to understand that when we ask, it is the Father's will—not ours—that we should desire!

How many of us, when we talk or pray, really want the Fathers will be done? I'm sure there are a lot of people who just said, "Well I don't know about anyone else, but that's how I pray."

You may say the words when you're reciting the Lord's Prayer, but do you really mean it? Do you really want The Father to do it His way, even if it's the opposite of what you desire or pray for? That is a deep, thoughtful question. Is our real desire to do the Fathers will?

You may not like what God has for you, or how he is going to go about getting His will to be done. Even Christ asked the pain and suffering be taken away from Him. He really didn't want the hurt when the whip cut His back. He didn't desire the pain of the crown of thorns cutting into His scalp. He wasn't looking forward to nails being driven into and through His feet and hands. He wasn't asking for the humiliation of hanging naked for everyone to see. He knew how the Romans put people to death, by letting them hang until they can't breathe any longer and die. It was a very long, humiliating, painful death. He was naked, alone, hurting, and in agony the whole time.

There are preachers, teachers, songwriters and singers who make a living with the praise, "When He was on the cross I was on his mind."

It sounds good and is a catchy tune, so these people believe that while He was in such pain, naked, bleeding and having a hard time getting a breath of air, they were on His mind. The salvation of mankind is the reason He had to die, the way He did.

Why did the Christ, the Son, God himself have to hurt, be humiliated, and suffer for our Sins? He asked the Father to take that from Him. In reality, He didn't want those things to happen to Him. Was He scared and frightened of the pain He was going to endure? I would say yes. Being a human, one would not look forward to any of that suffering. While in the flesh of a human, He still said, "Not my will but Your will be done."

He was like any child crying to Daddy for help. But few of us—if any—when we cried out for Daddy's help, added something like, "Don't do what I want Dad. Do what you need to do!"

Most people think about Christ being powerful, smart, and handsome. In our minds, He was a know-everything type of guy. We imagine that He never had a hair out of place, never did His sandals wear out, He really didn't need to eat, nor did He ever have to go to the restroom.

I wonder, did His Mom and Dad ever have to scold him? Would He be called a nerdy kid, just a few years ago? Of course not. He was perfect. He was also human, a teen. It is never told if he went through the terrible twos. Did He ever misbehave? Of course not. He was the Christ; God's Son. Did Joseph or Mary ever have to tell Him NO?

To us, those are a few things that seem interesting. There isn't any reasoning behind them, but they do show a point that He was human and just maybe He did those things.

In Matthew 6:9-13, Yeshua teaches a very strong, powerful, yet short prayer. Not only is it short, but when you concentrate on it, it's all that's needed!

We all know people, who when they pray, it's like a ten minute lecture, going on and on. Now I'm not saying they are doing it wrong. It's just long. It's not my privilege or responsibility to correct people who want to give a ten minute speech. But, don't blame me or anyone else, for a little day dreaming during your speech. Don't get upset, or think that a short prayer isn't good enough.

The way we look at it is, if a person prays and you don't appreciate their prayer, no one says you can't continue your own prayer in private. Maybe the short prayer filled the request, and you're the one trying to be used by Satan to throw in a little confusion.

In the end, it's your prayer, it's your request, not mine or anyone else's. Make it personal and let God hear from you!

We believe the Lord used a short prayer and it was good enough for the Father to hear and answer. We believe all prayers should start out with

Praise to the Father, for who He is. You shouldn't jump into a wish or want list and expect Him to give you what you want just because you may use a name that some say gives you a direct line to the Father!

If one would look up the Hebrew word for "to pray," it's l'hitpallel. The word means "to judge oneself."

THE CHRISTMAS HOLIDAYS

Being Christians and studying about Christmas has been very interesting and eye opening. The one thing we will start out with, isn't what most people will consider the Christian way of looking at Christmas. But if we wanted the watered down version of any topic, we wouldn't have had to study that long on most subjects. Here we go with the findings:

Christmas by itself, in all reality, is not a biblical holiday at all!

Chanukkah, the Feast of Dedication, has been celebrated since 164 BC. That celebration was because of the victory over Antiochus IV, King of Syria, by the Makkabim. We found that Antiochus IV was defeated in Egypt, so he attacked Judea, killing—even ruthlessly slaughtering—men, women, and children.

The king of Syria, confiscated the Golden Alter, Menorahs and Sacred Vessels. The King would only allow the sacrificing of pigs in the temple, no circumcision was performed, and the Jews could not observe the Sabbath (Shabbat) or even keep Kosher.

The King himself cooked a pig in the temple, and poured its broth on the Holy Torah Scrolls. The King poured broth on the Alter itself. The Syrian officers, being true to their king, overlooked this cruel and blasphemous ruling.

It is told that one time, a Syrian officer, in a place called Modi'in, told Mattathias, the Maccabee, who was the Jewish Priest, in the Tabernacle, to sacrifice a pig. He and his five sons killed the first Jews that tried. Then they attacked the officer and his soldiers, killing them. That is how the revolt or rebellion started, with the Priest and his five sons rising up against the ruling of the Syrian King.

After Mattathias (the father) was killed, his five sons kept the revolt going with what today we might call guerrilla warfare. It's been told that after getting the Syrian soldiers to the point of equality, then they confronted them in open battles.

The Hebrews won their country and their Temple back. On the 25th day, of the Hebrew month Kislev, they rededicated their Temple and consecrated a New Alter. (Kislev can fall between November 27 and December 27.) This Feast of Dedication is called Chanukkah.

When the Hebrews relit the eternal light (Nertamid), there was only enough consecrated olive oil to keep it burning for one day. It would take a week to prepare more. The light burned for eight days, until the new olive oil was ready. For this reason, the Jews celebrate Chanukkah for eight days, starting on the 25th of Kislev.

Since the end of the third century, December 25th on the Roman calendar, corresponds with the 25th of Kislev. The modern day Jews give a gift on each of the eight days of Chanukkah. We don't know for sure, but it might seem that the Jews don't want the Hebrew children to feel left out of the gift giving at Christmas time.

The Hebrews light one candle each night on a Menorah. The Menorah usually has nine candles to celebrate the eight days of Chanukkah. The Imagery is fantastic for the Messianic Jews, because Yeshua is the light of the world.

I'm going to ask you a question. When you celebrate the 25th of December, are you celebrating the Jewish Messiah? The one who stated he was here only for the Lost Sheep of Israel? Or are you celebrating a date to distance you and your beliefs from the Hebrews with gifts and ceremony?

It doesn't seem like a coincidence that the 25th of December was picked for the day of celebration for The Messiah. If you study scripture, you find out that was not his date of birth. It's not even close. It does, however, coincide with Chanukkah.

A little side note off the top of our heads:

Has Christmas become a mass of meaningless customs, such as Santa Claus, trees, reindeer, and the obligation of exchanging cards and presents?

We have Preachers having Santa as part of the celebration, who make sure the children get a gift from Santa. We are all in favor of celebrating Christmas with all that stuff at home. We see the eyes of the little ones showing their excitement at all the splendor. But that shouldn't overshadow the reason why we celebrate that date in the first place.

As far as we are concerned, in the place of worship, we should not be putting Santa in the place of the Messiah!

It looks like most adults seem to be losing any meaning of the Savior's birth. It has come to a question of, "What did I get?" instead of "How much did He give?"

They started celebrating Chanukkah because of an event. We also celebrate Christmas because of an event. We need to keep an eye on the celebrations. We need to stop and stay as far away as we can, from celebrating a pig to Zeus (The Greek God). Instead, we should be celebrating a biblical blessing from God, the Father!

WHO WROTE THE NEW TESTEMENT?

This is a very interesting topic. The real question is not only who, but when, and in what Language was the New Testament written?

Let's look at the book of Matthew (Mattityahu in Hebrew). We know he was one of the twelve disciples, a tax collector, a Hebrew who was doing work for the Roman Empire, and was despised by the Jews.

The timing of his calling is one of the more interesting points, to us. Here are a few topics that are good for people to consider during their studies or if you're having a conversation among friends.

1. Matthew wrote it around 60 AD. We believe that was about 25 to 30 years after the Messiah was crucified.
2. Even though most believe that it wasn't written in chronological order, the timing of his calling was after the Messiah's.

   a. Healing of the paralyzed man, the one that was lowered down on a mat. Matthew 9, Mark 2.
   b. The miraculous catch of fish, Luke 5.
   c. The healing of the man with leprosy, Matthew 8, Mark 1, Luke 5.
   d. Satan tempts the Messiah, Matthew 4, Mark 1, and Luke 4.
   e. The Messiah gives the Beatitudes, Matthew 5.
   f. The Messiah teaches about salt and light, lust, divorce, vows, retaliation, giving, prayer, fasting, money, worry, ask, seek, and knock.
   g. The herd of pigs, Matthew 8.

The reason for bringing those to your attention was to show that a lot of teachings and miracles happened even before the Messiah called Matthew. There are more than we have listed here. Matthew may have heard what this man was doing even before he was called. We can all speculate, but the one thing we are sure of is that Matthew was called by the Lord. It doesn't matter to us if he was called before or after those things took place.

There is much debate about what language the writings of Matthew were first in. There have been writings so interesting that they may jump off the page and take a hold of you.

Bishop of Heiro Polos (60-130) stated that the writings of Matthew were in the Hebrew language. Saint Jerome (347-420 AD) said the true way to study the Gospels is through the Hebrew language. That may not mean anything to you, but it points one thing to us: Matthew (or Mattityahu) talked, walked, and wrote in the Hebrew language. The people who wanted to distance themselves from the Jewishness of scripture have made great errors in their judgment of God's word.

Let's go to the other authors of the New Testament.

Mark (who was actually John Mark) traveled with Paul on a missionary journey. He was not one of the twelve disciples. His Gospel is believed to have been written between 55 and 65 AD. That would make it one of the first writings in what we call the New Testament. The book of Mark records more miracles than any other book.

We really do not know if he ever personally heard the Lord speak, but what is known is that he was a Hebrew, a Jew. He must have written what God put into his spirit to write. He learned about the Lord's power. Some may say that he must have walked with the Lord to know all this stuff, but that is not documented in any writing.

We believe that Mark wrote to those who we call Messianic Jews. Since he was a Hebrew writing about the Jewish Messiah, in our opinion, he wasn't writing to Pagan Greeks or Romans. What he wanted to do was lead his people to belief in the Messiah.

Concerning Luke: In Colossians 4:14, Paul wrote that Luke, the doctor and their dear friend sends his greetings. He was Greek and a Gentile, believed to be the only Gentile writer in the New Testament.

Luke, according to the beginning of Acts, wrote his papers to his friend by the name of Theophilus. Some believe he may have been a doctor also. At this point, that is pure speculation, we would say. He was most likely Greek and of the upper class of society. Luke addressed him as "Your Excellency." That may show respect, a great friendship, or maybe he held a high stature in Greek Society. It seems he wrote Luke, Acts, and even more that aren't recorded, to this man who deserved his respect. Luke thought so highly of him, that he wanted him to believe in this Jewish Messiah.

Through the other books, we find that Luke was with Paul on some of his trips. He may have been on the trips to perform medical treatments for Paul or the people they came in contact with. We believe he learned what Paul was teaching, and that brought him closer to the leading Paul had on his life.

John was a Hebrew. He was one of the five known fishermen that were Christ's Disciples. John was not a man of great schooling. His skill was to provide for his family by throwing a large net into the water to bring up fish to eat and perhaps sell. John and James, his brother, worked with their father Zebedee, in their fishing venture (Matthew 4:18-22).

The Bible states very little about John, except that he was in one of the inner core groups of followers. At the Garden of Gethsemane, John was one of the three the Lord wanted to accompany Him a little further to keep watch with Him. He is believed to be the one Yeshua asked to take care of His mother.

He wrote the book of John, 1st, 2nd, 3rd John and the book of The Revelation.

James, not John's brother, is believed to be the Lord's brother. Some people disagree, but that's their choice. It makes no difference to me which way you believe, that just happens with people. If we thought that by one person or even a few million people, who may not agree with us, would make the truth sway one way or another, we personally would go crazy. Some may say that any way!

Peter, The Rock, was a Disciple who wrote 1st and 2nd Peter. He was also one of the three Yeshua had go with him a little farther into the Garden, when the Lord needed that extra time in prayer. You remember they all fell asleep.

Jude, the Lord's brother, wrote to build up the people who were followers of his brother; the true believers in Yeshua, Our Lord. We believe he was trying to keep people from false teachings, like the ones we are bombarded with in this time. That problem has actually been around for over 1000 years. (We would have stated 2000 years, but he wrote the letter about 65 AD, therefore until 2065 that statement wouldn't have been correct.) If preachers, teachers, or Biblical scholars want to disagree, that's fine. It will not make any different to us.

Paul wrote most of the rest of the New Testament, although some of the letters were to and from certain people. For example, some were to an individual congregation or addressing a certain topic. Paul was a very learned man, taught by Gamaliel, a very prominent Pharisee. This Pharisee was the one who convinced the Sanhedrin not to kill Yeshua's disciples. He believed that if Yeshua was false, they would just go away. Otherwise, they would find themselves fighting against God. Paul was a Roman citizen, found the road to Damascus. As we all know, that was a very interesting and life-changing trip. It became a new road for him to travel and what he found on that road changed his direction forever.

I stated Paul wrote most of the rest of the New Testament, because no one really knows who wrote the book of Hebrews. There are no less than seven people who have been mentioned that may have been the writer. We know the translations have stated who they believe wrote Hebrews, but in reality it doesn't change anything. We guess you can make your own choice. That's up to you!

The individuals wrote what inspired them and what the Lord did while here on earth. You should study and learn what God wants you to grasp, not a denomination, a pastor, or teacher. They want to lead you to believe their way. That is why this book says to study. Study so you will come up with what God wants you to grasp! Not what we learned, not what they learned, but what you need to learn!

SUNDAY SCHOOL TEACHER

When we were Sunday school teachers, here is how we started our first class:

We are not Teachers! We are fellow learners of scripture and people who love to learn what the God of the Universe is trying to tell us. It is even better for us to learn the "why" and "who" He is referring to when He speaks.

We call this group a learners' group for adults, who happen to meet on Sunday. It covers the Assemblies' desire to have a Sunday school class. We will not always agree with your interpretation of the word, and you will not always agree with us. That's all right with us, if it gets you to study to prove your point.

Now we will start out with one of the wildest statements ever. We say to you, this group of people wanting to learn: Never, never, never read your Bible!

We know speed readers who can go from the first, "In the beginning," to the last "Amen," in a matter of a few hours. Then you have people who take months just to go through one chapter. A lot of times, perhaps even most of the time, they read and perceive what someone else taught them about the subject. When people tell us they went through a program and read the Bible in a year, we wonder if they understand what they read or did they understand what a preacher or teacher told them what was being said.

People get their knowledge from certain avenues: local church doctrine, church affiliation, TV, or denominations. They base what scripture says on someone else, usually a preacher or teacher. Maybe they feel their leaders have all the answers. That is basing your faith and knowledge on what someone else thinks, not by the Word itself!

So what we want from you are subjects you want to learn about, not what Springfield says we need to study to keep in line with what they need you to study, at this time of year. You need to remember no topic is wrong. You might bring up something others wanted to bring up but figured no one else would like to study that, or think it wouldn't be interesting to go over that one. Pick a topic, write it down, hand it in next week and the whole class will know what topic we will have the following week. You will then be able to study to find out your truth about the subject. We can't say we will go over one topic per week. Some may take a month to go over. We will go over each topic and see how you and the class look at each. This way we just might find out what is the correct interpretation.

You will be surprised how the answers are swayed by what others have taught us and not what is really said in scripture.

We know we started with, "Never read your Bible." We really mean that. You need to STUDY it because every topic is important, not only to you, but to your family. Your salvation hangs on the truth of the Word! It's not about what you read here or what your preacher or teacher says. Don't base your ETERNITY on us. It is your responsibility to hear what the Father wants His people to know!

STUDY, STUDY, STUDY!

OUTLINE TO BELIEF IN SCRIPTURE

The Bible's purpose is to show people the truth about God, themselves, relationships, the meaning of life, and for people to get the right response with the Father! The central Message is telling about God, His chosen people Israel, and Our Messiah!

The main point is humans need to be saved and God provides the Salvation!

God choose one man to start his chosen people, the Hebrews, and his name was Abram (Avram in Hebrew). Then God changed it to Abraham (Avraham in Hebrew).

Through His Servant Moses, God gave His people the Torah, which means teachings. It is the teachings or instructions from the Father, for His People.

Some of the Prophets have told the Hebrews what God wanted from them, but they often didn't want to hear what was said. Instead, they did what they wanted and at times they got into a lot of trouble.

There are people, a lot smarter than us, who disagree with the dating of Scripture. When talking about the writings of Moses, they seem to point to the importance of the dating instead of the instructions to the Israelites. Some people say if you follow the Old Testament, then you believe in the Old and you can't believe in the New Testament. Another group says that the New Testament somehow cancelled or changed what the Old Testament said or pointed to.

Isaiah 53 talks about what the Messiah would do for us. The thought of God sending a Savior for His people was truly a Jewish concept. It dates back to somewhere around 700 to 681 B.C., the dating of the book of Isaiah.

When you read Matthew 5:5, The Sermon on the Mount, you need to remember that Christ was repeating what was written in Psalms 37:10-11. "The meek will inherit the land." Through the misinterpretation of most English Bibles, it says the meek will inherit the earth. That is why most people believe it will be the whole earth. We believe that the Messiah was repeating what the writer of Psalms 37 wrote, which would instead refer to "the land." That would be Israel, and in reality Jerusalem, God's chosen People's Capital.

Matthew 5:17 (NIV) - *Do not think that I have come to abolish the law or the Prophets; I have not come to abolish them but to fulfill them.*

Compare that to the Complete Jewish Bible translation:

Matthew 5:17 (CJB) - *Don't think that I have come to abolish the Torah or the Prophets. I have come not to abolish but to complete.*

This one verse is so misunderstood that it pains us to think that most people, who confess that they are believers, don't have a clue how to take that one verse. We believe that's because of the misleading by denominations, churches, preachers, and teachers. They miss the whole concept of that saying altogether. A lot of the organizations who claim to be followers of Christ seem to be as misguided as any Jew, whom the Christian claims to be wrong!

Being that we are Christians and have been for a very long time, we see that the Jews and the Christians kind of think alike. They both look for the Messiah. One side thinks they want him to come and the other wants him back. So in reality, they both are looking for the same person. The difference is, only one of them has their belief in the One who has already been here.

They both have belief in scripture, they just have a different opinion of it. Both the Old and the New have stated what will happen. It says who will reject The Messiah, who will accept Him, and when the accepting happens, what will go on from there. We are by no means bright enough to figure out the exact time and the exact day. What we do know is, whatever will take place is already figured out by the Father. After all, He is the one who needs to be in control of our future. He has already seen our past. We can't hide from it, so we just might have to admit it and let it bite us.

The outline is in the Bible. It's already in the Book. The Scriptures say it all. Study to find out yourself. Enjoy the journey and enjoy the search!

THE BEGINNING OF TIME

There was a creation of all things: land, water, animals, trees, grass, light, and humans. The Bible starts with Genesis (B'resheet in Hebrew which actually means beginning or origin). How long it took the Father to do the Creation is up for interpretation. Some say each day, from the start until the end, was a 24 hour period. Others say that it was an indefinite period of time.

The "how" doesn't seem to be the main concern, but there are people who look at the time period and length of days as one of the primary points of concern and disagreement. We believe the time period has no impact on the Father in the least, so why worry or spend any time at all being concerned? You won't change what took place back in the beginning. Get over it, get past it, you won't change it. But if you fret about it, it just might change you.

There are a few things we know:

(1) We would have to say that Creation should be classified as undated.
(2) Up until Noah, the recording of history would most likely been destroyed in the flood.
(3) We know that around 2500 B.C. the tools of writing were brought into usage by Egypt.
(4) We know that Abraham, the Father of the Jewish Faith, was born around 2166 B.C.
(5) This tells us that from the time of Noah until 2166 B.C., people walked the earth. Gold was discovered and imported to Egypt from Africa and that was around 2400 B.C. Sargon, the first known world conqueror was around 2331 B.C. (We have to

remember that their world may have been only small villages, but that was their world at that time.)

(6) If you study Egyptian history and the dates of some of their inventions, it seems like they were an advanced culture, but intelligence doesn't necessary mean correctness or lasting for all time.

(7) One should acknowledge that God, The Father, is the Creator of all things. The perfect creation by the perfect Creator, but the creation walked away.

(8) It seems to us that, they walked away, the way we have from time to time. Though we have found very few individuals who would admit it, it is true.

One point of interest is that no writings have ever been found with the author's name of Adam. No book or letter from Noah was ever discovered, either. You can go down the list: Abraham, Isaac, Jacob, Joseph, until Moses. He was 640 years after Abraham, plus Abraham was about 330 years after the Egyptians came up with papyrus (today we call it a primitive form of paper) and ink for writing.

That means, from the time of ink and paper to Moses' writings were almost 1000 years. Still, none of those listed wrote a word that is in scripture today. Joseph may have some of his writings somewhere in Egypt, but they are not found in what we call scripture today.

To us, it's amazing to look back in history and find that the God of the universe has given so much without receiving anything in return. Think about this; He started everything, got mad, changed everything, He started over, got mad again, sent His Son to correct things.

However long it takes this time, you might say He will get mad and start over, at least one more time.

We have no idea what's on the Father's mind. He is the CEO, the Boss of it all. It's not our privilege to dictate to Him and tell Him what He is supposed to do. Most likely, like Adam and others, we would just make a mess out of it anyway.

We pray and it seems He doesn't listen. If it's not His will, what we should say is His will be done, not mine and not yours.

We have heard some preachers preach that you should not say "His will be done." That would be like saying, "We have done such a good job with life and what God has given us, we don't need to say, 'Your will' anymore, because we know what to do and we always do it." RIGHT?

THE FIRST DISCIPLES

In Matthew 4:18, we find Peter and Andrew casting a net. Yeshua says to them, "Follow me and I will make you fishers of men."

It's a similar scene in Matthew 4:21. James and John were preparing their nets with their father, Zebedee, when the Messiah called them.

Both stories are also recounted in Mark 1:16. The Lord calls Simon Peter and his brother Andrew by saying, "Follow me and I will make you fishers of men."

Shortly after, He sees James and John, sons of Zebedee, preparing their nets. He called them and they left their father with the hired men and followed Him.

Luke 5:10 also offers an account of the calling of the first disciples. It is very much the same as the other two, but Luke's account calls Simon Peter a partner of James and John, the sons of Zebedee. None of the other books point to that at all.

John 1:35 explains that two disciples of John the Baptist followed Yeshua. Speculation is that they were John (the author of the book) and Andrew. Verse 40 says that Andrew was one of the two. Andrew went to his brother and told him.

In verse 43, the next day, leaving for Galilee, Yeshua said to Philip, "Follow me."

In verse 45, Philip found Nathanael. Nathanael said, "Can anything good come from Nazareth?" That's when Yeshua said He saw him under the fig tree.

Those are four different accounts of the calling of the first disciples.

Matthew, Mark, and Luke did not see any of this take place in person. Each wrote a different account of how, when, where and who Yeshua called to be His disciples.

John was the only one who would have actually been there to see it happen, so we consider his to be the most accurate account. We hear preachers going off on each Gospel with the point they want to make or that fits their point of view.

We believe that only one account of the calling of the first disciples is correct according to what actually happened. Is it the one who would have lived through it, or one of the three who were told how it happened?

We see that Matthew and Mark are the closest to saying the same thing. Does that mean they are the correct ones in their account of the calling of His first disciples?

According to Luke, when Peter's mother-in-law was sick, Peter wasn't even a follower of Yeshua. At best, it seems he wasn't overwhelmed by what Yeshua said. Then one day, as Yeshua was by the Sea of Galilee, He sat down and taught from Peter's boat. He told Peter to go out and cast his net.

After the calling of Peter, James, and John, they left everything and followed the Messiah. Only in John's account were Philip and Nathanael listed. Remember, he would have been the only one who was there. It is important to note that John never wrote about when he personally started following the Messiah.

We know we stated this in another place, but it seems that it may need to be said again. Matthew wrote about things he didn't see. He must have been told by at least one of the first four, or he knew from Jewish History what would take place.

These topics include:

(1) The genealogy of Yeshua.
(2) Angel appears to Joseph.
(3) Visitors from the East.
(4) The Family went to Egypt.
(5) Their return.
(6) Yeshua being Baptized.
(7) Satan tempting Yeshua in the desert.
(8) Yeshua's first teachings.
(9) The calling of the first four disciples.
(10) Yeshua preaching in the synagogues in Galilee.
(11) The Beatitudes.
(12) Yeshua teaching about; Salt and Light, the Law, Anger, Lust, Divorce, Vows, Retaliation, Loving your Enemies, Giving to the Needy, Prayer, Fasting, Money, Worry, Criticizing others, Ask, Seek, Knock, Way to Heaven, The House built on Rock or Sand.
(13) Yeshua heals the man with Leprosy.
(14) The Roman Centurions Faith.
(15) Peter's mother-in-law being healed.
(16) The Cost of following Yeshua.
(17) The Calming of the Storm.
(18) Sending the Demons into the Pigs.
(19) The Healing of the Paralyzed Man.

Matthew was a Jew. He knew through the Jewish History writings what the Jewish Messiah would do. It was after all those things happened that the Lord called Matthew as one of His disciples. That doesn't take away from the spirituality of Matthew's writing, but it is interesting what He wrote.

We are not saying he didn't know what he was writing about. To us it is interesting.

THE BOOK OF JAMES

When you study the book of James, you read that he is a servant of God and the Messiah. He also says that he is writing the letter to the Twelve Tribes that were scattered.

First of all, "the Twelve Tribes" refers to Jews. It is not a metaphor for Christians. Too many preachers have the mentality that he was referring to the Christians of that day and the Christians now.

Here is a note to all teachers: We are sure hoping when you, the teacher, went over the first two sentences, you made sure everyone knew that it wasn't directed toward Gentiles, but toward the Jews who were scattered by either Saul's persecution or the persecution that took place in 44 A.D.

We recently heard a preacher say he thought the letter was written as early as 34 A.D., so that would point to a time of even before King Herod's persecution.

By James writing, we know it was after the Jews were scattered.

The scattering of the Hebrews(Jews) can be traced back to the Assyrian's invading the Land of Israel, somewhere around 732 B.C.

We read in Acts 9 that Saul went to the high priest for a letter to the synagogues in Damascus, so when he went to Damascus, he may take them as prisoners and bring them back to Jerusalem.

Saul was persecuting the Jews who came to faith in their Messiah. He wasn't chasing Gentiles around the area. He was after what we would call

Messianic Jews of the day. They were known, in those days, as "belonging to the Way."

The persecution in 44 A.D. was by King Herod. Both Saul and Herod caused the people of the Way (Messianic Jews) to hurry out of the area. That is why we believe James wrote to the Twelve Tribes scattered.

Another note to the teachers: The first twelve verses of James 3 tell the teachers that if they don't tell the truth, they will be judged more severely. You can't have the first twelve verses be "either-or." You have to tell the truth by what scripture says, not by your feelings, or what your desire is, or what you want it to say so it fits your need.

Verse 3 talks about who is wise and understanding. It also states if you have envy, selfish ambition, or jealousy, that wisdom does not come down from Heaven. They are attacking the truth with lies. We can't stress this enough; shame on the teacher who hears the truth and continues to lead people down their path to Hell, because of the philosophy of their church or denomination.

Chapter 4 starts out with fights and quarrels. James then says, the reason you don't have is because you don't ask God, or you pray and don't receive because you ask with wrong motives. In other words, your desire may not be The Father's desire for you. To us, he is addressing a certain problem of the day. This was a problem that was going through the Messianic community then, but if you look around in today's society nothing has changed. It's like a plague and the world has allowed this plague to grow out of control.

The worldly stuff, with the help of the church, has too often moved God out of the way. This happens because they want to make people happy, instead of telling truth. When you try to tell the truth and bring God back, you have a minority of people stopping you.

It is a shame that we allow the stupidity of the people who rule over the ones who are trying to know the true word of God. These congregations are doing this just so they can fill their churches. The denominations have convinced enough people, so instead of fighting against the minority of people, it looks like they may have the majority.

Wrong teaching is and will always be wrong teaching. In our society today, it looks like the minority has overrun the majority of believers.

NOT A NUCLEAR WAR

A Psalm by King David, Psalm 110, explains the credentials for the Jewish Messiah:

In this psalm, the King James and New International Versions start with, "The Lord says to my Lord."

The Complete Jewish Bible starts with, "Adonai says to my Lord." The word Adonai actually means "My Lord." In the Jewish Bible, Adonai refers to God.

In the KJV and the NIV, the city is called Zion, while in the CJB it is called Tziyon. Mount Tziyon was originally the City of David, south of the modern Old City Jerusalem, the hill may now be called Mount Tziyon. The word has a variety of meanings. It also may mean the people of Israel.

The phrase, in the order of Melchizedek, is in Psalm 110. It is also repeated in Hebrews 5 and 7.

Psalm 110 talks about the place, Tziyon. It talks about the youth willing to serve and fight for Adonai and their land. It also talks about Adonai shattering any King on the day of His anger, passing judgment on nations with dead bodies by shattering heads through an extensive territory. It refers not necessarily to the whole earth, but it would represent the extended area around Israel.

Psalm 110:7 says, "He will drink from a stream as he goes on his way; Therefore he will hold his head high."

With that ending, one would surmise that on the day of His wrath, the rulers of the whole earth will be crushed. According to the last part of verse 7, the water will still be drinkable. In other words, it will not be a nuclear war that contaminates the water.

Israel will hold his head high on that day. The Hebrews will have victory over the countries and lands that God gave them, however much that is.

That to us was a very interesting study. We found most preachers and teachers point to this victory as some kind of Christian victory. The country that will hold its head high will be Israel, not the United States, England, or any other. That is contrary to almost every sermon or class we've ever been in.

THE LORD'S PRAYER

What we call The Lord's Prayer was actually parts of other prayers that the Lord put in this order. The order He arranged them in brings out the beauty that we now enjoy as The Lord's Prayer.

After looking up Matthew 6:9, in five different translations, we found they mainly start out with "Our Father in Heaven." Some may have a few more flowery words added to it, but the bottom line is, they all addressed the Father and where he resides. That is, of course, in Heaven.

In the Hebrew language, the opening is (Avinu sh'baShammayim) Avinu (Our Father) sh'baShammayim (In Heaven). In the Hebrew language, there are a large number of prayers that start with "Our Father in Heaven."

The start of this prayer would have been considered standard in a lot of the Jewish prayers of the day.

We should address this prayer and all our prayers to "Our Father" and where he resides "In Heaven." Our Father doesn't roam up and down the Mississippi river or sit in the Arizona desert. We know the Father rules over them, but His domain is In Heaven.

Then we have, "Hallowed be Thy Name." Do we think about this part at all, or do we just recite it because we know it by heart? We just say it without any thought or feeling of what has just been said. We have to admit, for most of our lives, we knew and would recite The Lord's Prayer, but said the words without any concept of how, why, or what we were repeating. We just knew the words, like most people did. Then after we started studying, we came to realize, that the thought of just repeating the words is doing an injustice to God, the Messiah, and to our lives as well.

Some translations say, "Hallowed Be Your Name." We also found one that states, "May Your Name Be Kept Holy." With this one, we have to stop and think when we use it because it doesn't come out of our mouths from habit. If people, when reciting the prayer, had to stop and think on those two writings, it would give everyone a concept of how much we, as mere humans, should Praise the one and only Father with "Hallowed Be Your Name." We believe that if any person stops after each of those words and tries to grasp what you are saying— "HALLOWED BE YOUR NAME"– you will remember you're addressing The King of the Universe, the Great I AM, and honoring Him by saying, "Hallowed Be Your Name."

It's not a prayer to, or for, just anyone. It's letting The King of Everything know what you think of Him. Those first few words of the Lord's Prayer should make chills go up and down your back. You are addressing the King, the Great "I AM," and letting Him know what you think of Him. Or are you just repeating words that you learned when you were a little child? The start of The Lord's Prayer says to whom we are addressing our prayer. To put it another way, you are stating who He is, where He's at, how great He is and will always be.

Verse 10 (NIV) states, "Your Kingdom come, your will be done on earth as it is in Heaven." We are asking the Great "I AM" to have His kingdom come to us on earth. When this happens, things will change, the immorality of the human race will be so bright, it will not be able to hide any longer. All people will be affected. Those who try to walk the fence between the father's desire and their desire, their way of life, and how He would want them to live, will no longer be able to do so. They will have to make a choice between the Fathers' way of believing or their way of believing.

People get really excited when they get goose bumps during a song or a sermon. We guess they believe that's proof they are following God, or at least heard from Him. They may believe they are good enough to make it when the Lord returns, but are they?

We believe, by the way Scripture talks about Heaven, it is a beautiful place for the Father and eventually His Son's followers. There will be no sin, no pain, no suffering, just praising God! If those are a few of the attributes of Heaven, and we are asking the Great "I AM" for the same here on earth, when does the will of Our Creator start to be something more than just a phrase we say in a prayer? When does "Your will be done on earth as it is in Heaven" concept start to be a real desire for even the people who call themselves believers? Some in our churches today, say that is our main goal now. If it is, then when does it start to manifest into society, or for that matter in our churches?

There are people right now, thinking or saying that's what we do in our church. Is it really? Every individual would like to believe they know the truth, because that is what they have been taught for many years by a denomination. Do people really want the Father's justice and His will for everyone? Or do they just want Him to change the other guy because they think their church teaches the right way?

Verse 11 (NIV) reads, "Give us today our daily bread." That isn't asking The Father to give you a daily reading of the Word of God, like I've heard some preachers say. The Son is teaching His followers to ask for their needs, such as their substance for daily life. That means bread; food for the belly or food for the mind.

Verse 12 (NIV) says, "And forgive us our debts, as we also have forgiven our debtors."

The Complete Jewish Bible says it this way, "Forgive us what we have done wrong, as we too have forgiven those who have wronged us."

That sounds fantastic and most people would agree, but how many people hold a grudge for a very long time? If that is the case with you, then we would assume you want the Father to hold a grudge against you for a very long time, as well. That's what the Lord's Prayer states. We either forgive and are forgiven, or hold a grudge for a long time, hoping that through time we may forgive that other person. Is that how you want the Father to treat you? Maybe we should get over it, realize time is too short, and forgive. Even if the other party won't forgive you, you need to forgive them. If you do that, you have done what you should do, according to Matthew 6:12.

Most of the versions of verse 13 state something like, "And lead us not into temptation, but deliver us from the evil one (NIV)."

Consider James 1:13-14 (NIV) - *When tempted, no one should say, "God is tempting me." For God cannot be tempted by evil, nor does he tempt anyone; But each person is tempted when they are dragged away by his own evil desire and enticed.*

If what James writes is true, why would our Messiah tell His followers to pray that the Father lead them not into temptation?

The scriptures are full of testing. With that in mind, we like how the Complete Jewish Bible states verse 13: "and do not lead us into Hard Testing."

We believe The God of the Universe doesn't tempt anyone into doing anything. He has rules for people to live by and it's up to us to abide by them. We repeat what James wrote, "God cannot be tempted by evil, and He doesn't tempt anyone."

So with that in mind, why would The Messiah say, and lead us not into temptation? The Father doesn't lead, doesn't point, and doesn't guide us into evil temptation. We are lead by our own desires, not His.

Let's take a closer look at the second part of Matthew 6:13, "but deliver us from the evil one."

We've studied and read that the Greek word used there could also be translated evil. With it written that way, the King James Version's "but deliver us from evil" would be the more accurate version on that statement.

Using the word evil would mean, "deliver us from any evil caused by Satan or ourselves."

We believe that phrasing puts a more personal touch on that part of The Lord's Prayer. On the other hand, "deliver us from the evil one," would be saying you know who is causing the evil and he is the one to be delivered from. Those are good topics to study and think about while you are looking for the truth in scripture.

The King James Version says, "For thine is the kingdom, and the power and the glory, forever. Amen". You don't see that in some Bibles, or you may see brackets around this part. The oldest manuscripts didn't have that for the ending. It was somewhere around the third century before it was added.

If your Bible is a red letter Bible, and this portion is in red (meaning that the Messiah made this statement), then that is another example of "there is no translation that is perfect."

"The Kingdom, Power, and Glory" may sound like a perfect ending, but it couldn't have been said by the Lord, unless he came back in the third century and made that statement for the ending. The Catholic Bible doesn't have that last part added to the Lord's Prayer, but most Protestants do use it.

There is a shorter version in Luke 11:2. This version of the Lord's Prayer is more brief than Matthew's, but it contains the same topics for prayer.

The Lord's Prayer is a beautiful prayer, but most people recite it without any thought of what they are saying or what it means.

We are not saying to add anything, and we are not telling you to leave anything off. That's totally up to you. We wanted everyone to realize most writings are not—and should not be known as—a Catholic thing or a Protestant thing, the way we have been told by a number of people. As far as we are concerned, it is an interpretation thing. We do not have the authority, nor do we want the responsibility of telling you what you have to believe. That is something that you need to understand through your own studies, not ours. When you study and find the correct answer for yourself, Praise the Lord. Just try to leave out the denominational brainwashing of your past.

We would have to say that the main point, for any believer, should be, STOP and think what you're asking The Great "I AM" to do.

As Christians, we usually hear sermons that talk about an individual relationship with God.

The prayers by the Hebrew nation were more for the whole nation of Israel, and not usually for the individual person. The individuality is not found in this prayer.

"Give us our daily bread. Forgive us our debts, as we also forgive our debtors. Lead us not into temptation, but deliver us from evil."

When you study, you see it more as a group prayer. But, come to you own conclusion.

We pray you study, to find truth.

MELCHIZEDEK

Not much has been written about this individual. Genesis 14:18 is the first place he is mentioned. Most people have heard the story that Abram was blessed by Melchizedek with bread and wine, and Abram gave Melchizedek a tenth of everything.

Melchizedek said in Genesis 14:19-20a, "Blessed be Abram by God Most High, Creator of Heaven and Earth. And praise be to God Most High, who delivered your enemies into your hand."

Did you catch that? Melchizedek said Abram was blessed by God. Then, he said blessings to God, for being God, who by the way handed your enemies into your hand. What a great way to look at all the great conclusions in our own lives. To acknowledge the one who is blessed, then say a blessing to the one who is doing the blessing.

Hebrews 7 talks about Melchizedek and the Lord:

Hebrews 7:1a (NIV) - *this Melchizedek was king of Salem and priest of God Most High.*

Hebrews 7:2b (NIV) - *First the name Melchizedek means "king of righteousness"; then also, "king of Salem" means "king of Peace."*

The Complete Jewish Bible says, "king of Shalom," which means king of Peace. As far as we understand Shalom, it is more than just peace. It would also mean health, integrity, wholeness.

In Isaiah 9:6, it says the Messiah is called "Prince of Peace." (In Hebrew it would be Sar-Shalom.)

There are people who say such things like, "He was surely born of parents, we just don't know who they were. We have read that he was a son of Shem, and of course he died, but it seems no one recorded this king's death."

Others have said he was really the Messiah, that's why Abram gave him a tenth.

Well both of those may sound interesting to you and us, but here is one more interesting thing to think about: at the end of Verse 3, like the Son of God, it is stated that he remains a Priest forever.

Did you catch that? He was like the Son of God. He wasn't the Son of God, but he was like Him. He remains a Priest forever, for all time. He was and still is a priest, just like the Son. It says they are Priests for all time. There are only two people who the scriptures say are Priests forever; the Messiah and this King called Melchizedek.

Hebrews 7 talks about how neither came from Levi's descendants, which is the Priesthood in the Hebrew Nation. Then, when someone thinks they have things figured out, you read 7:8. In the one case a tenth is collected by men who die, while in the case of Melchizedek, it is received by someone who is testified to still be alive. (Does that really say, still alive? Not was alive but still alive? That he and the Messiah are still alive today?)

Here is one more Interesting thing to think about. We know Melchizedek was Priest of Salem, long before the Nation of Israel existed. We also know that he was King of Salem, long before the city of Jerusalem existed. In fact, it was long before the Jewish Priesthood or even the Hebrew Nation began. By studying, one would have to say he would have been a Gentile High Priest!

Let's take a little look at the Messiah and Melchizedek:

> Yeshua-A Hebrew-Lives Forever-He Died-He had a
> Beginning of Life-He had a Resurrection- A Priest
> Forever- Yeshua is in the Order of Melchizedek.

STUDY

Melchizedek-A Gentile-Lives Forever-No record of his
Death-No record of his beginning of days-Priest Forever.

The Bible states, "Yeshua is in the order of Melchizedek." It is not the other way around. The New Testament repeats what the Old Testament said over 2000 years earlier. Those are topics that people talk about. They mean nothing toward your salvation, but they are interesting to think about.

Now we are going to talk about something that some pastors have messed up for years. Genesis 14 talks about when Abram rescues Lot. It talks about the kings on both sides. One of the interesting parts is that, until Lot was taken captive by Kedorlaomer and the kings allied with him, Abram didn't pay any attention.

Kedorlaomer and his band of kings ran the region for 12 years. Where Lot lived (which was in Sodom), and what Lot was doing, was his own business. That was until Lot and his possessions were taken captive. That is when Abram took notice.

There are a number of interesting aspects of this. There were four kings against the five kings, and it would be like cities or areas having their own rulers. How large the city or area was would mean how much power or how little power the ruler really had.

Let's use a little example. Madison, Wisconsin wants the produce grown in the village of Potosi, Wisconsin. Potosi has the population of 800 people, so the powers of Potosi might try to make a truce with the powers of Madison, that way the powers of Potosi would still exist. Then the powers of Potosi and the villages around Potosi think they have enough power to rebel, but then the powers of Madison send their army to show Potosi and their friends, who's the boss.

Keep that thought in mind, as we go back to the part where most people get confused.

If you read Genesis 14, Melchizedek isn't one of the five or one of the four. When Abram returned after defeating Kedorlaomer and the kings allied with him, it does state that Bera, the king of Sodom, came to the Valley of Shaveh (that is, the Kings Valley). It may seem that Melchizedek came out to the valley not to retrieve any people, but to say a blessing for Abram and God. King Bera went out to pay honor to the man who brought his people back home. Bera wanted the people. After all, if there were no people, what would he be a king of? That's why Bera said, "Give me the people and keep goods and plunder for yourself." Melchizedek, The King of Salem, didn't fight or have any say so in the battle whatsoever!

When I first made that statement, there was a person in the group who knew almost everything about scripture. He more or less tried to show everybody how smart he was, when it comes to the word. He challenged me on what I just said, in front of about thirty people. He made the statement that I was wrong and where would I get an idea like that?

My answer was, from scripture, not from some denominational brainwashing or religious philosophy that people take as gospel without any in-depth study. This person said he disagreed with a number of things, but the main one is, that it was Melchizedek who was told he wouldn't be able to say he made Abram rich.

My reply was, let's look at scripture with an open mind and no preconceived ideas. I asked the person to look up Genesis 14:2 and read to the group what it said. When he got to Bera King of Sodom, I said now read Genesis 14:21-23.

> Genesis 14:21-23 (NIV) - *the King of Sodom said to Abram, "Give me the people and keep the good for yourself." But Abram said to the king of Sodom, "With raised hand I have sworn an oath to the Lord, God most High, Creator of Heaven and Earth, that I will accept nothing belonging to you, not even a thread or the strap of a sandal, so that you will never be able to say, I made Abram rich"*

I stopped the individual and asked him who made that statement, according to scripture? He said Abram. I asked him, and to whom did he make that statement? He said Melchizedek. I replied that Melchizedek was King of Salem, and according to Genesis 14:2, the scripture says, the king of Sodom was Bera. So in Genesis 14:17, Bera was the one who went out to meet Abram in the Kings Valley. Then after Bera met with Abram, Melchizedek blessed Abram and Abram gave The Priest of God Most High, a tenth of everything.

Most of the preachers and teachers we have ever heard say it the way this person did. That is why we should always study scripture ourselves.

This may have been a very small example of something being told over and over, until people read and understand it, the way they have heard it preached for years and years. It is not by Satan, but through our own laziness we are going astray.

Satan doesn't need to do much. He just sits back and lets you do the damage, all by yourself.

PREDESTINED OR PREDESTINATION

One of the first questions always asked is, are we predestined? And if we are, why do we need to pray for people to get saved? If they are predestined, then they are saved or already condemned and going to Hell, no matter what. So why pray if what is going to happen is already in stone?

We put it this way: the Bible says to Pray, the Messiah showed us how and what to pray, now it is up to us to understand and complete what the Lord instructed us to do.

Does the God of the Universe know everything? Does He know who will follow Him before we even realize it? Do we need to understand God's way and will, with our sinful lives? Does God answer to us, or do we answer to God? There are a lot of preachers and teachers who have that turned around. They preach and teach that everything is always roses, has been in the past, and will always be in the future, no bumps or bruises.

In our limited viewpoint, glorification is still in our future. From God's viewpoint, it is already accomplished. Therefore for us it can be a certainty that we can rely on.

The way we look at it is, we are trapped in an unredeemed universe. This earth and this universe will pass away. That's the unredeemed universe the scripture is speaking of when it talks about Heaven and earth passing away.

Are we robots that have no real control of our fate, our lives, or our death? We need to follow the King of All Creation, the Great I AM, and do what He says to do. Maybe then we will be able to stand in front of Him with our heads held high, because we have done the work we were instructed to do from the beginning of time.

If the Father already knows who will follow Him and who will follow Satan, then we need to do His will to be one of the ones that make Heaven.

What do we need to do? Live our lives the way we think we need to and hope that when we were formed by mom and dad, we were set aside for the Father's purpose.

Predestined or predestination is in reality up to God and we will not argue with Him.

PRAY

We need to look up and believe what the Old Testament teaches!

Deuteronomy 6:5 (NIV) - *Love the Lord your God with all your heart and with all your soul and with all your strength.*

In Matthew 22:37-38, we read that the Messiah said that was the first and greatest commandment!

Does God change His mind? What do you think? Does the Lord look down and when someone asks for anything, does that really change His mind or what He is going to do? Do you believe that a real Christian can change His mind? How about those part-time believers? Could they really change the way the Father was going to conduct business in this world?

We know that James wrote to the Twelve Tribes scattered among the nations:

James 5:13 (NIV) - *is any one among you in trouble? Let them pray. Is anyone happy? Let him sing songs of praise.*

And as far back as Genesis:

Genesis 18:20-21 (NIV) - *Then the Lord said, "The outcry against Sodom and Gomorrah is so great and their sin so grievous, that I will go down and see if what they have done is as bad as the outcry that has reached me. If not, I will know."*

We most likely know the rest of the story, how Abraham pleads for the people in that area, and how he went from fifty righteous people down to ten righteous people before he stopped. We have been told that is a true example of how God changes his mind. It never says he changed his mind, but what it does show is that Abraham was bold enough to ask! He still destroyed the area. The number of people who were destroyed never changed. But he did give Abraham a peace of mind when he asked.

> Isaiah 59:1-2 (NIV) - *Surely the arm of the Lord is not too short to save, nor his ear too dull to hear. But your iniquities have separated you from your God; your sins have hidden his face from you, so that he will not hear.*

> Isaiah 59:12-15 (NIV) - *For our offenses are many in your sight, and our sins testify against us. Our offenses are ever with us, and we acknowledge our iniquities: rebellion and treachery against the Lord, turning our backs on our God, inciting revolt and oppression, uttering lies our hearts have conceived. So justice is driven back, and righteousness stands at a distance; truth has stumbled in the streets, honesty cannot enter. Truth is nowhere to be found, and whoever shuns evil becomes a prey. The Lord looked and was displeased that there was no justice.*

We ask, is your country much different today? Over 2500 years ago, Isaiah wrote that about Israel. But consider the writing: The rebellion and treachery against the Lord, turning our backs on our God, justice is driven back, righteousness stands at a distance, truth stumbled in the street, honesty cannot enter, whoever shuns evil becomes the prey. All that pertains also to the society of today. We allow that to happen so we don't rock the boat of the minority of people who don't want to hear the truth.

People believe Isaiah wrote that around the year BC 681. It is amazing how every aspect of the wording lines up with what is going on today. Very few people want to hear the truth; they only want to hear what they already believe. In some way, they must feel better about their salvation, even though they put their heads in the sand and pay no attention to the happenings around them and the world!

This section is about Prayer. We believe that Praying would have controlled all those situations and none of that would be taking place if people would have been seeking God and not allow the evil that may look good control them. Society looks more at TV for direction than at the Bible these days. Isn't that the shame of our country?

Our Churches may say stuff like, "We know that it isn't right and we as a church must stand against it. Now go and watch what you say because you don't want to offend anybody. After all, we are true Christians, and we want everybody to feel good about themselves and that way we might get them into our church. Then we can work on them changing their ways. We may not see everything like they do, but we have to show love first, then show our way of thinking is the right path."

The problem is, you seem to be the ones that soften your way of thinking and your way of life, not the other person! We know that would never happen to your church or denomination. Now think about what you can say and not say these days and tell us that people and situations haven't changed your religion.

When you pray, do you have the faith to throw that mountain into the sea? If it doesn't happen, do you come up with an excuse why (or at least one you can make up) it didn't happen in your timing? Is it our actions that God pays attention to?

Belief, faith, and trust should be with our prayers. If we don't have those, we believe they're just words! But does that show how good of a Christian you are or how strong you are in the faith? After all, if you believe, then it will happen.

People look at the wording of 2 Chronicles 7:13-16 and use it like it is the United States or their country of origin or residence that he is talking about.

> 2 Chronicles 7:13-16 (NIV) - *When I shut up the Heavens so that there is no rain, or command locusts to devour the land or send a plague among my people, If my people, who are*

called by my name, will humble themselves and pray and seek my face and turn from their wicked ways, then I will hear from Heaven and I will forgive their sin and will heal their land. Now my eyes will be open and my ears attentive to the prayers offered in this place. I have chosen and consecrated this temple so that my Name may be there forever. My eyes and my heart will always be there.

Here is something you need to remember: It may sound great, may look good, it may make people happy and feel connected to the word... but God is talking to Solomon about Israel and His people, the Jews. Not us Americans or any other nationality!

THE TENTHS AND TITHES

Is there a difference or are they the same? While it's true that a tithe is 10 percent, according to scripture there were times for tithes and times for tenths.

> Malachi 3:8-10 (NIV) – *"Will a mere mortal rob God? Yet you rob me. But you ask, how are we robbing you? In tithes and offerings. You are under a curse-your whole nation-because you are robbing me. Bring the whole tithe into the storehouse, that there may be food in my house. Test me in this," says the Lord Almighty, "and see if I will not throw open the floodgates of Heaven and pour out so much blessing that there will not be room enough to store it."*

The New International Version and The King James Version both say tithes, while The Complete Jewish Bible says Tenth into the storehouse.

> Deuteronomy 14:22-23 (NIV) - *Be sure to set aside a tenth of all that your fields produce each year. Eat the tithe of your grain, new wine and olive oil, and the firstborn of your herds and flocks in the presence of the Lord your God at the place He will choose as a dwelling for His Name, so that you may learn to revere the Lord your God always.*

Leviticus 27:30-33 talks about the Israelites tithing grain from the soil and fruit from the trees. Then it talks about every tenth animal under the shepherd's rod will be holy to the Lord. Then it says they can't substitute a bad one from the good one. Then it says if a man redeems any of the tithes, he must add a fifth of the value to it.

Numbers 18:21 talks about giving the Levites all the tithes as their inheritance, for the work they do while serving at the Tent of Meeting.

Numbers 18:26 talks about the Levites receiving a tithe from the Israelites, then they have to present a tenth of that tithe as the Lord's offering.

We have looked up both tenth and tithe in the NIV, KJV, and CJB, we found over 50 in each interpretation. When you add all three together, it comes to 152 places in scripture that say either tenth or tithe. We are not saying those three are the only Bibles to use, but those were the three we used. You use the one you like or want to read.

While taking into account all those verses, we believe there is a difference between tenth and tithe. Like we said, even though a tithe is actually 10 percent. The difference comes down to what you are required to do with each. The scripture is really plain on this. According to Deuteronomy 14, eat your tithe in the place he will choose as a dwelling for His Name, a tenth goes to the Levites for him and their distribution.

Let's look at Tithe, Tithing, and Tithes. According to the Strong's concordance, Tithing = 2 times, and both in the Old Testament. Tithe = 12 times in the Old Testament, 2 times in the New Testament. Tithes = 18 times in the Old Testament, 5 times in the New Testament. That's 32 times in the Old Testament, 7 times in the New Testament. 39 times total.

That is the total number of times tithe, tithing or tithes appears in scripture. So few times and yet those words have such an impact on the people who say they believe. Do you tithe or not? Do you give 10 percent to the organization you belong to? Do you read scripture and believe that you need to get your instructions from someone else who knows more than you do? Maybe you call them your pastor, your Sunday school teacher, Bible study instructor, your Rabbi.

We didn't name all those leaders of your local place of worship so you rebel against them. But each person needs to STUDY and make sure that what they are being taught lines up with what God intended when He had

Moses, David, Isaiah, Jeremiah, Paul, Peter, James, John, Matthew and others write what we call the Bible today.

Can we tell anyone what or how much to tithe? NO! In the New Testament, the Messiah was proving a point (or chewing the Israelites out) because they were not doing what the God of the Universe had instructed them to do in the Old Testament regarding tithes. The tithe came from the grains, fruits, fields, animals, wine and olive oil. What we tithe today is a little different. We should use the same concept, though. Can we tell anyone to tithe or how much they need to tithe or command you to give anything at all? NO!

We have our personal opinion on the topic of tithing. That is, if we tithe from the head with the idea that we have given to get something in return, then it doesn't work. That tithing comes from the wrong place. It needs to come from the heart and expect, look for, or desire nothing in return. That is when God looks into your heart and the blessings start to flow! Not because of what someone else said, but because of what God, The Father, The Great I AM said!

Like we stated earlier, Malachi 3:10 says, "Test me in this" or "Put me to the test," depending on which version you read. We have found no other place in scripture that says to test anything God does, or will do in your future, if you follow what He told you to do.

> Malachi 2:17 (NIV) - *You have wearied the Lord with your words. "How have we wearied him" you ask. By saying, "All who do evil are good in the eyes of the Lord, and He is pleased with them" or "Where is the God of justice?"*

> Malachi 3:1 (NIV) - *"I will send my messenger, who will prepare the way before me. Then suddenly the Lord you are seeking will come to His temple; the messenger of the covenant, whom you desire, will come," says the Lord Almighty.*

We believe he is referring to John, The Baptist.

Chapter 3 talks about the Day of Judgment, His messenger, purifying the Levites, those who are sinful but do not fear the Lord, robbing God, and the faithful few. Chapter 3 ends with, "and you will again see the distinction between the righteous and the wicked, between those who serve God and those who do not."

"Test me on this," says the Lord. But if a person tests on one's head knowledge, or what someone else says, then it's not a test but more of an ultimatum to God.

Do we tell you that you have to tithe? As we stated before, we don't have that authority. What we do ask you is, what does The Father of the Universe and The Messiah say to you?

DO REALLY, REALLY GOOD PEOPLE DIE?

Some translations state Genesis 1:26 as, "God said, 'Let us make man in our image.'"

In the CJB it says, "Let us make humankind in our image."

Also consider:

> Hebrews 13:8 (CJB) - *Yeshua the Messiah is the same yesterday and today and forever.*

> John 14:6 (CJB) - *Yeshua said, "I am the way and the truth and the life, no one comes to the Father, except through me."*

The Bible doesn't lie! That is and always has been the only way to Heaven. Our question is, in Old Testament times, when a person died, where did they go?

God sets the rules in place and doesn't change them! Same rules yesterday, today, and forever. Was it always that way? Did man know good and evil, right from wrong? Who were Adam and Eve supposed to be?

Those may sound like dumb questions to the people who know everything, but for us who have to STUDY, they seem like a topic for a great study! Let us explain why we call this a great study.

> *Genesis 3:22 (NIV) - and the Lord God said, "The man has now become like one of us, knowing good and evil. He must*

not be allowed to reach out his hand and take also from the
tree of life and eat, and live forever."

Did you stop and absorb what the scripture was really saying? Or did you, like the two of us did for years, read it the way someone else told you to? So often we simply read the what and why of the way their church believes.

What is God really saying? Before they ate from the tree of the knowledge of good and evil, did they know right from wrong? Did they need to know about good and evil?

It would seem that, in the garden there was no such thing as good or evil. There was no such thing as having to know about right or wrong. It was God's place, set up for man. We are sure that your whole life you have been told how great a place the garden was, but have you really thought about why it was such a wonderful place, and why they were banished from the garden?

> Genesis 3:24 (NIV) - *after He drove the man out, He placed on the east side of the Garden of Eden cherubim and a flaming sword flashing back and forth to guard the way to the tree of life.*

Because of Adam, both had to leave the garden. It seems that the reason they had to leave was because of the Tree of Life. Adam had already eaten from the Tree of the Knowledge of Good and Evil.

> Genesis 3:6 (NIV) - *When the woman saw that the fruit of the tree was good for food and pleasing to the eye, and also desirable for gaining wisdom, she took some and ate it. She also gave some to her husband, who was with her, and he ate it.*

We know that some biblical scholars will not agree, but the writing says her husband was with her. Adam was there. He didn't try to stop her. He didn't put his foot down and say we can't do that. No, he let the woman be tempted. That is why Adam should be blamed for the fall, not the woman! To us, it would seem that the two were just living. They were to look after the garden.

After studying this section a number of times, we must say this next piece. This may sound like a very unusual statement, but here goes: It doesn't seem like they were that bright.

Adam was with the woman when the serpent was talking to her.

The woman gets the blame for eating the fruit, then telling Adam to eat, but Adam is the reason they had to leave. At least that is what Genesis 3:24 states.

After that, God drove the MAN out! Stop blaming the woman. I said the woman, because she didn't get a name until after the eating of the fruit.

We had the woman made from Adam's ribs, the serpent talked to the woman and tempts both, the Lord God comes to the garden and can't find them, God's told what happened, confronts the serpent, the woman, the man, then the woman gets a name in Genesis 3:20.

God sets the rules in place and doesn't change them. We break them, bend them, ignore them, we even try to explain them in a way so they fit our situation. But the Father who is in control of everything doesn't change.

One rule is that man dies. We will see death, even if we are here when Christ returns. The Bible says you will be changed in the twinkling of an eye, at the last trumpets call.

We don't believe that the Father will look down and say, "See that couple, I made George lose his hair, get fake teeth, and hearing aids. I'll change the rules for him."

No. The rules are the rules, and they must be followed! There are no exceptions! We need to be that good to please the Father. Are we, or do we just think we are that good? Some believe that if our good outweighs our bad—because we have more good than bad—that must mean we will be good enough for Heaven. For those people, here is a shocker: That doesn't work. It never has, and never will!

Our question is, in the Old Testament, where did people go when they died? We know the most advertised answer is Heaven or Hell. Let's take a look at what some of the Word says.

Did the Father change the rules?

Genesis 5:24 (NIV) - *Enoch walked faithfully with God; then he was no more, because God took him away.*

Hebrews 11:5 (NIV) - *By faith Enoch was taken from this life, so that he did not experience death: He could not be found, because God had taken him away. For before he was taken, he was commended as one who pleased God.*

Now we know someone is thinking, that means God changed the rules. How about when Elisha saw Elijah, go in a whirlwind up to Heaven, taken by a chariot and horses of fire in 2 Kings 2:11? Is that changing His rules?

After all, Noah saved mankind. Joseph helped the children of Israel from starving, King David was a man after God's own heart. Solomon was so wise, he had seven hundred wives of royal birth, and three hundred concubines. (I really don't know how smart that would be.) Yet, Noah, Joseph, King David, and Solomon all died.

That makes Enoch and Elijah that much more interesting. We still don't believe God changed the rules, we believe He blessed those two. Can you imagine what those two were really like, for the Father to bless them in that manner? We look at people we respect a lot and the people who influence others in their way of belief, yet they all have already died or will die in the future.

Now to our original question, where did the individuals go when they died in the Old Testament? We believe the answer needs to fit the Old and the New.

Look at Luke 16:19-31, the story of the rich man and poor Lazarus. One interpretation says that it's a parable, others say it's just a story. Make up your own mind and conclude what you want. The Christian in us says it's a parable.

Could it have been a true event told by the Messiah? Yeshua was a Jew, and as far as we have found in the Jewish faith, both the Old and New Testament times, The Hebrew word Sh'ol (in Greek Ades) refers to a place of the dead.

It is a place of not only punishment, but also a place of Gan-Eden. That means literally, Garden of Eden. In the Old Testament, the Hebrews referred to Gan-Eden as Abraham's side, or Abraham's Bosom!

Most people will not agree because they have already heard or read somewhere, that what the Children of Israel, God's chosen People, believe and accept is wrong.

You can make up your own mind. What you believe one way or the other about Abraham's Bosom will not get you out of Hell or into Heaven. What we will say is, that if The Messiah said today you will be with me in Paradise, then to Paradise you go. Like we stated before, the Hebrews say Abraham's side (which is Paradise).

We are not here to change your way of believing. We're not here to say believe the way we believe. But what we want is you to look into scripture and learn. We don't want you to believe the Pentecostal way, nor the Baptist way, nor the Catholic way. We believe you need to study to find your way. We hope that you study with an open mind, to what the Word is really saying, not being lead down that large interstate by some denomination. Again, study to find truth!

We don't study the New Testament without studying the Old Testament. In our opinion, that would be ignoring the rest of the Book! It does take a lot longer to get an answer, because we won't tell you what a certain denomination wants you to believe.

STUDY

In the Old and the New did really, really good people die? Yes they did. Do really, really bad people die? We know they do. Did they go to Heaven or Hell before the Messiah was here the first time? That is what we are trying to get you to study.

We believe that the original holding place was Abraham's Bosom, where one could see some sort of torment and see some sort of paradise. In our opinion, Paradise and Abraham's Bosom were one and the same. That is what Christ was referring to when he told the thief, when he was dying, "Today you will be with me in Paradise."

HATRED TOWARD THE
JEWISH NATION

It is a shame that the people who hate the Jewish Nation have such an influence on the people and culture of today! We still have countries whose main goal is to wipe out the Jews all together, while other countries look the other way. What is the difference between those countries and what Hitler did, or tried to do? The evil people of today get most of the headlines and TV programs. Why is that? Because the evil headlines sell TV time and newspapers.

Why do the people who say they back Israel, most of the time just sit on their hands? It's as if they are saying, "That's their business, not mine!" While the people and countries who want the destruction of Israel also want the destruction of the United States, England, and most of the free world if you don't see eye to eye with them! Will these countries, that don't want to help Israel, want the United States to help them when they are attacked? Will they stand with America when they come after us? They already want our destruction. It's just we're a little bigger and stronger than Israel, so the haters want to get Israel out of the way first.

We have people of influence trying to bring division in the United States right now. We have so called leaders who like nothing better than to condone breaking the law. We have politicians who count on the people who break the laws to get themselves elected. Corruption has taken a toll on the people who say that the laws should be carried out. Fast talking people get others to follow a philosophy that has only self-gratification as the main goal. We want self-gratification in our lives, but not at the cost of others or the destruction of our society, country, or our freedom!

People get so distracted by outside activities that they lose focus on the goal. Winning becomes the only thing, even if one has to cheat or break the law to achieve it. It's that way in religion, government, and sports. In sports, it seems that people don't care if their team or favorite player cheats, as long as their team wins. You may win the match, tournament, playoff game, but where is their integrity? Do they have any integrity at all if they had to cheat in the first place? The football game, golf tournament, or even the president of the United States winning the election by means of not telling the truth... we ask the individual, at what cost is the prize won or the election counted as a victory, if you are, and always will be labeled a cheat or a liar?

Life is too short. We need to stand for what is right! We need to stand with individuals who have integrity; the ones who don't and won't cheat! They are hard to find in our society but there are a few.

Individuals or corporations are influencing the youth of today by making it look good, even profitable, to cheat as long as you may win a large amount of money, get a ring, or are praised by people who have the same kind of integrity as you do. Remember, cheaters are still cheaters and liars always will be known as liars! The result is what we have today: an over abundance of arrogance, people building themselves up with self-pride, and a society with no integrity at all!

The selfish attitude is why and how individuals and countries can turn their backs on Israel. The people have taken their eyes off the prize, off the chosen people, off the Messiah and His leading. All they are achieving is wood, hay and stubble that one day will burn up. Then they will find they have achieved nothing but ashes! We need to start with the Glory God has given us, and that starts with INTEGRITY!

DECEPTION: SATAN'S MAIN WEAPON!

It started in the garden. It keeps growing each and every day, week, month, and year. It keeps growing as time goes by.

The Jews were deceived by other countries. The deception came in the form of those other countries' riches, size, beauty, and lifestyle. The Jews had it all, and at times lost it all, for various reasons. They wanted a king, like other countries. Maybe they thought that would make them stronger or at least look that way. They wanted what other countries had, instead of just a number of leaders for them and their religion.

We think of people who were and are what we call religious. We think of a meek, mild, soft pushover in life. What a deception we have! (1) The leaders of Israel had to be great warriors! They fought for respect all the time. (2) Abraham got mad enough to fight for his relative when Lot was taken. (3) Moses led the Hebrews in a lot of dangerous situations. (4) Joshua attacked places all the time while leading the Jews into and toward the Promised Land. (5) David became a great king, was a warrior, and won many battles.

There are many more but we have decided to name just one more:

(7) Yeshua was a great Son, a fighter against Satan, a man with lots of power, and strong enough to whip people when they were doing wrong. He confronted evil and won, with all authority, wisdom, and he knew when to use it! We wonder why some call religious people weak. Could it be the philosophy of today, or that we are looked at, in that manner. The meek

shall inherit the earth. We haven't found where it say let the immoral run over the believer so you won't hurt someone's feelings.

The deception of interpretations is that they seem to want to powder puff religion.

God is the God of love and He shows that all the time. When your child does something wrong, you need to correct him and need to punish him if he doesn't listen, just like our Father does His children. In our society today, the deception is, you shouldn't punish your children. Look what we have now! There are people who say that the next generation is better equipped because they were not corrected when doing something wrong. We don't know how else to put this: how much more bull do we have to put up with… when the criminal has more rights than the victims do, and the people we have elected go right along with it?

Our opinion is our opinion and everyone has their own! If you correct your child and punish him when he deserves it, he will grow to the point where he will correct himself before he does the wrong he shouldn't do. If you train a child when they are young, the child will grow with respect for authority, respect themselves, and respect other persons and property. If this were to happen, society wouldn't be in the mess we have today with young people getting into trouble with police, school, and families.

There is a difference between correcting a child as a teaching tool and doing an abusive act of violence! We know that the parents who abuse their children get all the publicity. They should go to jail for their act of violence toward their child. However, to take the correction out of the hands of the parents who want the best for their child's upbringing—to teach the child right from wrong—is one of the stupidest intrusions possible by the government into our family lives. The government is telling us how to raise our children. They want us to follow their rules and their "norm." That hasn't worked very well, plus it has turned into one of the most undermining acts of parenting in the world. Look how it has changed our society!

When you undermine the parents (and we can also include the teachers), how do the smart people in government plan on bringing up the child? Did they want the street gangs to take over parenting? How about the sex that seems to be running wild in schools now? This one act of stupidity by the government has brought about the demise of a whole society of young people!

If you look at our country today, with all the deceptions towards the undermining of authority, it looks like a weapon from Satan. It may bring the downfall of our society from within! We know that there are people who say that it can't happen here; we are too big and strong for that to take place! All we have to say is, that is what every country must have believed before their fall. A good example is Russia. It seems that we are running away from God, the Father, like Israel did a number of times in the Old Testament. Do you remember what God let happen, even to his Chosen People, when their leaders decided to go their way and turn their backs on His leading?

The Government should stop interfering with the Family and the raising of our children! We should punish the ones who abuse, but let the parents take control back. We need to take our hats off to the young people of today when they don't turn to drugs or gangs. With the lack of real leadership in our country and the court system we have today, it's no wonder. With the peer pressure in the schools and on our streets, they seem to be the ones influencing our young people. They follow someone that shows a strong authority figure!

The Supreme Court should be embarrassed on a lot of their decisions. They seem to go down party lines, yet they are sworn to uphold the laws that are made by Congress. The court has no authority to make the laws, so stop trying to change history to make a certain person or political party look better!

Remember: GOD doesn't need us, but WE need him!

WHEN JUDAH WAS IN TROUBLE, GOD SENT JEREMIAH

People of today, as in the past, have double standards. They want to receive from God, without God Himself! They want God as long as He doesn't interfere with their daily life or interrupt their life style. Most believe that we live for God as long as we enter a building that's called church.

> Jeremiah 2:21-22 (NIV) - *"I had planted you like a choice vine of sound and reliable stock. How then did you turn against me into a corrupt wild vine? Although you wash yourself with soap and use an abundance of cleansing powder, the stain of your guilt is still before me," declares the Sovereign Lord.*

Society has taken the choice vine and twisted that vine, to almost exclude truth. At the same time, they are including a corrupt wild vine as their truth. They believe (and some preach) that you can believe how you want, you can use any name, follow any individual, walk any path, as long as you read a certain version or use enough soap while taking a bath, and that atones for turning away from God.

All you are really trying to do is make yourself smell better here on earth. But let us inform you that the stink still reaches the One in control. We know that most people are saying, "I would never do that!" Most people will adhere to the truth in Jeremiah 2:27:

> Jeremiah 2:27 (NIV) - *They say to wood, you are my father; and to stone, you gave me birth; They have turned their backs*

to me and not their faces; yet when they are in trouble, they
say, Come and save us!

Most people believe in the last part, but you still live your lives in the first part. Some will say that was in the Old Testament.

Now we know none of Jeremiah 2:21-22 or 27 make you think of what society has become today, and surely not to those church people, or not in MY church. GET REAL. The only things that have changed might be the names of the people, the way they pretend to follow God's commands, what the so-called God's people call themselves. All worship a god of money, wood or stone.

The god of materialistic venture (wood), the god of stone (church building), and the god of greed (money) are just a few. But the point isn't that we can't have nice things. The point is, do we put anything before our God? The Children of Israel's lifestyle during the Old Testament times aren't the model we should be following, but we seem to do as bad or even worse in our society today.

It would seem that the level of corrupt living has now been raised to a new high standard. In far too many cases, God has been escorted out of our society, out of our churches, out of our schools, and into the forgotten realm of our existence. God's not done with us, even though we act just like Jeremiah 2:20

> Jeremiah 2:20 (NIV) - *long ago you broke off your yoke and tore off your bonds; you said, I will not serve you! Indeed, on every high hill and under every spreading tree you lay down as a prostitute.*

That is just what the world has done now. You think that people would have learned through history what not to do, but like a dog we seem to keep going back to our vomit!

The time is coming when you will see and want to serve, but who will be the One that really accepts your sacrifice? People have already chosen their leader, who will be served by them, who they will follow into everlasting joy or everlasting torment!

A bigger house doesn't mean God has blessed you. A new vehicle doesn't show His love for you. More money isn't Adonai (the Lord) paying you back for something. The quiet time doesn't mean He's taking a break. Peace isn't what you should always desire, although most of us do. We believe that there is such a thing as peace before the storm.

People take certain verses and say, "Peace be with you." That's all fine and good until it's time for the storm. When you take a look at society today, do you really believe, the Triune God of the Universe, is smiling and saying I love what you're doing? Maybe he is saying, "Do you even try to keep my commands? Do you call on the true name of My Son? You worship me with all your being, as long as it's your way!"

Even considering nations, people, society, and everything else that has happened in the past, we haven't learned from History. They seem to put their heads in the sand and believe if it looks good, then God must be behind it.

Everyone is in a time of their own. There is a time to be born and a time to die. We believe it's time to follow Adonai (the Lord), The Triune God of the Universe. It is time to put God in front of ourselves, time for family to be second, time for God to not be in the center, but to be lifted to the head. It's time for everything to be no more than second best in our lives: our homes, our families, our jobs, our outside interest, our investments. Everything has to take a back seat to Adonai, our Lord.

Most people will say that's what they already do. When tax time comes, how many take this little deduction that everyone gets, even if you didn't really deserve it? We have seen people who will stretch the truth or not tell the whole truth to get rid of something or to buy something, as long as the Christian gets the best deal! Then they say something like, "That must have been God!"

No. It's being deceitful, it's cheating, not the way God would want you to act or how he would want you to handle it! But wait a minute! The Christian got the best deal! What we ask is, at what cost do you put your claim?

Remember if you lay down with a prostitute, you're a prostitute! God plants a sound reliable vine, but when we prostitute ourselves, we become the wild vine going our own way and doing our own thing. We believe and convince others that our wild vine is an offshoot of His vine.

We are trying to convince others that we are being accepted by Adonai as being His chosen, when in reality we are leading more and more people into the wild vineyard to walk their own way, to commit adultery, steal, murder, or puts other gods before The Lord. Then we come to God and say that we know we are safe, even though we have condoned and do detestable things.

This might be a good time to read and learn what God told his Prophet in Jeremiah 11:14.

> Jeremiah 11:14 (NIV) - *Do not pray for this people or offer any plea or petition for them, because I will not listen when they call to me in the time of their distress.*

That just might be a good study. Jeremiah was told what not to do for God's chosen people because of their wicked ways. With the way our government and churches have gone, we need to take a good look at their wicked ways. We might just be getting close to our wicked ways right now!

God told Jeremiah, "Don't pray for them, I've had enough I won't listen to them or you, if you pray for them!"

Now that is scary! To have The King of the Universe tell you don't even pray for them because they have gone far enough, then one would have to wonder how far off track they must have gone for God to do such a thing?

Do you think they kicked God out of their schools, off the public buildings, permitted anything to go on? But if you bring up God you may be offending someone, so you must be quiet about that kind of stuff.

What about some of the churches who have permitted this to happen in their congregations? Their denominational bosses must have instructed their preachers, what and how they should preach as to not offend anyone. They decide who they let preach and why they let them preach. The list goes on and on, but we hope you get the picture before it's too late!

TEMPLE

Through the centuries, people have had the feeling of great joy, because they feel they know The Lord personally. The time for the joy of the Lord is complete and full in this time. Each individual is responsible for his own sin!

We believe the time is near for The Temple to be rebuilt in Yerushalayim (Jerusalem in English). WHY? Because the individual has done what the individual wants with scripture. They have taken the Word and modernized it to the point that it has become a show for certain people. The Temple is God's desire for Jerusalem, for mankind. It is a dwelling place for each follower of the Father.

God's chosen people messed up and were sent into exile. They came to the Promised Land, built a temple (a permanent place of worship), it was destroyed, and they went into exile again. In 538 BC, the Persian King Cyrus let the Jewish people return to rebuild the temple, but they didn't get it accomplished. The Hebrews again received the right to rebuild the Temple in 521 BC, after King Darius Hystaspis made his decree that the Temple was to be finished!

Now, Christ is the Temple. He is the one we go through. But the scriptures state that the Temple in Jerusalem will be destroyed. It also says the Temple must be rebuilt for the worship of His people.

Man overlooks the importance of that one small point. Why does the Temple need to be rebuilt, why can't we just stand on the street corner and beg God for the fulfillment of history? Because the House of God in the Holy Land of Israel, the Temple in Yerushalayim (Jerusalem) has to be rebuilt. Those are not my words. They are God's words!

Many of the houses of worship have become social clubs. They are a place to get together and eat, play bingo, listen to some feel good message, so you can go home and be happy. Far too often, you hear a message where the preacher has an "I syndrome" in most of his sermons. If you listen to some preachers, you will always hear the sermons tell you if you're poor, it's your fault. They will say God wants you blessed and maybe rich like them.

There are far too many preachers who must feel they do not need to tell the whole truth! Their job must be to bring up some point that will get you to come forward, whatever that means. They teach that if you feel good about yourself or good about what you're doing, then that must be God.

Now we see why the scripture says that the Temple needs to be rebuilt. The True Temple for Yeshua Worship. A Temple of Pure Worship without the influence of the world.

Do we believe that it will ever happen? YES! Do we believe that we will see it? NO! That's our personal opinion. We rather doubt we will see it. It would be nice to see, but will it happen in our lifetime? We don't think so. The fact is, according to scripture, it will take place before the Lord returns. The Temple is the Temple. We, as believers, need the Temple in Jerusalem so we can get back on track with the King of the Temple in Heaven!

To get things right, we do not need the feel good stuff that most preachers are spreading throughout the world these days. We do need to believe scripture and look forward to the Temple being rebuilt.

The time for The Temple could be very close or it may be a long, long way off. That's God's timing, not ours. We do believe that we need to remember the one thing that will get the ball rolling is the leaders of the Hebrews, the Jews, must accept and ask for the Lord's return.

WEARING A HAT WHILE PRAYING

There have been a number of sermons about men wearing a hat while praying. One verse they point to is, 1 Corinthians 11:4. Let's look at two translations of this verse:

> 1 Corinthians 11:4 (NIV) - *Every man who prays or prophesies with his head covered dishonors his head.*

> 1 Corinthians 11:4 (CJB) - *Every man who prays or prophesies wearing something down over his head brings shame to his head.*

That brings us to write about the Jewish Kippah (the skullcap). It is worn by a large number of Jews. What we have been able to find is that there seems to be no scriptural basis for wearing one. In the Orthodox Jewish viewpoint, the Kippah itself didn't become mandatory until the 16th century. As a matter of fact, until the 12th or 13th century, kippahs (skullcaps) weren't worn very often at all.

In the Jewish faith, the Tallit (prayer shawl) is like a veil to provide intimacy and create privacy between you and God. Remember, in verse 4 it states that, "Every man who prays or prophesies with his head covered or wearing something down over his head brings shame to his head."

There may be something about those two wordings that don't really see eye to eye. In one, "with his head covered" may mean that you are wearing a hat. The other states that you shouldn't wear something down over your head. Most of us look at those writings and think they mean somewhat the same thing, but they are totally different. To us, they both seem to be man-made customs. They may sound spiritual and may look spiritual, but in reality they are man-made customs only.

During the time when the Lord walked on the earth, Jewish men did wear what is called a Tzitzit on the fringe of their garments. These fringes on the corner of their garments were to remind God's people to obey his commandments. Today, Jewish men wear tzitziyot on their tallit gadol (large tallit), which is not an article of clothing. Instead, it is a ritual cloth donned primarily for synagogue worship. Yeshua wore His on His robe, which was a small heavy blanket made from a piece of cloth.

Paul was talking to the people who worshipped in Corinth. They may have had questions for him and wanted him to straighten things up in their order of worship. They wanted to know why certain people did certain things in their service, and maybe even how men and women should dress or wear their hair. We need to remember that in Paul's time, if a woman had her arm exposed, it was considered flirting.

> 1 Corinthians 14:36 (NIV) - *Or did the word of God originate with you? Or are you the only people it has reached?*

We need to remember that in the Corinthian place of worship, there were groups of Gentiles and Messianic Jews. In our opinion, Paul was asking the Gentiles, "Did the Word of God originate with you?" The answer is no, it originated with the Jewish people!

In other words, don't make up your own practices and force others to believe that God changes so you have a feel good religion (like more and more churches in this day and age are doing). God set the rules in place and the Lord followed the rules.

God also told the leaders of the Jewish faith when and how they were wrong. We need to understand that the feel good stuff we keep getting from a lot of the Christian teachings are just fluff to make you feel better about yourself and what you are doing. The Lord followed the rules made by the Father, not the rules made up by man. We should do the same. Paul was a Hebrew, and he kept the original Hebrew rules.

This next part may make a lot of people uneasy. Paul wanted everyone to follow the rules about what the Father wanted for us. It was not to start a new faith, but to embellish on God—the One we all should be looking for. That doesn't mean the Christian faith is wrong, but it does hint that the people who look down on the Jewish faith should be ashamed of themselves. Not because they are wrong, but because the Hebrews are God's Chosen People and will always be God's Chosen People.

> 1 Corinthians 14:40 (NIV) - *But everything should be done in a fitting and orderly way.*

Paul was saying that there should be order in the service. If you don't have that, there will be people who miss out because of the disruption. The problem isn't what is preached or the timing, but the other activities going on around them.

There are too many people who get caught up with the role of women, because Paul wrote that women should be silent in the church. 1 Corinthians 14:34 most likely that was for the place of worship in Corinth.

FROM THE GRAVE

What would the people who molded our history say about the world right now? Would they say that is why we did what we did? Or would they be saying that's not how we instructed, guided, lead, swayed or pointed any of you? What happened to you? Did you feel that you were too smart to believe the way we instructed you?

Here are a number of thoughts that we came up with, for the fun of looking at the comments these people may be saying right now in this time in history:

ADAM- "Look at what we started!"

ENOCH- "Boy am I glad I left when I did!"

NOAH- "We can't build another boat! What do you want the Father to do, start out all over again?"

ABRAHAM- "I walked by faith, but the people now seem to walk with a blindfold on. What happened?"

JOSEPH- "You had your beautiful fat cow. If you don't change, be ready for some ugly ones!"

MOSES- "After the firstborn and the Red Sea, don't drown on ignorance!"

JOSHUA – "Listen people: If you want the walls to fall, you have to be willing to trust the One who can!"

STUDY

DANIEL- "If you expect to get bit, whether you're in a lion's den or in the world of today, you better have a lot of band-aids to cover the marks!"

SHADRACH, MESHACH, and ABEDNEGO- "Fire burns and purifies, but faith preserves!"

ELIJAH- "Either you believe or not, I still like chariots and horses!"

ELISHA- "Look around you and see the people. From what I see, you better not pick on us bald people!"

JAMES- "If you believe in him or not, my brother was AWESOME!!!"

JOHN- "You wouldn't believe what I saw with my own eyes!"

SAUL- "Change my name and call me home!"

GEORGE WASHINGTON- "I lead you into battle… but I won't be, nor do you need, a dictator! You have had some who have held this office, they think they were, the dictator this country needed, but that also came at a price for you!"

ABRAHAM LINCOLN- "One thing this country doesn't need is more actors!"

POLITICIANS OF TODAY- "Talk is cheap. Our promises were hollow and quite far from the truth!"

ABRAHAM: A GREAT MAN IN SCRIPTURE

Let's start at the beginning with Adam. In Genesis 1:26, God made man. By chapter 3, Adam was blaming God for his own fall because He gave Adam the woman. Adam avoided responsibility and blamed others (sounds like the politicians of today). It took until Adam was 235 years old for people to call on Adonai (my Lord, in the English language). In other words, it took longer for people to acknowledge the Lord, than the length of time the United States has been a nation. Interesting, isn't it?

Adam and Eve talked and walked with God, but they didn't call on the Lord. Cain talked with God, but he didn't seem to worry about his doing wrong or ask for forgiveness. Cain only worried about what may affect him. Genesis 4:26 says that some 235 years after the creation of man was when people began to call on the name of the Lord (Adonai).

Abram's name was changed to Abraham, and he became the father of the Hebrew Nation. We believe he was also the father of the Arab Nations. Remember, his son Ismael was the father of twelve tribes, believed to be the tribes of the Arab Nations (Genesis 17:20).

Back to Abraham: he lied, or you could say he distorted the truth. Sometimes he would stand up to defend what was his. He also met Melchizedek and he rescued Lot. It seems Lot was the relative who was always in the wrong place at the wrong time.

Abram was born about 2166 BC. The Egyptians came up with ink and parchment paper around 2500 BC. From time of 2500 BC and back to the beginning of time, we would have to say would have been a long, long time, either with evolution or creation. We would say that Noah building the Ark would have to be classified as undated.

Creation itself is undated. We like to think we know, but like so many other things, we would have to admit it's nothing more than a guess. Maybe some people want to call it an educated guess, but it's still a guess.

The time between Adam and the flood can be somewhat counted in ages of men. Yet some say their ages overlap. Do we really know? Does it make a difference to you or history if we are right or wrong?

History is still history, the past is still the past, and the future is still the future. Even if no one agrees with you or us, it doesn't change those events.

God didn't tell Adam to take a rock and chisel out a 0, then count 365 nights and days, then chisel a 1 for the first year. Then he would have had to chisel out a 4000 or 6000 then go down to 0. If they would have done that, then you could live like the devil all the time and when year 5 came you could have started to live like the Father wanted you to. We said 5 just on case someone forgot to chisel a year or two during those 6000 years.

Here is something interesting to think about. Ask yourself, what are the names of the Gentiles of the past who you would have liked to have met? Here are a few people: George Washington, Abe Lincoln, any President, maybe the King and Queen of England.

How about this group of people: Adam and Eve, Abel, then there is Enoch.

> Genesis 5:24 (NIV) - *Enoch walked faithfully with God; then he was no more, because God took him away.*

It says he lived 365 years. Can you imagine, having lived up to God's love so much that the God of the Universe would take you so you never had to die?

Methuselah lived 969 years, according to scripture.

Then there is Noah. Now there is a real great guy. He's not in the same category as Enoch, but God told him how to save himself and his whole family from the flood that was coming, 8 people in all.

Shem was another Gentile. He was Noah's son, and that tribe was where the Hebrews came from.

By the way, so was King David. He was a guy after God's own heart (but he died).

How about our Messiah? He also came from the ancestral line of King David, who was a descendant of Shem, a Gentile until Abraham!

After King David, we get the smartest man alive, Solomon. In 1 Kings 11:3 it says he had 700 wives of royal birth and 300 concubines. He may have been the smartest person alive, but what would anyone do with that many wives and concubines? We would not want to be that smart.

YESHUA

Many people have a vague belief in God, but refuse to accept YESHUA as anything more than a great human teacher. The Bible does not allow that option! Most do not even recognize that if you want a true Messiah, you have to call on the true Messiah.

This may sound like a kind of a repeat, but it is the most important message of this whole writing.

Most people have never heard the Messiah's name. They may have heard of a name to worship other than the Father's one and only son. There have been songs written about Him, religions have used a name in their organizations, they pray to the other names, and their beliefs are in the other name.

The God of the universe is a stern God. He will not tolerate wrong. He will not say, "Oh well, they may get it right next time." We don't believe He thinks, "Sooner or later they will come around." It's not a waiting game for the Father. It's now or never.

Imagine you had a son who died at the age of 33. When he was born you named him Mark, but after his death people always called him Fred. Now, Mark was your only child and you loved him more than anyone or anything. Would it upset you that people disrespected you and Mark so much that when talking to you they would use Fred, even after they were told by someone that the name they are using is disrespectful to you, his parent?

Then you have people who say, "It's OK, because you know they are talking about Mark when using Fred." Would you want to listen at all when people used the name Fred? Don't you think the Father is the same way? When the children of Israel did stuff wrong, even though they thought they were doing right, the Father didn't say, "That's OK. They're just a little confused on the word to use."

Do you think the Father thought that if the children of Israel had been doing something wrong for hundreds and hundreds of years, maybe *He* should change *His* rules or terminology so what they say will be fine, as long as enough people believe in Fred?

Our answer is NO! You wouldn't like it. We believe the God of the Universe doesn't like it either. His NAME is and always will be Yeshua; by no other name can one be saved.

It isn't Yeshua today, Jesus tomorrow, Iesous yesterday. It's YESHUA today, tomorrow, and forever. There's no substitute name and no other name means the same! There is only One Son, with one name. All others are just names.

People can pretend the other names are the ones that the Father calls His Son. You can even worship one of the other names. You can pray to him, bow down to him and even die believing you're worshiping the Lord every time you use Fred or one of those other names.

Even if hundreds of millions of people believe a certain way, that doesn't make it right. If it's wrong, it's wrong. Even if your parents, wife, husband, child, grandchild, or you follow Fred, then they all follow an imitation of the Real Son.

If a loved one has gone by the way of the grave, like both of our parents and my five brothers have, without this concept, there is still time for people to come to the truth and believe in only "YESHUA."

We may have failed them by not getting this message to them soon enough, or maybe we didn't stress it strong enough. We told each of our brothers, whether they believed it or not. Now that's up to them. Like everyone else, even if no one accepts this, that's their choice.

We read that when Jeremiah spoke to Judah, nobody listened to him either. We, in no way, put ourselves up to the status of Jeremiah. However, knowing that about him makes us feel a little less of a failure, because not many want to listen to us when we speak about the Son's only name.

Does the Father look down and say, "I know who they mean." Or does the Parent look down and say, "That's not the name I gave My Son, you might as well use Fred!"

THREE TOPICS

1) The Separate
2) The If
3) The We

(1) The separate. A preacher stated in a Wednesday night service, that the reason the Lord hasn't come back yet is His love for mankind, because the Father wants as many people as possible to get saved first. He is waiting for the people to accept Him, so out of love for us, He is waiting. He thinks that's the reason The Lord hasn't returned. We still have no idea where he came up with that notion, or why a preacher would make a statement like that. He stated nothing about the Father having set times or dates, like in the Messiahs statement. It's only based on Christians and how many Christians, according to him. It was another feel-good service, that gets his congregation feeling good about themselves. In our opinion, if the Father is waiting for anyone, He is waiting for the Jewish leaders to accept the Lord!

(2) The If. If people overly serve any person, then who is their real God? Respect is one thing, but worshiping a man (or person) is what makes Satan happy! When Satan influences a pastor (or any person), then Satan gets what he wants. Other things have that individual's attention, be it money, size of a congregation, a TV ministry, the kind of music, missions, traveling for God, staying in one spot for God. Many try to make what they really desire most look like it's God's will in their life. Examples of this would be making motorcycles a ministry, trucks a ministry, or cars a ministry. A very convincing person is able to get others to see God in whatever makes them happy. I said, makes *them* happy, not necessarily makes *God* happy. We believe God likes it when you take Him with you, but not as a billboard to what you have done.

There are people and preachers who get what they desire by schemes. They can convince the church board they need to have more time away from church. They say, that's Gods calling on their life. The person may have figured out a way to make money, and at times a lot of money, by just getting others to do the work for him, by taking advantage of the brainwashed congregation to do their work for him. While it's true other people may have been helped, the real big benefit goes to the pastor. The real misconception is that when the person says stuff like, "It's because of you people, I can do this or that." The real point is, he is getting cheap labor and is getting what he needs and wants, while you are buying into his idea. Even if, in the grand scheme of things, it's helping others, who is the one who is being helped the most?

The Preacher may be able to brag about everything that has been accomplished; the food, shoes, and blankets, whatever the gifts are. Then they make all the people who did the actual labor feel good with a comment like, "I couldn't have done that without your help! It's because of you I did this or that, if you weren't serving God, I wouldn't be able to do what I do for those people or God." We call this the "I syndrome."

There is truth that people in our country and other countries were blessed by food, shoes, and blankets while the preacher got most of the acclaim of the job well done. There is a sense of pride that people get while helping others.

God does bless a cheerful giver. Some people really give until it hurts, and then there are people who convince the person who gave until it hurts, the more you give, the better off you will be, while they themselves are lining their pockets and their future on the backs of the giver. What a shame! We guess the term slave labor doesn't fit IF people are convinced that it's what they should do to serve God, while other people prosper on the backs of good-hearted individuals.

If Satan is smart enough to let people get the blessing they want when they worship a savior other then the true Messiah, then isn't that his Job? Since there is only one Messiah and people worship many messiahs, isn't

Satan getting the job done? If you worship any of the other messiahs, does Satan have to do anything more? Can't he just sit back and let you worship anyone you desire? Are you brainwashed to believe a certain way of interpreting scripture? If you pray to the Father and He answers your prayer, does that mean you're saved, or does it mean He heard your prayer and answered it? Do you believe that Christians are the only ones who get their prayers answered? If you believe that, then what about before you called yourself saved and something went wrong and you prayed. Did He answer your prayer, or was it just a coincidence?

(3) The we. We are not Jewish and don't pretend to be. We realize that our Messiah was Jewish and His name was Yeshua. We do have a corner of our dining room that has our Jewish symbols in it, which we picked up while visiting Israel. We acknowledge that some of the things the Jews and Messianic Jews do seem to be more in line with the Word of God than some of the stuff we have been instructed to do by the Christian denominations we've learned from. We believe the Father has forgiven us and looks past our faults. Why? We believe the real reason is we worship His son, Yeshua! People need to learn that His Son is on the other side of a very small gate. He stated very few people will find it, and the path to Hell has a very large gate for the ones who don't know Him, or they worship a made up messiah. The scriptures are full of people who follow made up saviors, and even imitation gods. Scripture talks about God's chosen people being lead astray by the lust of the flesh, the look or beauty of the eyes, the desire of money or the power that comes with it. Are we saying money is wrong? No! Are we saying that a beautiful person should be shunned? No! But don't let money or beauty lead you down the wrong path, to that very large gate.

There is only One God, One Son who is our Savior. If anybody has already gone through the small gate, they need to keep walking, feeling the grass between their toes. There are so few on that path the grass still grows along the way! Not like the path to the large gate where the grass would be worn down by the multitude of people, working for the desires of the world, while thinking they have found the truth while worshiping a made up name, person, or religion!

It's not our job or duty to preach to people so they don't go to Hell. We feel it's our mission to tell the truth and just maybe someone will get their eyes opened and feel that grass between their toes on the path to that small gate. After writing and talking, we believe it's not our responsibility to drag you onto that path! Choose your path. It's totally up to you where your final home is.

Most people—we would have to guess about 98% – don't like what we say. That's fine with us, because most likely it's where or what they want, be it a feel good sermon, or a song that brings goose bumps. Maybe if they believe something different, other than what their brainwashed ideas are, they feel like they turned their back on their loved ones who have preceded them in death. The place of damnation is going to be a very crowded place after Yeshua returns!

Do we have all the answers? NO! We don't think or pretend to have all the answers. What we have done over the last 30+ years is to search for truth, not some feel good part of a sermon or a preacher with an "I syndrome." The focus shouldn't be on what he has done, or how successful his scheme seems to be. The trouble is, he can make everyone feel good about him getting very wealthy.

We are blessed and would love to be rich, would love to get wisdom beyond measure, would love to have each of our sons and their families get in line about this truth. Like everyone else, that's their choice, not mine or my wife's. The message is for them, just like everyone else. Which path they take is totally up to them. We can't make that decision for them!

WHAT ABOUT THE END TIMES?

Most religions of the world don't know about the end times, or they just choose to ignore it. They don't believe in the Jewish Messiah. What is even sadder is the fact that the majority of the Jews don't accept the Jewish Messiah. The scriptures do state that the Jews will reject their Messiah. They may accept him as a good or great prophet, but not their Messiah.

We have found that most people who call themselves Christians have very little knowledge about the Messiah. There seems to be a lot of people who think because they're Americans, that means they are Christians. There are people who believe if they are good enough, they will surely be awarded Heaven. Then you have the people who believe if their good outweighs their bad, then they will enter the pearly gates. There are people who believe that once they say yes to the Lord, they have clear sailing to Heaven no matter what they say or how they act afterwards. We have met a few who believe everyone will be in Heaven. They say that God is a loving God and a loving God wouldn't send anyone to Hell. There are people who believe your life is predestined, and no matter what or how you act, you're going where God wants you to go. There are people who believe in order to really be forgiven of sin, you have to go to a human and confess what you've done wrong. Only then are your sins wiped clean. There are people who say, "I'm going to eat, drink and be merry, no matter what because this life is all there is." There are people who believe that you must speak in tongues to really receive from the Father. There are people who say it's too hard and they don't want to try. There are people who think that if all you have to do is believe then it's too easy. There must be more or harder things to do to be really saved from sin, so they get discouraged and don't try at all. There are people who say, "Why pray? God's going to do what's best for Him anyway. If a prayer is answered, it must have been a coincidence that something happened the way you prayed." There are people who believe that the Father won't forgive them because even after believing, they have been doing things they knew were wrong. And then there are people that don't believe the world will end by some religious war at all, but only when man messes things up so bad, the world can't take another billion years. (We guess we should have named this part, "There are people who believe…")

Now that we've tried to bring up as many beliefs as possible, here is another: The Father is in control and He already notified us, in scripture, what's going to happen!

Let's look at a couple places in scripture, Zechariah 14:1-8, and Revelation 19:11-21.

> Zechariah 14:1-2 (NIV) - *A day of the Lord is coming, Jerusalem, when your possessions will be plundered and divided up within your very walls. I will gather all the nations to Jerusalem to fight against it; the city will be captured, the houses ransacked, and the women raped. Half of the city will go into exile, but the rest of the people will not be taken from the city.*

In other words, the nations who want to destroy the Jews will attack Jerusalem, others will fight with them, send their approval or stand by pretending it's not their fight.

The city will fall into the hands of their enemies again. The city will be in turmoil, houses will be ransacked, and their things will be stolen, or taken for the worship of some pagan god. The Jews try to flee from the destruction. The Jewish women know that scripture states they will be raped. The strength of the women in the Jewish faith is amazing. We believe this doesn't necessarily refer only to the ladies over 18, but girls most likely as young as 8 years old. The rapist won't care the age, only that they can humiliate the God of Israel, by taking virgins and passing them around for multitudes of savages for their pleasure.

Stop right now and think about the courage of the women and the girls who are Jews, knowing that their prophet Zechariah wrote in 480 BC what will take place to them, if they are alive at that time in history. By that count, it has been about 2500 years ago, when their prophet saw what is going to happen. When you look at the brutality of that war and the things that have already been written about it, the price of being one of God's chosen will be very costly!

Most people in America worry about nothing compared to the truth from that prophet. We know there are people being raped everyday in the U.S. and around the world, but these ladies and young girls know it's coming when this war starts. Even though half the Jews will go into exile, there still will be Jews in Jerusalem. We know there have been wars in Jerusalem before, and some will say that has already happened. You're half right. It has happened before in Jerusalem up to that part, but in verse 5, it says, "The Lord my God will come, and all the holy ones with him." That hasn't happened before because it wasn't the last time!

In the book of the Revelation 19:11-21, it talks about a warrior on a white horse. The war is when all of Christ's enemies gather in one spot. This rider on the white horse is different than the rider of the white horse in Revelation 6:2. In 6:2, the white horse is one rider among many. These may be called the four horsemen of the Apocalypse, and they bring judgment, not relief. In other words, these riders bring judgment by war and conquest. But the rider in 19:11 is believed to be the Messiah. This rider brings God's covenant promises to all.

We would say that this may be the Battle of Armageddon. When you study 19:20-21, consider the part where it says the false prophet signs had deluded those who received the mark of the beast and worshiped his image. We ask, could it be that the diluting of the word leads to following an imaginary image of the Messiah himself, for the feel-good religions of the day?

With this in mind, look at the falsehood of the followers of today! If you say a certain phrase, it means you're saved. If you talk in tongues, it means you're saved and accept his gift. If you confess your sins to some man, you're forgiven. If you listen to certain songs, then you're a believer. IF, IF, IF.

The IFs are gaining ground with society today and the more IFs there are, seem to distract from the true word. People don't hear what the Lord stated in Matthew 7:23: "I NEVER KNEW YOU!"

Stop the IFs, right now! In your life, start your study with an open mind to the truth. Receive what the Father has already instructed. The preachers and teachers of today are leading people to follow their belief, philosophy, and their denominational doctrine—with their Ifs—and what they want you to hear!

MISCONCEPTION!

When a person studies Isaiah 59:20-21, they might get two different ideas. There is the Christian finding and then there is the Jewish finding. Please let us explain that last statement.

> Isaiah 59:20-21 (NIV) - *The redeemer will come to Zion, to those in Jacob who repent of their sins, declares the Lord. As for me, this is my covenant with them, says the Lord. My Spirit, who is on you, will not depart from you, and my words that I have put in your mouth will always be on your lips, on the lips of your children and on the lips of their descendants - from this time on and forever, says the Lord.*

We have read and heard some preach that this means Christians today are heirs of this prophecy, because of the Holy Spirit. Jews say those in Jacob who repent of their sins are Hebrews, therefore it pertains to the Jews.

If one studies Isaiah 59:20-21, you will see that the Father's Spirit was and will always be with his chosen people. Even if they turn away for a while, there still will be a group who believe. When a person studies, we find that the Big Misconception is that Isaiah was writing to the Gentiles or about them.

He makes it very clear while writing between the years of 700 BC to 681 BC, that out of Tziyon (Zion), which is the Old City Jerusalem, will come a redeemer to those in Jacob who repent. What most Christians miss is, that he said this is *my* covenant with *them*. When he talks about *them*, he was referring to the ones in Jacob. They are the Jewish Nation! Isaiah 27:2-13 talks about the time that is coming when Jacob (the Hebrews) will take root, Israel will bud and flower, the whole world will harvest, the Jews will be sent into exile, then one by one the Jews will be gathered, and the people of Israel will come back to the land of their Promise.

> Romans 11:28-29 (NIV) - *As far as the gospel is concerned, they are enemies for your sake; but as far as election is concerned, they are loved on account of the patriarchs, for God's gifts and his call are irrevocable.*

If 28 is written about the Jews, then so is 29. That means it is referring to Jews, not Christians at all. The question is, why are God's people so loved? It is not because of the phrase so often used by some misled Christians: "God is Love, that's why He loves us Christians."

You might say this sounds a little unspiritual, but the answer is in the scripture, "For the Patriarchs." Not because you say a few words and are convinced you're saved, not in your belief, not by how good they are, or how bad they were at one time. It is on account of the patriarchs, nothing else. It is because "God's gifts and his call are irrevocable" for all time. God promised this to his people, His Chosen People, the Hebrews!

The Hebrews were totally driven out of Jerusalem or they were killed in the war of 70 AD. The Jews scattered to places like Yavneh, Tiberias, Tzippori, and other locations throughout the land of Israel. While they were not in the city of Jerusalem, you could say they were in the land of Israel continuously since the time of King David.

When Yeshua returns, He will establish a literal Kingdom on this earth. Yes, on this earth! His Kingdom is here now in part. We, the believers in Yeshua, represent Him here now. But later, all real believers, those trusting in Yeshua, will be here with Him in His restored Kingdom of Paradise!

GOD'S MAIN GOAL

This may sound like a strange statement, but stay with us. God's main goal isn't to get us out of here with something called the rapture. God's main goal is to get Yeshua back to Jerusalem in all His fullness!

> Luke 21:24 (NIV) - *They will fall by the sword and will be taken as prisoners to all the nations. Jerusalem will be trampled on by the Gentiles until the time of the Gentiles are fulfilled.*

Yeshua made that statement when He was here. At the time, Jerusalem was under Roman control with their rules.

Consider the Prophecy in Psalm 79:1.

> Psalm 79:1 (NIV) - *O God, the nations have invaded your inheritance; they have defiled your holy temple, they have reduced Jerusalem to rubble.*

In that prophecy, the nations represent Gentiles.

> Isaiah 63:18b (KJV) - *our adversaries have trodden down our sanctuary.*

"Adversaries" represent Gentiles.

Take a look at Daniel 9:26.

> Daniel 9:26 (CJB) - *Then after the sixty-two weeks, Mashiach* (Messiah, the Christ, Literally Anointed, the

Anointed One) *will be cut off and have nothing. The people of the prince yet to come will destroy the city and the sanctuary, but his end will come with a flood, and desolations are decreed until the war is over.*

Each of those writings talks about Gentiles being in control, killing the Jews and destroying the Temple. That has taken place a number of times, but the Jews returned and rebuilt, because there were always Jews in the city of Jerusalem.

In the 66-70 AD rebellion, the Romans killed or enslaved over 1,200,000 Hebrews (we know that the Assyrians and the Babylonians each had their part in the Hebrew captivities). We believe they expelled only part of the Jewish Nation.

In the rebellion of 132-135 AD, the Romans expelled all Jews from Jerusalem (Jerusalem will be trampled down by Gentiles until the age, or seasons of the Gentiles has run its course). The Romans wouldn't leave one Hebrew in Jerusalem, the whole city was Gentile, they even changed the city name to Aelia Capitolina. Even the name was Gentile.

Luke 21:24b (CJB) - *until the age of the Goyim has run its course.*

We realize that there have been a number of nations that have had control over Israel and Jerusalem, and this might be the time we bring up a few: the Romans until 324 AD, Byzantines until 614 AD, Persians until 629 AD, Muslim Arabs until around 750 AD, Abbasid Arabs until 878 AD, Egyptians until 1096 AD, the Crusaders until 1187 AD, Egyptian Mamluks in 1250 AD, Suliman the Great in 1517 until 1917 AD, then under British control.

After the Nazi Holocaust, Israel became a nation again in 1948. (We may have left out a nation or two, but we hope you see the picture. It was all Gentile rule.) The Jews were back in Jerusalem and after the six day war, in June of 1967, thus liberating Jerusalem from the Gentiles!

THE TIME OF THE GENTILES HAS RUN ITS COURSE! Before long the blinders will come off and the Jewish leaders will call and believe in the Messiah, Yeshua.

As far as we are concerned, The Messianic Jewish persona isn't a new concept. That's what the first believers in Yeshua (that was the real name of the Jewish Messiah) would have been called in our language.

Somewhere around the 1970s, the Messianic movement started up again. The terminology in our day would be called Messianic. The Bible isn't anti-Semitic! The New Testament has no form of anti-Semitism whatsoever! The Hebrews are and will always be God's Chosen People. The Church hasn't replaced the Jews. The land of Israel was promised to the Jews. Jerusalem was where the Messiah left, and in Jerusalem he will come back. Acts 1:11 states, "He will come back in the same way you saw Him go into Heaven."

Too many people, preachers, and denominations get caught up with what some perceive as the rapture. Are you waiting to just get out of here, or are you believing and looking for the one who is going to return? Yes, you may die. You may be alive when He does return. That just might be your rapture. Either way, we will be with Yeshua.

Paul wrote in Romans 11 about the Jews stumbling, but not being permanently rejected by God. The Natural Branches and the Cultivated Branches, all Israel will be saved, for God's gifts and His call are irrevocable to His chosen people, on account of the Patriarchs!

Some key places in scripture to point to, as God's plan from the beginning are:

1. Genesis 1- God created Heaven and Earth.
2. Matthew 6:10- during the Lord's Prayer.
3. Mathew 28:18-Yeshua states all authority in Heaven and on earth has been given to him.

STUDY

Ephesians 1:10 (CJB) - *and will put into effect when the time is ripe, His plan to place everything in Heaven and on earth under the Messiah's headship.*

This verse describes the dispensation of the fullness of time, when all comes together in Heaven and earth.

Revelation chapters 20 and 21 (STUDY) see clearly the New Heaven and the New Earth, and the Bride comes out of Heaven.

If one studies Revelation 21:9-14, you see that the bride—who is the wife of the lamb—is the Holy City Jerusalem. The Bride is The Pearl, The Glory of God, The brilliance of God. His Holy City Jerusalem! (in Hebrew it's "The Holy City Yerushalayim.") God's intent is to bring His Glory to the Earth with a New Jerusalem!

God is not some mystical spirit floating around in the clouds somewhere. This may be a surprise to some people, but God has a body! Genesis 3 states, "God was walking in the cool of the day and called out to the man." Nowhere in the scriptures does it state we will be floating around. The New Heaven and New Earth will come down and then we get new bodies. People may assume that it seems more spiritual to think we're floating like some angel. However, when you study, you find that is more of a cult theology than biblical.

The Hebrew mindset is that you don't go to a place called Heaven. They are waiting for the restoration of Paradise, in the Garden of Eden. It was God's presence that made it Paradise. If we Christians think about that, it's kind of a neat way of looking at God's Presence, isn't it? The Bible begins with the Garden of Eden, and the ending is Yeshua fixing what was destroyed in the first few chapters of Genesis. The Garden is restored with the New Heaven and the New Earth. God's plan is to reverse the fall by restoration.

We know that some people believe Christ was here in a spiritual form, not with a physical body. If that's the truth, then Yeshua wasn't here in the form of a man to die for our sins. Their sins are not forgiven. It doesn't matter what they do or believe in. It is an interesting study, but in our opinion misleading.

There are 3 things a person needs to live by:

1. Yeshua's Birth
2. Yeshua's Resurrection
3. Yeshua's second coming to establish a literal Kingdom on earth.

This is our opinion. You need to have your own.

There will be a 1000 year period during which people who die at 100 years old will be considered young. This was the way it was when God started with Adam. Note the ages of the people in Genesis 5.

We believe Heaven shouldn't be our Final Goal. You are not complete if you are in Heaven. Our ultimate goal is when Christ returns and we live with him here on the earth. God's ultimate goal is to bring the New Heaven and New Earth! Yeshua's return is in Jerusalem. Why? Because the final battle is over Jerusalem and Israel. While Jerusalem is central for the return of Yeshua, it is also very important to the events after Christ's return.

In Zechariah 2, it states that the Lord will return to Zion with great zeal and dwell in Jerusalem. In the Old Testament, they saw the importance of the Holy City with all of the Glory, Jerusalem!

Covenant means linking or yoking together, a covenant between God and Man. Abram was called by God to leave his land and go where God instructed him. The land is now known as Jerusalem. The man making the link or fulfilling the covenant between God and Man was Abraham, the father of the Jews. The land represents Gods intent for the whole earth to be restored. The phrase, "The natural then the spiritual," is referring to the Jews returning to Jerusalem—the natural. The spiritual will be when the Jews receive the Messiah, and their leadership asking for Christ return while acknowledging Yeshua as the True Messiah!

That will truly complete the covenant between God and His chosen people. The process of reconciling started with the Jews returning to their land. The land was unproductive, a literal wasteland, after the Hebrews left. After they started coming back, it became very productive again. You would have to say Gods promise and blessings are being fulfilled on the land. It seems the more Jews that come back, the more rain the land of Israel gets.

Therefore, when The Covenant order of God is fulfilled the more He releases His blessings. We are seeing the people of the covenant, with the land of the covenant, coming together. The Land, the Jewish People, and the move of Yeshua will be the fulfilling of Matthew 23:39.

> Matthew 23:39 (NIV) - *For I tell you, you will not see me again until you say, Blessed is he who comes in the name of the Lord.*

In that verse, the Messiah was stating that only when the leaders of Israel (which will again be the Sanhedrin) acknowledge Christ, then and only then will He return to Jerusalem. The Sanhedrin are 71 men who are responsible for the rules for their religion and country.

The Orthodox Jews are very stern about not accepting Yeshua. They can be shown all the prophecies that point to Yeshua, but they will tell you He can't be the Messiah unless the Sanhedrin says so. Until the Sanhedrin reverses its decision and accepts Yeshua, He won't return. Why the Sanhedrin? It is based on the Covenant, where Christ's return is to Jerusalem and the Sanhedrin will be the body of Authority in Israel.

No other country or group of people are so important in the return of The Messiah. He is returning to rule Jerusalem and the Earth. The Lord is waiting for the rulers of the land in Jerusalem to say, "Blessed is he who comes in the name of the Lord."

David would not accept his call as the king, as long as King Saul was still on the throne. He may have had a lot of followers, but he would not acknowledge his own Kingship until Saul was dead. He said that he would not kill God's anointed one, who was Saul. Even though he was anointed king by Samuel in 1 Samuel 16, he still waited for his time in 2 Samuel 2:4.

> 2 Samuel 2:4 (NIV) - *Then the men of Judah came to Hebron and there they anointed David king over the tribe of Judah. When David was told that it was the men from Jabesh Gilead who had buried Saul.*

That is the way the Sanhedrin will be. They need to call on the Lord, then Christ will accept their call to Him and return. Yeshua will not, nor can He, return any time He wants. He may know the time it will be, but it all is connected to the leaders of Israel, the Sanhedrin, to do their part and receive The Lord. We didn't just make that up, that's what the Lord said in Matthew 23:39.

There will be a massive war, which we believe is to try to stop the Messiah from being called and His feet touching down on the Mount of Olives. Right now Israel is surrounded by over 20 countries, and a lot of them are much bigger. Yet Israel is looked at as the bully. We haven't figured that one out yet, but we aren't the ones in control. Thank God for that!

Israel must be only under Jewish control. It's not a political issue, it's a Covenant Issue! Yeshua isn't returning to any other city or to a land that used to be Jewish, but now is lost. It won't happen that way. The Sanhedrin must be in control for them to call on Yeshua!

Most Jews have no problem with Christians believing in Yeshua, but there seems to be a huge problem when a Jew says he believes in Yeshua. This will happen until their leaders accept and call on Him. If we as Christians have a movement and do everything right (that won't happen, but let's say it did), we still will not help The Messiah's coming one minute earlier than when he told Jerusalem in Matthew 23.

If Prophecies are talking about the same event, they don't contradict themselves. When talking about the Old Testament, it must mean the same thing in the New Testament. The same activity means the same in both. They may have been written at two different times in history, and may be looked at two different angles, but the outcome will always be the same. They may look like two different events but in reality they are the same event, from different angles. That is the same with the Testaments, New and Old. Way too many people believe that the Old isn't relevant to us, or the Old was done away with after the Messiah left and the writers penned the New. If that is how you believe, we feel sorry for you. If you add to or take away from this book, God will take away your share in the Tree of Life and in the Holy City.

In Acts 1:4, the disciples were told to wait in Jerusalem for the gift the Father promised, but the disciples asked, "Are you at this time going to restore the Kingdom to Israel?" Think about this: it may seem logical to ask this, since they were waiting for a mighty king to take control of their land, restoring David's literal kingdom. There are people who say that they should have known after 40 days of teachings, after His death, His return, and with all those miracles, they should have seen that He was going to leave and not restore King David's kingdom at that time in history. They lived in the moment. We have the privilege of seeing the past and to analyze what was taught.

Yeshua added something new to their thinking and religion: being filled with The Holy Spirit. Then He told them to take this new concept, and be witnesses in Jerusalem, Judea, Samaria, and to the ends of the earth. After studying, you will see that they are filled with the Spirit. They took their new teaching (the gospel) to the nations, and now the Jews who believe in Yeshua are brought back to Jerusalem, bringing the Jews back to Israel from the ends of the earth. What no one understood is that by the blindness of the Jewish Nation, Israel blesses the Nations. Eventually, the Nations bless Israel by bringing back the blessing to Israel in the last days. In other words Jews (Israel) took the Gospel to the Gentiles, and Gentiles bring it back to the Jews (Israel).

In the Jewish people's mind, prior to King David, they had no concept of a Messiah. It was more of an Internal Destiny. The Israelites were the people of God, and they came from Abraham and were in the line of God's blessings. After King David and Solomon, the kingdom of Israel went into a decline with their leaders (their kings) dipping into sin and walking away from what God had set up with King David. When Yeshua performed miracles, the Jews would ask, "Could this be the son of David?"

The Nation of Israel wanted an ideal king, but they seemed to be growing more corrupt as time went by with most of their kings. By the time of the Roman rule, the prophets were starting to confront the people about their sins. The prophets knew they needed a Messiah, and a special king to lead that Kingdom.

Here is an interesting thought: the leading from God directs His people to a literal reign of our King (Yeshua). Therefore, it becomes a group salvation instead of an individual salvation. His reign will be here on earth, with Jerusalem being the center. We claim the Gospel today, preparing for His return.

When we have an individualistic society, it becomes a system of "all about me." It's my everything, it's not our part of the Kingdom, it's me, me, me. Our purpose should be, "What's my role in your Kingdom Lord?" Not, "What about me and mine!?"

We, who believe in Yeshua, are trying to acknowledge Yeshua's authority over His Kingdom on the earth. Yeshua will have all authority when He returns, but He gives that to us now to help usher in His Kingdom and His Ultimate Authority.

Here is what people should be hearing from the pulpit:

Preach the Gospel for the central event. That event is Yeshua. It's not the rapture, the Anti-Christ or the tribulation. They are not and should not be a major focus in the teaching of what is important in the Bible. This is so important, we need to repeat it: our focus shouldn't be on the tribulation, rapture, or the Anti-Christ. It has to be on Yeshua and what the scriptures say about Him, not about the end times. We need to focus on The Kingdom, The Messiah, and His Kingdom!

The Second Coming, Revelation 19 and Zechariah 14, must fit together. They are the same event, one description from the New Testament and one from the Old Testament. We heard someone say they are like a snap shot of the same event and that would be The Second Coming, from different perspectives. They are like two pictures, one from the front and one from the back. They are the same picture but different angles.

The central event, about the end times, is Yeshua's second coming. Zechariah and Revelation describe this event. With studying you will see they do line up. There are two parts of this battle, the earthly and the spiritual. The earthly battle is fighting against Jerusalem, the spiritual is the battle against the Messiah's return. The battle between the mountains may be the battle of Armageddon. Yeshua comes back in the middle of this battle, which is a satanic battle against Jerusalem and Yeshua!

The reason for the Jewish exile, from the land of Israel, was because of their rejection of Yeshua. When they accept Yeshua, then their victory will be complete over Satan! First the Natural, then will come the Spiritual. They came back to Jerusalem (Israel). That's the Natural, now is the time for them to accept Yeshua (their Messiah). That's the Spiritual.

> Romans 11:11 (NIV) - *Again I ask; Did they stumble so as to fall beyond recovery? Not at all! Rather, because of their transgression, salvation has come to the Gentiles to make Israel envious.*

The Lord told Zechariah in Chapter 8, "I am very jealous for Zion. I will return to Zion and dwell in Jerusalem, I will bring them back to live in Jerusalem: they will be my people, and I will be faithful and righteous to them as their God. Speak the truth to each other. In those days' ten men from all languages and nations will take firm hold of one Jew by the hem of his robe and say, 'Let us go with you, because we have heard that God is with you.'"

Those are just a few of the highlights of Chapter 8 in the book of Zechariah. In reality, both Romans and Zechariah go hand and hand. In Romans,

Paul wrote even though they fall they will not fall so far, as not to be able to recover. Zechariah says that the Lord will return to Zion and dwell in Jerusalem. The Hebrews will recover and live with the Lord IN JERUSALEM. That's where He is returning and that is where Christ sets up his Kingdom!

The Jews are more like the Messiah than what we Christians want to admit. The Jews left Jerusalem and did come back. The Lord left Jerusalem and He will come back to Jerusalem the same way He left!

There are a number of things that need to happen. The Temple must be rebuilt, peace in Israel is no more, and the nations turn against Israel. What seems to be kind of odd is revival increases (that is why most people who call themselves believers, will not accept the Jews stance). The Christians will say, if the Jews will follow us then they are following the truth. That is a false statement, but it will sound like a logical direction. Then Yeshua says, "Now is the time for My Return!"

Before the very end, we hope God will open people's eyes. In the midst of judgment, we believe God will open people's eyes. However you want to state it, God is the one in control, WE ARE NOT! People will try to help God out with some formula of theirs, but praise God, He doesn't listen. He already has everything under control. We may be blind to His instructions, His directions, His leading, and in most cases, we are not smart enough to see the forest for the trees. That is a sad statement, but we must be on guard for a forest fire. We're not just talking to you. We are talking to ourselves as well.

No people, after losing their identity for at least two generations, have come back to their homeland and regrouped into a nation of prominence as Israel has. Only by the power of God did this happen. Abraham had a son with Hagar. In Genesis 17, it states that Ishmael will be blessed and be the father of twelve rulers. It also states that the covenant will be established with Isaac, who ends up with twelve tribes also. If you read Genesis 17:18 (NIV), you read that Abraham pleaded with God, "If only Ishmael might live under your blessing." When you read verse 19, you see

God does honor Abraham and his request. Then God said, "Yes, but your wife Sarah will bear you a son, and you will call him Isaac. I will establish my covenant with him as an everlasting covenant for his descendants after him." Did you catch that? God said Yes to Abraham's plea to bless Ishmael with twelve tribes just like his younger brother.

What about Israel being constantly rebellious? You might say, except for a very small amount of time, Israel didn't walk in favor with God. We look at it this way, just because Israel didn't hold up their end of the promise, doesn't nullify God's promise to His people. He let them go their own way, then after a period of time, they returned to Him. It seems that replacement theology has tried to correct God for making a mistake. That is what it looks like when they say that God has given the promise to the Christians now and taken it away from the Jews.

Ezekiel 36 talks about bringing his people back to their land, Israel.

> Ezekiel 36:28 (NIV) - *Then you will live in the land I gave your ancestors; you will be my people, and I will be your God.*

All of chapter 36 talks to and about Israel. It's not for your sake, O house of Israel, that He does things. God says it's for the sake of His holy name. His covenant will always be to his people Israel!

The ending to this part is very important to all Christians and Jews alike.

Israel is the homeland of the Jewish people because of Gods covenant with Abraham. This land is the key to establish the fullness of His kingdom here on this earth! That is why it's such an important issue. It's not about the Jew. It's about the covenant and it being passed down. It's about where, why, and how Christ returns. The demonic worldwide outrage is against Israel. It was foretold and it looks like it is now coming to pass in our day and age. We shouldn't be afraid, but we should be praising The Father for the fulfilling of what scripture says.

Yeshua will return to earth, but where will be his return? In Jerusalem, and the word will go forth from Jerusalem. Jerusalem is the key for the Messiah.

The Misconception is how we look at the Jews and how important they are to our salvation!

SIN

What was the original sin? If you're talking about the first sin ever committed or the first sin by mankind, they just may be two different events. Does the word sin refer to each person's individual act? Maybe it's the sinful inclination behind the motive, or the personal act itself?

Is it our nature to fight against God's rules? If it isn't, we sure go out of our way to look like it is. How about what our society dictates as being good or evil today? You may hear someone say, God is love, and therefore, if it's against the law of today, then it must not be from God. We must live in harmony with our fellow man.

Here's one: God would never have you hurt anyone else physically. If that is your philosophy, then you must not have read the Old Testament (that wouldn't surprise us because most people only skim over the Old Testament just to say they have read the whole Bible). We have heard the argument, "That was then, but now God is the God of love."

Doesn't the scripture say God is the same Yesterday, today and forever? We believe Yeshua made a whip and drove the money changers and the people selling things out of the temple. Maybe He just circled the whip over His head without really hitting anyone with it. If God is only the God of love, did the Lord sin by using the whip on the business people of the day? Was He using anger and the whip to impose the Father's desire for His house? If that's the case, then anger, the making of the whip, then using it isn't the sin.

How about you? Would it be a sin for you to go into a place of worship with a whip and drive out the false believers? How about the people who go to your church because of the pastor or what they can get from him? Would it be a sin against you if the ones you drove out were putting the pastor's desire first and their desire for what God wants for them second? If you set the pastor on a pedestal, and you put the pastor's desires first, then you just may be a false believer. If you fall into any one of those three, then aren't you using the temple like the money changers or the businessmen? We know there are a large number of people saying, "NO, we just honor our leader." OK, believe what you want. It's your eternity!

Some preachers use the pulpit to say, "Look what I've done. Look at all the people I've helped."

Maybe they should get some credit, but they repeat it over and over and over again for what seems like months. It is like their act of kindness puts a feather in their cap if he lets more people know how good he is. Was it an act for the people in need, or a sounding board on how good he is?

If it's an individual desire, is God the center? People may receive some needed things, but wasn't the person exchanging money doing something that people needed? The people coming to worship had to have a certain coin for the temple. Yet the Lord wasn't happy with them. So why would the Lord be happy with the self-centered individual actions by some today!

Do you believe that the ones selling the coins for the Temple were looking at it as an act of kindness to the unfortunate ones who had the wrong coins? They knew everyone's need for the right coin to worship at the Temple in Jerusalem, their place of business. Their motives and most likely their actions seemed to be wrong.

Should we judge the act as sin, or let the one who is in control be the judge? That's not an easy task for most of us. After all, we always know exactly what the Father is doing. Or we act like we know what He should have done. It seems we can always see what He was supposed to do according to His will, so why doesn't He do it the way we see it? Well, you go ahead and tell Him He messed up. We won't! We're not His boss. You might say, we may be a little afraid of upsetting the CEO of Heaven!

Here is just something to think about: In the Old Testament times, when God told the children of Israel to go into a country and kill every man, woman, and child, what would we call them? What if God instructed them to do the same thing today? And if they did and said it was an act of God, would we judge God's instructions as sinful? Or would you say that maybe the Father told them to sin? Now you better watch out, you just may be telling the Father you know best when it comes to sin. That is something to think about when we judge any person or country's act. We all do it, but in the end, who are we to judge the when, what, or who the Father will use for His good?

There is no reason to expect New Testament ethics to differ from Old Testament ethics. God doesn't change! He is not like the wind, one direction one day and the total opposite the next. If it's one direction Monday then Saturday, it is still the same direction. He is not a politician, who seems to be able to go both directions in the same sentence. They can lie and people act like that's all right. Where is their ethics? Or should we say, do they have any ethics at all? We guess that was a stupid statement. It is obvious, that person has no ethics at all!

The original sin: was it Lucifer's rebellion or Adam eating the fruit? We would have to say, original would be the first act recorded. That would be Lucifer when he rebelled against the Father! If you say that Adam imposed his desire to eat of the forbidden fruit without thought of God's will, you're right. Adam did do that. But Lucifer did the same thing when he imposed his will ahead of the Father's, before anything here on earth existed.

Our way of looking at it would be, the original sin is Satan's. The first recording of humans going against God's commands would have to be Adam's sin.

We know a lot of philosophers and biblical scholars will have a lot to say about that one, but that's what makes this book so important. If they disagree and you believe their way, that's your business. We hope that also gets you studying more, so you find the real truth.

STUDY

Are we that bright? NO way. But we are the only ones (that we have found) who will admit it! The real question shouldn't be how smart we are. The real question is, how smart are you? Do you follow someone without really knowing his philosophy and just take his or her word for it?

IN OTHER WORDS, STUDY ON YOUR OWN AND FIND THE TRUTH!

YEAR OF JUBILIEE

What an interesting study! We have to admit, we know very little about this topic. We will be trying to find as much as possible through a number of ventures.

> Leviticus 25:10 (CJB) - *and you are to consecrate the fiftieth year, proclaiming freedom throughout the land to all its inhabitants. It will be a yovel (jubilee) for you; you will return everyone to the land he owns, and everyone is to return to his family.*

How interesting is that philosophy? Consider the fact that the Israelites would return not only their land, but the Israelites who sold themselves or were used as slaves would go back home as well. In other words, they would be set free from their time of servitude to someone else. The land was to go back to the landowner. In this day and age, it would be like a fifty-year lease of the property. No matter if it pertained to people or land, they would return home. Very Interesting!

There are so many theories about this Biblical writing. We hope to stir your interest, without getting you too confused about it.

We do not have all the answers, nor would we pretend to have even one answer to any of your questions. We wrote what we have been able to find out about the topic, and hopefully you will have your own interesting ideas, which we hope will get you into studying more.

That is what this book is called and the main reason for this adventure of ours!

WHAT IS SIN?

What really is Sin? Is it doing things that God doesn't want you to do? Does the Father of the Universe care if you follow the rules set up by man? Does He look down and see everything with holy eyes? Does He see you no matter where you are or what you're doing? Does He know everything you have done in the past?

There are teachers and preachers who say that God sees everything. He knows what you're thinking, what you have done, and where you are. Has He ever changed?

When God walked in the Garden of Eden, He called to Adam and Eve. Did God call them because He didn't see them? He looked for them because He didn't find them. Were they hiding from God? In Genesis 3:9, God asks, "Where are you?" Why would He ask that?

Back to Sin, Adam did what he wasn't supposed to do. Cain was the first recorded murderer. Noah got drunk after the flood. Ham saw his father's naked body and made fun of what he saw. (Ham was the father of the nation of Canaan.) Abraham distorted the truth (in other words, he lied). King David had sex with another man's wife. Then he had her husband, Uriah, murdered, so he could take Bathsheba as his wife. She was already caring King David's child when he had Uriah killed. Those are just a few of the things that may have been looked on by the Father as sin. But in reality, we shouldn't put those words in God's mouth. They seem to be sin to us, but are they in the Father's eyes? Of course they are!

Have they been forgiven for eating the forbidden fruit, murder, getting drunk, having an affair and impregnating someone else's wife? He even had her husband carry his own death sentence to his boss. How about the one who actually followed the order to put Uriah on the front line, then leave him alone, knowing he would be killed?

We are not in the position to tell you what the Father of the Universe forgives, forgets, or overlooks. We have enough preachers, teachers, denominations, and religions that tell you that already. We're not here to work out your salvation. We have a hard enough time with our own!

What we will say is, we're not really sure society has it right yet. We read about Adam and Eve being cast out of the Garden and then having to do work in the fields. (Now we know who to blame for us having to work for thirty years to get to our retirement. Sorry, just a little sense of humor.) Anyway, back to Adam. If Adam was the first chosen one, then that means the Messiah even had a choice.

If Adam had made the choice not to eat the fruit (in other words, not to sin against God's command), would there have been death on earth at all? We know preachers and teachers may say something like, "They would have died physically, but there would not have been a spiritual death."

Why, if the God of the Universe gave a direct command to Adam, do we analyze it to take it apart? Let's take a look at what the word says:

> Genesis 2:16-17 (NIV) - *and the Lord God commanded the man, you are free to eat from any tree in the garden but you must not eat from the tree of the knowledge of good and evil, for when you eat of it you will certainly die.*

We humans look at that statement, and it seems inconceivable that Adam would never have died. Our logic doesn't fit that terminology at all. We are not God, and we haven't the capability of reading God's mind, like so many pastors and teachers seem to think they are able to do. We guess they must be more spiritual than us.

While death may have been possible before Adam sinned, had he chosen not to eat from the tree of life, it apparently was not a necessary consequence of being human. Think about that one. Had Adam not eaten from the tree, would death have entered human existence at all?

The prophet Ezekiel wrote in 18:4 (NIV), "the one who sins is the one who will die." Or, in the CJB, "so it is the person who sins, himself, who must die." The prophet wrote each person dies for his own sin. If Adam had not allowed himself to sin with that fruit, think about how life would have been changed for all of us, in the past and right now!

> Romans 5:14 (NIV) - *Nevertheless, death reigned from the time of Adam to the time of Moses, even over those who did not sin by breaking a command, as did Adam, who was a pattern of the one to come.*

Adam was the pattern of the one to come. What is really said with a statement like that?

(1) Both made perfect.
(2) Both had a choice.
(3) Both had direct fellowship with God.
(4) Because of their choice, both died.

This is our logic: we see a father who had two sons. One He made human, from the ground. The other He made through a human, who came from the first son's descendants, for the purpose of His death. Imagine the pain one would feel watching both of His own die, knowing that the older one had the choice to obey and cause life forever or disobey and cause his younger brother to be put through a painful execution. Also consider what it was like for the older brother to see the pain the younger one had to go through because of him and for what he had done.

Here is the most interesting outlook on sin. Any individual can—or we should say, must—work his or her way into Hell. You have to work for it. If someone dies and never did anything (possibility an infant), would you say they worked their way into Hell? We know there is no way to work your way into Heaven! No matter how good you think you are, or how many people you bless, how many you preach to, or how much you pray, you won't work your way to Heaven. After all, why wouldn't all those good things you do put a feather in your cap to get you to the Heavenly Promised Land?

We believe the free gift from God is the free gift of eternal life. It's free. You can't obtain it with anything, or through how many things you do. If you believe Yeshua was the Messiah our Lord, then you have received the free gift. Once you believe, it's yours and you didn't do one speck of work to obtain it. In conclusion, there is only one thing you work to obtain and that's Hell. Heaven is a free gift in union with Our Lord!

We guess our next statement should be for us and you: STOP WORKING SO HARD!

COMPARE

(WARNING)

Matthew 24:4 (CJB) - *Yeshua replied: Watch out! Don't let anyone fool you!*

Revelation 22:19 (CJB) - *and if anyone takes anything away from the words in the book of this prophecy, God will take away his share in the Tree of Life and The Holy City, as described in this book.*

(FALSE CHRIST)

Matthew 24:5 (CJB) - *For many will come in my name, saying, I am the Messiah! and they will lead many astray.*

Revelation 6:1-2 (NIV) - *I watched as the Lamb opened the first of the seven seals. Then I heard one of the four living creatures say in a voice like thundering, "Come!" I looked, and there before me was a white horse! Its rider held a bow and he was given a crown, and he rode out as a conqueror bent on conquer.*

(WARS AND RUMORS OF WARS)

Matthew 24:6 (CJB) - *You will hear the noise of wars nearby and the news of wars far off; see to it that you don't become frightened, such things must happen, but the end is yet to come.*

Revelation 6: 3-4 (CJB) - *When he broke the second seal, I heard the second living being say, Go! Another horse went out, a red one; and its rider was given the power to take peace away from the earth and make people slaughter each other. He was given a great sword.*

(FAMINE)

Matthew 24:7 (CJB) - *For peoples will fight each other, nations will fight each other, and there will be famines and earthquakes in various parts of the world.*

Revelation 6: 5-6 (CJB) - *When he broke the third seal, I heard the third living being say, Go! I looked, and there in front of me was a black horse, and its rider held in his hand a pair of scales. Then I heard what sounded like a voice from among the four living beings say, "Two pounds of wheat for a day's wages! Six pounds of barley for the same price! But don't damage the oil or the wine!"*

(PERSECUTION)

Matthew 24:9 (CJB) - *At that time you will be arrested and handed over to be punished and put to death, and all peoples will hate you because of me.*

Revelation 6: 7-8 (CJB) - *When he broke the fourth seal, I heard the voice of the fourth living being say. Go! I looked, and there in front of me was a pallid, sickly-looking horse. Its rider's name was Death, and Sh'ol (Hades) followed behind him. They were given authority to kill one-quarter of the world by war, by famine, by plagues and with the wild animals of the earth.*

STUDY

(MARTYRS)

Matthew 24:9 (CJB) - *At that time you will be arrested and handed over to be punished and put to death, and all peoples will hate you because of me.*

Revelation 6:9 (CJB) - *When the lamb broke the fifth seal, I saw underneath the altar the souls of those who had been put to death for proclaiming the Word of God, that is, for bearing witness.*

(ANTICHRIST LIMITED)

Matthew 24:22 (CJB) - *Indeed, If the length of this time had not been limited, no one would survive; but for the sake of those who have been chosen, its length will be limited.*

Revelation 6:11 (CJB) - *Each of them was given a white robe; and they were told to wait a little longer, until the full number of their fellow-servants should be reached, of their brothers who would be killed, just as they had been.*

(SUN, MOON, STARS DARKENED)

Matthew 24:29 (CJB) - *But immediately following the trouble of those times, THE SUN WILL GROW DARK, THE MOON WILL STOP SHINING, THE STARS WILL FALL FROM THE SKY, AND THE POWERS IN HEAVEN WILL BE SHAKEN.*

Revelation 6: 12-14 (CJB) - *Then I watched as he broke the sixth seal, and there was a great earthquake, the sun turned black as sackcloth worn in mourning, and the full moon became blood-red. The stars fell from Heaven to earth just as a fig tree drops its figs when shaken by a strong wind. The sky receded like a scroll being rolled up, and every mountain and island was moved from its place.*

STUDY

(DELIVERENCE)

Matthew 24: 30-31 (CJB) - *Then the sign on the Son of Man will appear in the sky, all the tribes of the land will mourn, and they will see the Son of Man coming on the clouds of Heaven with tremendous power and glory. He will send out His angels with a great shofar and they will gather together His chosen people from the four winds, from one end of Heaven to the other.*

Revelation 7:3 (CJB) - *Do not harm the land or the sea or the trees until we have sealed the servants of our God on their foreheads!*

(WRATH)

Matthew 24: 37-38 (CJB) - *For the Son of Man's coming will be just as it was in the days of Noach. Back then, before the Flood, people went on eating and drinking, taking wives and becoming wives, right up till the day Noach entered the ark.*

Revelation 8:5 (CJB) - *Then the angel took the incense-bowl, filled it with fire from the altar and threw it down onto the earth; and there followed peals of thunder, voices, flashes of lightning and an earthquake.*

These writings came from the book of Matthew and the book of the Revelation. They work together as the Bible does throughout scripture. Most people try to make sense out of Matthew, but look at Revelation as a very hard book to understand. When one studies the word we must acknowledge that it is one book, one word, we have one God, and He is looking for people who believe in His True Son!

There are parts that you need to study more to grasp the true intent. You should also follow through with a more in-depth reading, to grasp what the writer wants for you. It is important to understand what he wanted for the people of his time, as well. The goal is for everyone to understand God's Word before the end time comes!

Do people look at it as letters from the Father to His children, or just a bunch of letters that a number of people wrote from their own experiences?

That is a sad statement, but in most cases we believe it is true for far too many individuals today!

NOAH

Noah's sons (Japheth, Ham, and Shem) were the ones who helped him build the boat. There are a number of things that people overlook about these three and their father.

Most people who go to church, know a little about Noah and his sons. But how many sit down and really look at what Noah had to do and go through while here on this place called earth?

> Genesis 6:11-13 (NIV) - *now the earth was corrupt in God's sight and was full of violence. God saw how corrupt the earth had become, for all the people on earth had corrupted their ways. So God said to Noah, I am going to put an end to all people, for the earth is filled with violence because of them. I am surely going to destroy both them and the earth.*

That meant he lived in a time when people didn't follow God or live with any morals. They had followed their own desires and felt proud about it. Kind of sounds like the world today, doesn't it? Really, stop and think about the world today—even the United States.

We have people who call themselves Christians, but it's OK to fib to another person if the truth might hurt the other person's feelings. Isn't that a lie, no matter what you're trying to cover up? If a person doesn't want the truth, then don't ask the question. What does the Father think about you, when you feel, for some reason, you have to lie to cover up the truth? Do you think that he overlooks your lie and says something like, "I understand and you know what, I will look the other way just for you?"

You must believe you're really special to get that special treatment from the Father. You must really have an in with the God of the Universe.

The time period has changed, but the corrupt world is still thriving with the people who live on this place we call earth. There are people who seem to enjoy figuring ways to get others to follow them instead of God. They are smart enough to get individuals to follow, learn and then teach other people their way instead of God's way. Somehow, they get people to follow their ideas. They may ask questions like, "If God made everything, then who made God?"

Let's look at Noah's sons.

Japheth was the oldest son. It is believed that from Japheth came the Greeks, Thracians, and Scythians. Japheth's descendants settled in Europe and Asia Minor. This was where Paul ministered, and the areas where John wrote to the seven churches. In that area, there where cities that were noted for open immoral sexual practices in the worship of Artemis.

Ham was the youngest son. It is believed that from Ham came the Canaanites, Egyptians, Philistines, Hittites, and the Amorites. All became corrupt and enemies to their relatives. Ham's descendants settled in Canaan, Egypt, and in other parts of Africa.

Shem was the middle son. It is believed that from Shem came the Hebrews, Chaldeans, Assyrians, Persians, and the Syrians. Some of his Hebrew descendants were Abraham, King David, and Yeshua! While those may sound impressive, we need to realize that the Chaldeans, Assyrians, and Persians all became enemies of the Hebrews. Shem's descendants were called Semites.

This becomes really interesting when you study about Noah and his descendants. We need to understand that after Joseph helped the Egyptians through the famine, the Hebrews became slaves to the Egyptians. The younger brother's descendants became the overpowering ones for a while.

STUDY

As one studies, you find that not only do brothers fight, but after a number of years relatives forget who their family was. They think only about the now. You need to remember that they didn't have the internet to look up who their relatives were or where they came from. It would have been more like, we have this spot of land and these other people must want it also. They didn't want anybody to take their land from them so everyone became their enemy. Their land and what they produced was more or less all they had.

It wasn't like today. If you don't want to work, you expect the government to bail you out. You shouldn't have to work for thirty years to get your retirement, it should be given to you right from the start. After all, you deserve it because other people get it, even if they worked those thirty years so they could enjoy the latter years of their life. This has become a "give me" society, where people think because where their ancestors came from they deserve a free ride.

My skin is white, I deserve the best. My skin is black, I deserve the best. I came up from Mexico and broke the law by doing it, therefore I deserve to get overlooked for doing things that break the law.

This is just an opinion, but if you are breaking the law to get into a country, then you are doing an illegal act. You are not obeying their laws.

YOU ONLY LIVE ONCE

There are a lot of feel-good preachers on TV. The preacher that stands behind the pulpit at your church may not be that different, if at all! They know the right things to say to put you in a mood of believing whatever they say. Most people believe that while the preacher is behind his own pulpit, he is always right. They even get goose bumps whenever they hear him preach on certain topics.

Our question is, are they goose bumps, or should you categorize them as chills? Chills that your subconscious knows that if you really studied you would come to the truth.

The other day we were with a group of people, four preachers and seven followers. The single verses that were flying around made some feel good, then others joined in with more single verses and that brought joy to most of them. The real problem was most of those verses were stated totally out of context to the whole Word of God in scripture.

Oh, they were from the Bible, but that was as far as it went. The total concept of where and what was happening at the time of its writing was ignored by the preacher trying to get another feel good mood in the group. They sounded so spiritual. We know those words are in the Bible, so we guess these messages from the preachers must have come from God for that group, even though they were totally out of the original reason for saying any one of those statements.

One preacher stated that he had eight people come forward and accept Jesus last month, and now their names are written in the book and are on their way to Heaven. That saying brought out the best in all the preachers, let alone the followers grabbing each (out of context) one liner that was stated after that.

One should enjoy God's word, be lifted up by it, but one should also study to find the true meaning behind each saying. The joy one gets should be from God's word, and that should come from the true meaning and format, when it was stated. We believe a problem arises, when those individuals who hear and the ones who repeat those one liners, go on the knowledge of someone else's studying and some other person's acceptance of it.

We have no problem with one liners. The Bible gives so many places where you can use one liners to get your point across. The problem comes when those one liners are taken out of context. In most cases, the one reciting them knows very little about the history of the verse, or WHY it was stated in the first place. Each one of us should know the context before we assume we really know the true meaning behind the statement.

We guess that's why we never enjoy hearing a preacher or teacher brag about how many they got saved. Now if we are in a private conversation with one of them and they state they were overjoyed when so and so came to Christ, without putting the emphasis on himself, great. But when the focus is on whatever he did that prompted that person to come forward, that's a problem. Then the back slapping seems to point to the preacher, not Christ!

What people need is a more in-depth study of the Word. Most people feel like they don't have time for that. After all, they pay the preacher and maybe even their teacher for that. But the problem comes when the person being taught is influenced. Who influences them? When they were learning, was it by someone who has more of a "name it and claim it" philosophy? Or was it from someone who feels that if you accept Christ you are on your way to Heaven, even if you do or continue to do stuff wrong? How about the snake people? You know there is a verse that states something like snake venom won't hurt you, but we guess if you die after the bite, you must not have been doing enough to charm that snake.

Our point here is not to point fingers at any of those who want to believe that way or any way. Our point is, believe by way of your studies, not what someone else studies. Study to show yourself approved! Don't believe because they said to, believe because *you* learned that God is good and His word will never come back void. (His word; don't believe because of some preacher, teacher, or us.)

This statement needs to be repeated. Never believe what we say, but study to prove us wrong. If you study with an open mind, without the brainwashing of your past or the teachings of another brainwashed individual, you just might find truth, not the watered down learning of the left or right. Those are two paths that we all go down, to those two doors, one almost everyone uses and then the one only a few find and walk down.

DON'T GET LOST IN THE CROWD. REMEMBER YOU ONLY LIVE ONCE!

MATTHEW 5:17

Matthew 5:17 (or Mattityahu 5:17 for our Jewish friends) does not contradict itself, unless you read it the way we have been taught by our Christian leaders. Hopefully you will be able to understand our explanation.

> Matthew 5:17 (NIV) - *Do not think that I came to abolish the law or the Prophets; I have not come to abolish them but to fulfill them.*

If a person looks at A and B, you may come away with mixed up feelings. If a person reads that the Messiah came and did away with the law or the prophets, then one would have to say, the law and the prophets are no more.

If you read MATTITYAHU (Matthew) 5:17 from a Jewish perspective, you may have a different understanding.

> Matthew 5:17 (CJB) - *Don't think that I came to abolish the Torah or the Prophets; I have come not to abolish but to complete.*

That statement is true in both A+B. In other words, Christ was the aim of the law (Torah in Hebrew) and the prophets were shooting for. To us, that is a logical statement!

As it states, He has NOT come to Abolish, but HE IS THE GOAL the whole Old Testament points to! Some Christians have interpreted Matthew 5:17 so it would say what they really wanted to do, and that was to render the Torah and the Prophets obsolete!

We have stated this in a number of places in the book, but we believe that it is such an important statement that it may need more attention.

What Most Christians refer to as the Law of Moses, should in all reality be called, "The Teachings of Moses, from The Father." One should say that it is a doctrine from God, through Moses. The Christian faith seems to lead people in a way to interpret it as obsolete. Do we as Christians really want to do that? Do we believe that Christ did away with The Torah and The Prophets? Remember, Christ said, "I have not come to abolish but to complete."

Are the Christian leaders so brainwashed that they must gather their congregations together to go against the Hebrew writings? Consider Romans 3:31.

> Romans 3:31 (NIV) - *Do we, then, nullify the law by this faith? Not at all! Rather, we uphold the law.*

Paul wrote Heaven Forbid, God Forbid, or Not at all, (depending on which version you like to read), with each one of those forbids, we need to understand that neither Christ nor Paul did away with the teachings of Moses or the Prophets.

Think of this: the faith of Our Father isn't the faith of the person who started your denomination! The Faith of Our Father must be the Father, God!

There are rules the Father gave for His people, and then there were rules for mankind. We understand that there are a great number of teachers and preachers who are saying, the rules are the rules for everybody. Or they say, the rules by way of laws are done away with, in Christ's death and His resurrection. Christ was the aim, and there were some rules the Father set down for His people, not for the pagans, not the gentiles, not unbelievers. They only pertained to His people, the Hebrews!

It didn't and still doesn't mean anything if an unbeliever doesn't tithe, pray, or for that matter accept Our Messiah. He may still want to go to a better place in the end. He may even go to a place of worship, gives large sums of money, or spends ten hours a day in prayer. But even when he prays, it's to an enemy of the Father and the Son. Even though he is going in the wrong direction, that person would still feel edified, wouldn't he?

Do you believe, like so many millions of people, that you can and will call the Father's Son any name you want and the Father has to listen to you when you pray?

Are there special words a person must say? Do you believe that the Torah of God was done away with because of the person it pointed to when He died? If one stops and thinks about that kind of brainwashing, it doesn't make any sense whatsoever! The Father gave the rules. Maybe they were through Moses, King David, Jeremiah or some other person in Old Testament times. Now there are people who believe that the Father does away with the rules after his one and only Son kept every rule His Father made.

There are rules that could be called laws to the Hebrews, but to lump all the rules into that one word, law, that does an injustice to the rules, the writers, to the Son, and to the Father!

While trying to study this one, we came across a lot of explanations that sounded logical to us. But after a lot of soul searching of our past and the brainwashing of the replacement theology in most of the denominations these days, we have come to believe that we, like most, have had a total wrong idea about God and the rules He gave.

Look at it this way: in your religion, denomination, church, or in some school (Sunday school, bible class, etc.), have you ever been taught that Christ did away with the Torah? By Christ, who kept all the Torah, keeping all the Laws and rules, then when he died and rose from the grave, we are lead to believe now that we, who are following Him, we do not need to keep the rules any longer? Do you believe that after all that, we are free from all the rules that He had to obey?

If you really believe that, and now you are not bound to any rules that were in the Old Testament, we would have to say, you have stepped into one of these:

(1) Replacement Theology
(2) Dominion Theology
(3) Kingdom Now Theology
(4) Covenant Theology

All those, plus a couple more, try to point to a reconstruction of all religion to fit their way of thinking, their belief, or at the very least, so you see it in their way of understanding. In other words, all want you to believe like them, even if they differ or have to change the meaning to fit their denomination, church, or their religion. All those theologies are based on them being the head. They also believe they are the trunk of the tree. You would have to say, they must believe they are the reason for the season.

If you believe they have all the correct answers, then you already know you are right, no matter what scripture says. So believe in one of those theologies and land on that large road going to that huge door. But when you are asked, don't deny that you were told the truth about the misleading of some of the religions of your day.

Why are we saying this? Why are we trying to get individuals to study to find truth? Why wouldn't every person who reads this want to be on that small path that leads to that little gate? By the way, it says very few people will find that gate.

Don't believe us because you read this and now you feel you need to find the real truth. Believe scripture because of your own study.

Study to find your fate! Study to find the truth, even if it takes you to that day you draw in that last breath of air, or that last beat of your heart! Do It!

STUDY

Like we have said before, we are not always right. We don't make claims like so many teachers and preachers believe. We want each person to study without any brainwashing of your past, and start to do it with an open mind to what the Father God wants for you! There isn't any better day than today to get started, is there?

There is joy in study, when you finally get to the mindset that you are following the real truth, for you and your family.

WAS IT REALLY A VIRGIN BIRTH?

Miriam (Mary) as "almah" in the Hebrew language always refers to an unmarried woman of a good reputation. In other words, a virgin.

The Greeks translated the Old Testament from the Hebrew into Greek, some two centuries before the Messiah was born. The Greeks used the word "Parthenos" in place of the Hebrew word "Almah" and the Greek word Parthenos unequivocally means "Virgin." Even though the Greek translation uses a word that pertains to her being a virgin, we should really look at the Hebrew writing to make sure.

B'Tulah refers to a virgin. B'Tulah was used in Genesis 24:16:

> Genesis 24:16 (NIV) - *The woman was very beautiful, a virgin; no man had ever slept with her. She went down to the spring, filled her jar and came up again.*

That was referring to Isaac's future Bride Rebekah, a virgin.

We have the word "Almah" being used in Genesis 24:43 where he is explaining why he picked Rebekah. Now we have Rebekah being referred to in 16 as a B'Tulah, and in verse 43 she is referred to as an unmarried woman of a good reputation—an Almah.

Through our studies, we believe the Hebrew writings, using either word must refer to a virgin.

Our Messiah's birth was from a woman who never had sexual relations until after the birth of Our Messiah. There was a rumor of a Roman soldier, but we believe that was just another cover up.

The best we can come up with is that Our Messiah was born in the month of September (not December), because of the activities that were going on at that time and the census.

The Messiah would most likely have been over 1 year old, when the Magi got to see him. Most scholars disagree, but Christ's birth would have been around 2BC.

If a person celebrates Christ birth in September or December, and you want to believe in that date, then that is totally up to the individual.

The date and month are of little value, if you are worshiping a date or month.

WHO YOU ARE WORSHIPPING IS THE IMPORTANT PART. YOU MAY NOT WANT TO GET THAT WRONG!

PSALM 5:9

David wrote the fifth Psalm. He was a shepherd, soldier, scholar, and king. By this writing, we can see he was a prophet also.

As you read Psalm 5:9, think about the people of today.

> Psalm 5:9 (NIV) - *Not a word from their mouth can be trusted; their heart is filled with malice. Their throat is an open grave; with their tongues they tell lies.*

> Psalm 5:10 (KJV) - *Destroy thou them, O God; let them fall by their own counsels: cast them out in the multitude of their transgressions; for they have rebelled against thee.*

> Psalm 5:12(11) (CJB) - *But let all who take refuge in you rejoice, let them forever shout for Joy! Shelter them; and they will be glad, those who love your name.*

> Psalm 69:34-36 (NIV) - *Let Heaven and earth praise him, the seas and all that move in them, for God will save Zion and rebuild the cities of Judah. Then people will settle there and possess it; the children of his servants will inherit it, and those who Love His NAME will dwell there.*

We used three different versions to show you that they all point to using the right name. All were originally written by King David, the prophet. We had to change two words because of the copyright laws. Originally, we had used the terms "Tziyon" and "Y'hudah" for the Zion and Judah, which would have been the Hebrew names King David would have used.

STUDY

We will stress this over and over in this book, because we feel that this one point is the worst and most used misunderstanding by preachers, teachers, and so called biblical scholars since the time of Christ. The difference is that, if you disagree, that's all right with us. When you study to prove us wrong, please use the scriptures instead of some doctrine of your denomination. Then spread your word and get your truth out there. Remember, in the end, false doctrine hurts your future in eternity.

Will we be always right? Heavens NO, but don't take our word for that either.

OUR PRAYERS EVERY DAY

Dear Heavenly Father, Forgive our sins. Forgive our lack of understanding. Forgive us for all the wrong ideas that we have allowed into our lives. Help us to turn totally toward you and your leading. Open our eyes as well as the eyes of the people we are sent to and the ones you send to us. May we read your words. May you speak through us. May we write only your words to give life and guidance to people. Give us strength to look on others as you would. We pray we are forgiven through your Son, Yeshua, and strengthened by your Spirit. May your angles be helping us every day in our walk and talk for you!

Heavenly Father, show others and ours the blessings that come from following "YESHUA", your Son! We also ask that only by the true name of Your Son, comes the blessings from THE FATHER! Help us to bless others with the blessings you are giving us!

Remember us, O Lord, when you show favor to Your people. Come to our aid when You save them. Help us enjoy the prosperity of Your chosen ones so that we may share in the joy of Your nation and join Your inheritance in giving praise. - AMEN

WORK

What is work? What some people believe is that doing something you like is not really classified as work. We disagree with that statement. There are people who never get to do any activity they enjoy, yet they seem to be very successful in their endeavor. Then you have people who are very happy with what they are doing and never get past the point of poverty. Which one would you consider successful?

> 2 Thessalonians 3:10 (NIV) - *For even when we were with you, we gave you this rule: The one who is unwilling to work shall not eat.*

Then it talks about people who are just idle, not busy. It says to settle down and earn their bread they eat. Then it says to never tire of doing what is right.

When you look at those writings in 2 Thessalonians, it seems that Paul must be talking to someone else and not you right! He doesn't know the trouble we have or the trouble our family went through. How dare he tell us we need to work? We deserve everything handed to us because of what our ancestors had to go through. If that is how you look at things in your life or your pastor tells you stuff like that, then he isn't leading you to that Promised Land in the afterlife. Very few people can make you feel better about yourself unless you feel good already. If you don't like yourself or the situation you're in, then maybe you need to change your ways! The concept that God will provide no matter what is very easy to misinterpret. It's not that he doesn't provide, but there are far too many people who handcuff The Father and bring nothing to the table. It's a two way street, not a one way for The Father only! When Paul wrote to the church in Thessalonica, they were idle. They were not busy; they were busybodies. Such people we command and urge in the Lord to settle down and earn the bread they eat. *And as for you, brothers, never tire of doing what is right!* - 2 Thessalonians 3: 11-13 (NIV)

Ecclesiastes 6:12 really says a lot and we have heard no one say it: *For who knows what is good for a person in life, during the few and meaningless days they pass through like a shadow? Who can tell him what will happen under the sun after they are gone?* (NIV) In other words: if you spend all your time working for riches, after you're dead you will have no idea what will come of all your money. So when you are supposed to work, then work. Don't expect a free ride for any reason because he who does not work should not eat! There seems to be far too much of that, in the United States these days. Work as you want the Lord to bless your being, not that He or anyone else owes you a lengthy and prosperous life or time on earth. That may be one of the benefits that comes along with following Yeshua our Lord!

THE DEATH PENALTY

In far too many eyes, it seems like the scriptures do not fit today's society but this next unpopular statement is true, OUR SOCIETY HAS TO FIT SCRIPTURE!

> Genesis 9:6 (CJB) - *Whoever sheds human blood, by a human being will his own blood be shed; for God made human beings in his image.*

> Exodus 20:13 (NIV) - *You shall not Murder.*

> Exodus 21:14 (NIV) - *But if anyone schemes and kills someone deliberately, that person is to be taken from my altar and put to death.*

> Deuteronomy 19:21 (NIV) - *Show no pity: life for life, eye for eye, tooth for tooth, hand for hand, foot for foot.* (This is about false witnesses, but look at the court system, people lie every day in our courts. You can see it when two people go after each other with totally different stories about the same event. Then some judge has to figure out which one has a more convincing story. They were in the same place but one didn't get what they wanted, so it's wrong.)

The Death Penalty isn't something new. According to scripture, it's been around a long time. Only now we have people who want to make it their life's ambition to do away with the death penalty. That way the taxpayers can support the person who did the crime for the rest of their life, even if that person took more than one life himself. But the lawyers will still get their money, even if it has to come from the taxpayers themselves!

We hear some say that the Ten Commandments say, "Thou shalt not kill." Well, Exodus 20:13 in the King James Version says that but, in the earliest writings and most of the versions we have found, the wording is properly "Thou shalt not murder." We know there are a lot of individuals, preachers, and denominations that say these ideas are the same. Well, as far as scripture is concerned, they are totally different. It doesn't matter what a denomination, preacher, teacher or rabbi says. They are not the same! One may kill someone else by accident or in a war. But for killing to be murder, then you need to plan it or go out of control and murder someone for one reason or another. The only thing that is in common is the death. Do we condone killing? No, but there is a difference according to scripture. That doesn't come from us. We need to address it as a sign of the times (which we believe is the wrong sign). The judges and lawyers seem to have gotten together and figured out that the believers aren't smart enough to fight them on this one. They can milk the taxpayers to pay for the murderer's crime for life. We who pay taxes can foot the bill! Shame on the Lawyers and Judges for their unjustified attack on God and His word!

COMMUNION

What we call communion is an example of what the churches of today want. We are not down on communion or the remembering of the body and blood of Christ. There are at least five places in the New Testament that talk about the Lord and the Last Supper. Each one is a little different.

> Matthew 26:26-28 (NIV) - *While they were eating,* (Yeshua) *took the bread, gave thanks and broke it, and gave it to his disciples, saying, "Take and eat: this is my body." Then he took a cup, and when he had given thanks, he gave it to them, saying, "Drink from it, all of you. This is my blood of the covenant, which is poured out for many for the forgiveness of sins.*

> Mark 14: 22-23 (CJB) – *While they were eating, Yeshua took a piece of matzah* (unleavened bread), *made the b'rakhah* (blessing), *broke it, gave it to them and said, "Take it; this is my body." Also he took a cup of wine, made the b'rakhah and gave it to them; and they all drank.*

> Luke 22:17, 19-20 (NIV) - *after taking the cup, he gave thanks and said, "Take this and divide it among you." And he took bread, gave thanks and broke it, and gave it to them, saying, "This is my body given for you: do this in remembrance of me." In the same way, after the supper he took the cup, saying, "This cup is the new covenant in my blood, which is poured out for you."*

John 13 never really talks about the Last Supper, except that he dips the bread and gave it to Judas.

In 1 Corinthians 11:23b-25, most versions say something like: The Lord Yeshua, on the night he was betrayed, took bread, gave thanks, broke it and said, "This is my body; do this in remembrance of me." In the same way, after supper he did the same with the cup, saying, "This cup is the new covenant in my blood; do this whenever you drink it, in remembrance of me."

The people of today seem to think that in the church is the only place to have communion. We disagree. Genesis 14:18 says: *Then Melchizedek king of Salem brought forth bread and wine: and he was the priest of the Most High God.* (KJV) When you study that verse, you see that Melchizedek took the bread and wine to Abram and blessed him. There are pastors who give communion to people in hospitals, homes and almost anywhere. Therefore, to state that you need to go to church because there is communion today is really a ploy to get people in their church. We really don't care if they want to use communion to get people into a church, but when you have them in your building, tell them the truth. Teach them what the word says, not what your denomination instructs you to say. A lot of people recall the Last Supper in Matthew, Mark, Luke and John, but the oldest record of the Last Supper is in 1 Corinthians 11:17-34. 1 Corinthians was written around 55 A.D., some years before the Gospels. Therefore, the earliest writing was by Paul.

How often should communion be taken? The question isn't that hard to grasp. It was the last supper the Lord had on earth and it seems that they were doing the same stuff they always did. However, this time the Lord was telling His chosen friends what was about to happen to Him and what they could expect as a result of their belief in Him.

It was a supper, the same kind of supper they enjoyed every night. But it was only known by the Lord that it would be his last supper. Christ said the blessing for the bread, just like every supper, only this time He explained what the bread would mean in the future. *After* supper, Christ gave the usual blessing for the wine and, like He did for the bread, explained what the wine would represent from then on. So the bread blessing and the wine blessing were the ones given at every supper. The Lord brought His friends to the realization of what every supper should represent. So every supper we have should be just like their supper. We should bless the bread before the meal and then, after supper, bless the wine. If you really want what the Lord was telling his disciples to do, we should do likewise.

Study the verses and come to your own conclusion, don't take our word for it. If you call your pastor we are sure they will convince you that their denomination has it right, even if it doesn't line up with what the word really says.

While proof-reading our writing, we came across Matthew 26:28: *"This is my blood of the covenant, which is poured out for many for the forgiveness of sins."* (NIV) When we read this, something jumped out to get us thinking again: "for many." The bread was given with "take eat this is my body," but the wine was "for many." This is interesting to say the least. His instructions about bread and wine were different. Do the right thing and try to dig deeper yourself. Maybe you can let us know what you have found out!

GENESIS 1 & 2

Let's look at this with open eyes, not the brainwashed eyes of your past.

The Hebrew title for Genesis is "B're sheet," which means "in the beginning."

Now the first word is rê'shîyth, pronounced ray sheeth. This word means the first, in place, time, order or rank, beginning, principal thing.

The next word is bâ râ, pronounced baw-raw'. It means to create. It could also refer to the Creator.

Next is Elôhîym, pronounced El-o-heem. In the Hebrew language, it can be used to refer to the supreme God.

Now the pessimist would read that and say something like, "It says in the beginning whatever the higher power was created God." The pessimist could influence a lot of people by saying or interpreting a falsehood with ignorance. That misconception, told over and over, would grow in certain circles until it became their truth. It's not our truth, but they would get their point across and deceive many people. They would accomplish what they wanted to do: distracting people from the word of God! Most people want someone to tell them what they already believe in order to build up their ego, confirm their way of life, or make them feel confident so they don't have to study the real word. By going along with someone else, they believe they already know what's right.

We have two words for you if you fall into one of those categories: hypocritical Pharisees!

How do you think a lot of people were and are lead astray? A lot of preachers, teachers and professors have a huge ego trip because they have the higher education and they have been taught a certain way. In their opinion, they already know the right way to believe and interpret the word. Don't try to tell them by using scripture that they are wrong because their denomination has everything already figured out! Doesn't that sound like what some of the Pharisees did in the time of Christ and right after He died? Now we have people who sound just like the Pharisees influencing people and trying to get individuals away from what The Lord is trying to get across to the good people of today. To us they sound just like the Pharisees!

Some followers get lazy. You know, "the preacher said it so it must be true, even though it wasn't scriptural." That is what we call dime store psychology, which leads to comic book philosophy! But instead of Pharisees we have preachers, professors, and teachers of Sunday school classes or bible study classes who fall into their own trap. They would never agree with any of this because they would have to admit they have instructed people wrongly for however long they have been spreading their Philosophy!

> Genesis 1:1 (CJB) - *In the beginning God created the heavens and the earth.*

God started with earth, animals, and man. What we want you to do is study Chapter 1. Read all of Chapter 1, not Chapter 2 yet, just Chapter 1. When you study, try to look at what Chapter 1 says without Chapter 2 influencing you. Try not to use any preacher's directions and especially not a teacher's classroom instruction on how you have to look at what it says! Again, read Chapter 1 by itself. Don't think about any brainwashing of your past. Just grasp what Chapter 1 is saying. That is very, very important!

Now that you've read Chapter 1, as far as we've been able to grasp, you've just studied something that is undated with any accuracy whatsoever! Some teachers guess and some preachers lead without any real proof whatsoever. In other words, they use what they want you to believe so you align yourself with them. After reading it again, without any preconceived ideas, the reality is that there is no way of dating Chapter 1! You may disagree, but that's most likely because an individual led you to read it and interpret it their way!

Before we go any further, we know there are people who are saying, "That's just our way of looking at it" or maybe they're saying something like "That's the Old Testament, not the New, so we don't have to pay that much attention to it any longer." There may be some saying, "So what? I believe what my preacher, teacher, and denomination say and they bundle Chapter 1 and 2 together. That's how our preacher preaches, that's how they teach and believe, that's how I learned it, and that's how I believe no matter what!" Well, that's your choice. It's your choice what to believe and what not to believe. Some say it's your choice where you spend eternity. It's your choice to follow someone's brainwashing instead of what the Word really says. Some people preach and teach that you chose, heaven or hell. (We don't believe that, but some do. If it was that easy, then everyone would say HEAVEN wouldn't they?)

You could say that those statements are only true if you line up with what God says. What if the Father's meaning was for instruction and that only now denominations turn fact into a misleading concept. Then it's not your choice. They have not only led you in a direction, they have made that choice for you, right or wrong. They make it, not you. But you are just one of the many who will suffer because of it!

God gave us the ability to understand, interpret, and grasp the Word. We just need to observe what the Word really says and not be led down that large road to that huge door that leads to damnation!

> Genesis 1:1 (CJB) - *In the Beginning God Created the Heavens and the Earth.*

We believe the main point is and will always be GOD CREATED! But what about the big bang theory? What about the single cell that crawled out of the slime somewhere, and reproduced by itself until that one cell became an ape and then a man? As far as we are concerned, if that's how you want to believe, that's up to you. It changes nothing with our studies or how we look at "In the beginning God created." Now, in your theory, it took a lot longer to get to the point of man and the growth of civilization. It took a very long time with the creation theory also, but not quite that long.

In verse 2, the earth was formless and void, just water. In verse 3, God said "let there be light." In verse 4, light was good. In verse 5, God called light day and darkness night. And there was evening and morning, the first day. (When you read that, did you notice it starts out with the evening first?) In verse 6, there was just a mass of water. It doesn't say anything about ground or sky. There was nothing except water. In verse 7, God changed all that by separating that mass of water, some above, some below. God, The Father of the Universe, had a plan all along! In verse 8, God called the expanse "sky", and there was evening and morning, the second day. In verse 9, God said, "Let the water under the sky be gathered to one place, and let dry ground appear." And it was so. (NIV) In verse 10, God called the dry land "Earth", the gathering together of the water He called "Seas", and God saw that it was good. (CJB) In verse 11, Then God said, "Let the land produce vegetation: seed-bearing plants and trees on the land that bear fruit with seed in it according to their various kinds." and it was so. (NIV) In verse 12, They all say, God saw that it was good. Verse 13 states "so there was evening and morning, the third day." (CJB) In verse 14, God said, "lights in the dome of the sky to divide the day from the night; let them be for signs, seasons, days and years." (CJB) Verse 15 says "and let them be lights in the vault of the sky to give light on the earth, and it was so." (NIV) Verse 16 states "God made two great lights, the greater light to govern the day and the lesser one to govern the night, he also made the stars." (NIV) (That way there was a separation. The sun, moon, and stars never collide with perfect tilt, perfect rotation, and perfect distance from the earth for life of any kind to exist!) In verse 19, there was evening and morning, the fourth day. Verse 20 shows the water teeming with living creatures and birds flying over the earth. Verse 21 says that God created the things of the sea and the birds of the land according to their kind. (God saw that it was good.) In verse 22, God commands sea life to be fruitful and increase in number and fill the seas and for birds to increase on the earth. Verse 23 states that there was evening and morning: day five. Now we have day six. It seems God was busy on that day. The interesting part to us in verse 24 is the wording. There seems to be a distinction between cattle and wild animals. If there were no humans to take care of the cattle, wouldn't they be wild animals until humans came along? It also says he made different kinds of livestock plus creatures that move along the ground. In verse 25, all three, the livestock, wild animals, and ground crawlers were also to reproduce according to their kind. It doesn't say how many he made of each. It just says, the birds, fish, cattle, wild animals, and the ground crawlers. But it does say he made them male and female. It states they were created by the Word of God, not the number or amount of them The Lord had made. They were to just reproduce according to their kind. And God saw that it was good.

Then we have Verse 26 where it depends which translation you read. Some of them say "let us make man in our image." Others may say something like, "let us make humankind in our image." Now read Verse 27 without the influence of your past. God created human beings in His image, he created them male and female, he created them, and then God gave everything to the humans He just made! In verse 28 God commands them to be fruitful, increase their numbers, and rule over them. (This one is the most Interesting to us!) In verse 29, Then God said, "I give you every seed-bearing plant on the face of the whole earth and every tree that has fruit with seed in it. They will be yours for food." (NIV) (Did you catch the interesting point? NO forbidden tree! There was NO tree that God said they couldn't eat from at that time in history!)

Chapter 2 states that God rested, even though when Moses wrote it wasn't divided into Chapter 1 and Chapter 2. Chapter 1 does state that God rested from what He created. How long did He rest? No one knows the answer to that one!

Here is another interesting aspect: up until after the flood, time was really undated! Now we know a lot of biblical scholars are flying off the handle complaining about that statement, but it's true! We know that Abraham was born around 2160 BC. The Egyptians used paper and Ink around 2500 BC. Moses was born around 1526 BC. We believe that Moses wrote what God wanted him to, but we still say that from before the flood to 2500 BC time was and will always stay undated!

People have tried to make their logic fit the scriptures by saying that there were 2000 years from Adam to Abraham, 2000 years from Abraham to Christ, and that there will be 2000 years from Christ to His second coming. Sounds great, but it seems to be pure speculation! We really don't know the date of creation. Heck, we don't even have an accurate date of the flood without guessing, flipping a coin, or some other imaginary pretend fact-finding method! Our point is that, without people putting their imagination in high gear, no one can date Creation accurately!

Now that all you biblical scholars are twisting in your chairs, think about this: Genesis 2:7-8 (NIV) – *Then the Lord God formed the man from the dust of the ground and breathed into his nostrils the breath of life, and the man became a living being. Now the Lord God had planted a garden in the east, in Eden; and there he put the man he had formed.* Here is the interesting point: if it was to the east of Eden, there was already an Eden! There was a land already there by the name of Cush and the river Tigris runs along the east side of Asshur. So we have four rivers, the Pishon, Gihon, Tigris, and Euphrates. We have the lands of Eden, Havilah, Cush, and we have Asshur. All those lands where there before creation. So we have established countries, cities, and named rivers. Who did that? It seems that the lands and rivers were already there.

Could there be a time when God made everything (Chapter 1) but the people didn't follow God totally the way they were supposed to. The time lapse or the number of days wouldn't really be affected by reading Chapter 1 as the beginning of man-kind and the beginning of the world as we know it, but the instructions are clear on what we are to do: reproduce. Then after the God of the universe rested and the people of the earth started to be a very unlikeable existence for the Father to put up with, God made a man out of the dust of the ground and placed him in a special garden that was perfect. God put the garden East of Eden and it seems that, if they would have followed The Fathers instructions this time, they would have stayed in that protected place and been safe from the people of Eden,

Havilah, Cush and Asshur! Adam and Eve didn't follow the instructions either, they were sent out of the protection, security and the perfection that God set up for them.

Interesting tidbit: look at the wording in Chapter 4. We have Cain killing Abel and by Verse 14 Cain says "whoever finds me will kill me." He was the first-born, so who would kill him? Verse 16 says he went to a land called Nod. If he went to the land of Nod, there must have been people already there! Who were they if he was the first?

Now is this theory perfect? No. When a person studies, the object should be to get to the truth, even if it doesn't line up with a certain religion, a denominational doctrine, church, synagogue, or philosophy. If a conclusion is reached that lines up with none of them, but is the truth, that's all it takes. If you study what the Word says by the Word instead of with some preconceived idea that your church, synagogue, preacher, rabbi or teacher must say to prove their point of view, then you just might find truth. No matter what you've been taught, read, believe, follow, or reject, The Truth will still always be truth! It doesn't change, people do!

Genesis 6:2 (NIV) states, *The sons of God saw that the daughters of men were beautiful, and they married any of them they chose.* We would like you to think about this. It just might give you something to ponder. The "daughters of men" were from the people in Chapter 1, "the sons of God" came from Adam and Eve's descendants in Chapter 2.

Have a look at Genesis 2:24 (NIV) - *That is why a man leaves his father and mother and is united to his wife, and they become one flesh.* Read with the Chapter 1 theory in mind. Then study Genesis 1:28a (NIV) - *God blessed them and said to them, "Be fruitful and increase in number; fill the earth and subdue it."* You will find there were already people coming together, having sex, creating children, and becoming parents. When the child grew, he or she would leave their parents for the one they were in union with. Even if they weren't married, they still would have had to have two people, even if either or both had more than one mate. The mother would still have been a parent to the child, cared for the child, helped it grow. After a time the child would find their own partner for reproduction.

We believe that the way of life as scripture says is to reproduce and fill the earth. Why are we here? To do what The Father says: reproduce, increase in number, fill the earth, and subdue it. Like everything else, we are to reproduce according to our kind!

Vegetation reproduces vegetation.
Fruit trees reproduce fruit trees.
Fish reproduce fish.
Wild animals reproduce wild animals.
Livestock reproduces livestock.
Birds reproduce birds.
Snakes reproduce snakes.
Humans reproduce humans. Our first instruction from God was to reproduce according to our kind!

Elephants didn't come from mice! Apes didn't come from penguins! Whales didn't come from minnows! Everything is to reproduce according to its kind. Humans have stepped in and messed things up a bit. They have crossbred trees, plants, and animals. Why? They say it is to make a better animal for the field or so people could have a different kind of fruit. From Genesis 1 and Genesis 2 we are given one instruction: TO REPRODUCE!

GENESIS 3

Genesis 3:6 tells us that the fruit looked good and Eve desired to gain wisdom. She desired to be smarter and she thought that by eating the fruit she would gain wisdom. Then she gave it to Adam. They both ate and found out that going against the Father's commands changed things!

You could say they did get smarter, smart enough to know they were naked. At first, like little children, being naked wasn't something they had to worry about. They were both without any clothing, like some tribes around the world today. But as the fruit brought knowledge, it seems their innocence was separated into a desire to know more. Here is an interesting thought - Scripture never says that they felt sorry for what they did, only that they knew they were naked. They must have been shocked with this newfound knowledge to think they had to hide from God because they were naked.

At first they were like little children who put their total trust in mom and dad. That's how it seems they lived. They put their total trust in someone else and that was in God. This went on until they were influenced by another "someone else," the serpent!

This special civilization fell because they disobeyed God! The man listened to the woman, the woman listened to the serpent, and they both acted on their impulses. They didn't keep the rules that God gave them. Unlike the civilization in chapter one where they could eat from every tree, these people were not to eat from the tree in the middle of the garden! Now before some biblical scholar writes me, those are not my words. They came directly from scripture, Genesis 1:29 and Genesis 2:17.

If a person studies Genesis 3 without those preconceived teachings of your past, what do the verses 1-15 say? The serpent was more crafty than any of the wild animals the Lord God had made. It doesn't say the serpent was Satan. Now it does say that the serpent talked to the woman and she talked back. Was the serpent walking around speaking in a language that the man and woman understood? It seems that he not only could speak, but he was also most likely not a ground crawler or what we would call a snake. In other words, it would not have been a punishment if he already were a ground crawler.

The woman admitted that she talked to the serpent and the serpent talked to her. When Adam and Eve were in the Garden, could they actually talk to all the animals? Could the animals talk back to them with a language, they both understood?

When you read Genesis 2:8-17, you find there were two trees in the middle of the Garden, the tree of life and the tree of the knowledge of good and evil. The command was that they were free to eat from any tree in the garden; but they must not eat from the tree of the knowledge of good and evil. It doesn't say they couldn't eat from the tree of life, just the tree of the knowledge of good and evil. However, after the couple had eaten from the forbidden tree, God didn't want to give them the opportunity of taking from the tree of life and live forever. Maybe that is just our way of looking at that part, but it is an interesting way to look at it, isn't it? Maybe we are wrong, maybe not, we have been wrong before, but unlike most preachers and denominations, we will admit it!

We believe mankind runs wild with these verses! That part of scripture doesn't say the serpent was Satan. It does say the serpent was more crafty than any of the wild animals the Lord God had made. It says they talked to one another. God, the serpent, man, woman and maybe all the other animals were speaking the same language at first. Who knows? Maybe the other animals weren't crafty enough to speak. But why would only the serpent be given that ability? Is that what should be understood, when the word says, "the serpent was more crafty." Was he was the only one given that ability? We really don't know and it wouldn't change anything in our point of view anyway, but it is an interesting thought, isn't it?

Satan may have used the serpent, but the serpent wasn't Satan. The serpent may have been a crafty son of a gun. In those days he might have been a speaking, influential, smart type of creation. Snakes are not usually people's favorite pets, but they still seem to be crafty, cunning, and smart in many ways. As far as we know, they don't seem to be able to talk any longer. They must communicate with one another, like everyone else, according to their kind. Would you say that Adam and Eve were really any different than our society today?

We guess one of our points would be to ask are we really any different from them? Think about these: (1) After a while, would curiosity get the best of us and would we take a bite out of the fruit, maybe just to see what we were missing? (2) When you took the bite, would you own up to your actions or would you get some lawyer to prove it wasn't your fault? (3) Would you blame someone else so you would look better to the boss? In other words, it's someone else's fault too. At least you could share the blame. Maybe the penalty wouldn't be so bad if you were able to share it with someone else or cast some of the blame to someone else! Sounds like society today doesn't it?

We bet there are people who are saying they wouldn't have taken a bite out of the fruit. Let's see what they may say to just a few rules to be followed today by God and Man. These are for the people who say they would obey all the rules and not ever take a bite. (1) When driving, do you ever go over the speed limit? If you do and get caught, do you try to get out of a ticket by blaming someone or something else? Interesting. You wouldn't take a bite if no one was watching, yet you can't even be trusted with a simple thing as the speed limit! (2) Would you invite a friend to participate in an activity that may not have been the smartest activity you've ever done? Then, when it was over, you say something like, "that was your choice to participate, and I just put the invite out to you." (3) When you got caught, would you complain the punishment was too harsh on you? In your mind, you're just the one who got caught. After all, everyone else is doing it too, so why blame me or penalize me for what everybody is doing? Doesn't it sound like Adam, shifting the blame? Why are we any different than Adam and Eve were?

We say this a number of times in the book, but we also feel we can't stress it enough: What is needed is TRUTH! If we can stand on a house top and proclaim the truth, if we teach only what The Father wants, if we never lead people down the wrong path, if we are never right, if we are never wrong, if everybody listens to the truth, if no one believes the truth... all those ifs still don't change one word of TRUTH! Study to find TRUTH because that is the only thing that doesn't change! The truth will always be there. Whether you find it or not, it is still truth. Study to find TRUTH, not denominational doctrine of any kind!

The truth will always be truth no matter how many believe it, reject it, add to it, or take away from it. Everyone should aim at truth. The fact is that most people go more for the feel-good feeling a preacher, teacher, or singer may give them. We guess that they believe if they feel good, then it must be God making them feel that way and therefore it must be truth that they are experiencing. If that statement is true then, with all those denominations and religions, the real truth must change with time and therefore must not have been a real strong truth in the first place! If that's how you look at it or how your religion views truth, we feel sorry for you and everyone aligned with you and your religion. The Truth is just that, THE TRUTH. It hasn't changed with time! It can't be twisted to fit your wants or to fit your denomination! It doesn't change with society. It hasn't ever changed and it never will!

Do the hardest thing an individual can do - study without any preconceived ideas or denominational brainwashing. Everyone needs to find one thing - THE TRUTH!

THE MAIN REASON FOR THIS BOOK

This may seem like a repeat of some of the writings, but we feel the main topic doesn't change, it just gets better. So bear with us, please.

The main reason for this book is to respond to the misleading interpretation of God's Word by teachers and preachers who want to dictate the Bible instead of guiding the people who are looking for truth! There is a big difference between guiding someone with the Word and leading someone down the path to their denomination or their religion. Most people, when talking scripture, talk their denomination and it doesn't even seem to matter what religion you call yourself. When people do that, it fails the person speaking and the person or class who is listening!

This book is neither down nor high on any religion, but it does and will point out where we feel a certain belief or practice doesn't line up with what scripture says. If your religion practices a certain way or believes something contrary to what is written about as scriptural, then we believe it's up to the individual to find truth! We would suggest that *you* study to find truth. If you go to the teacher or preacher that leads you in a certain direction in the first place, then you may end up with what you have already been taught and you will always fall right back into the practice you had believed before, even if it's just a denominational way of looking at a long standing ritual. Right or wrong, you are still in it.

In this book, you may well find different ways and ideas to try to get teachers to follow the Bible instead of what they were taught or a philosophy that they heard their preacher or someone else point to for many years.

STUDY

There is a certain amount of brainwashing in every religion on the face of the earth. That's how they get their religion and denominations to grow and their philosophies to spread.

Here is the most important advice we will be able to give you. While reading this book, please stop and think about what we have written. If it gives you a new way of looking at a certain topic, ritual, denomination, your religion, or any religion, then you need to study to find TRUTH!

That is an easy statement, but it is the hardest thing to do. Most people go back to what their denomination has taught them on any topic and they look at the topic with a closed mind. You might as well say that you never really studied it at all and that you just followed someone down that huge road to that large door. If you study with an open mind to truth, then you have to divorce yourself from the practices and the brainwashing of your past. What some people don't realize is that at times you may find out what you believe has a hint of truth. If that is all you want, then go for the hint. There are many times when you study with that open mind that you find out that you're following a denominational ritual and philosophy. In reality, it doesn't line up with the Word unless you take a part here and a part there. Then, by God, it fits! We believe your religion should fit the whole part, not bits and pieces!

This book has writings on a number of topics that people have actually asked us to research. In most cases, when we gave them the Biblical answer, they would not accept it because that's not how their religion viewed it or practiced the topic. So, in most cases, we started writing them down and filing them in categories. The amount of study to find truth about one little topic can take weeks or months for just a little topic, not the larger or more intense questions.

We never really thought about chapters, it's more about topics. We are trying to give each topic the space and time each topic requires. In most cases, we try to bring out the biblical place to find the answer, or at least point you to where you can start. We can't have all the fun of finding truth!

STUDY

We have told you before and repeat it again: we are not what you would call biblical scholars. We never went to seminary school or to a certain college to be brainwashed on how we need to read and believe the way they want you to.

We believe this way: A teacher teaches a class. Then the future preachers and teachers come out of the class believing the way the instructor taught, otherwise their grades wouldn't be high enough to brag about. Then they spread the philosophy of what they have been taught. Whether it's right or wrong, they pass it on down to their students. The preachers and teachers send their children to be taught by the same ones who taught them and the cycle starts all over again!

Everyone should read this book with an open mind and an open bible. Study to find truth. The real truth just might surprise you!

WISDOM

There are many verses in scripture that relate to wisdom. Here are a few that caught our eye. They may just get you into studying or at least looking a few of them up for yourself. All scripture passages are taken from the NIV unless otherwise indicated.

> Psalm 111:10(NIV) - *The fear of the Lord is the beginning of wisdom; all who follow his precepts have good understanding, to him belongs eternal praise.*

Does "the fear of the Lord" mean you're scared to go to him? No, but you had better remember who is the one in charge! When scripture says "The fear of the Lord" it doesn't mean you tremble every time you think of Christ, or do something wrong. When you lose the concept of who is the boss, you start thinking you're in charge and you're number one!

> Proverbs 11:2(NIV) - *When Pride comes, then comes disgrace, but with humility comes wisdom.*

Does this verse say that you shouldn't be proud of what you have accomplished in life? No, but when you get so prideful of yourself, you just may have a fall in this life or the one after.

The verse states that one gains wisdom with humility. That doesn't mean you believe everything someone else says just because they said it. Neither does it mean that you accept it without spending your own time in studying the same topic. When you're in the process of learning, you might say you're humble to the one who is doing the teaching. That could be anyone who knows more about a topic than you or maybe you're humble to the leading of God.

Proverbs 13:10(NIV) - *Where there is strife, there is pride, but wisdom is found in those who take advice.*

Think about that one for a while. If you are closed minded on getting your way and you will not listen to anyone about anything, then your pride takes over. It becomes your religion. You are right, no matter what the Bible says! To us, that sounds like a number of religions of today. They are right even if you have to look at it with your eyes partly closed to find their point of view.

If a person thinks he knows it all, you will always have strife, quarrels, and a person who is arrogant! He can't be taught anything, new or old. If someone takes advice, you may find one of two things. The other person has a point worth looking into, or that other guy doesn't have a clue about the topic. You may be repeating what someone has brainwashed him about. In both scenarios, you learn something. We will always advise against jumping on anyone's bandwagon because it lines up with your church or denomination. We know we repeat this over and over, but it is the most important thing we can pass on to you - STUDY! You can take advice from anyone. But remember that is all it is, their advice to you about what they believe or what they have been taught. If you study the topic yourself, you just may have gained valuable wisdom, one way or the other.

Proverbs 16:16(NIV) - *How much better to get wisdom than gold, to get insight rather than silver!*

That Proverb goes against most people's way of looking at life. One should gain wisdom first. About what? Our answer, as you could guess, would be God. People may say something like whatever catches your attention, such as your business, your passion, or your desires. There are people who say your desire is your passion. That's not always true. You may have a desire to learn the truth about God but want everyone else to do the footwork. Truthfully, you could say you learned the passion of someone else. When you turn your learning over to someone, it really isn't your passion. It's theirs!

Does Proverbs 16:16 mean you shouldn't have gold? Not at all, but when your gold becomes your God, you just might want to rethink your opinion. We believe Proverbs 16:16 talks about the gold or money, when it becomes the main desire and God becomes second place in their life.

What is it about wisdom that scares people? If a person learns the truth through wisdom, does it change their belief, philosophy, outlook on life, or their view on their religion? Wisdom just may open people's eyes to truth. If a person sees their walk is not as spiritual as it should be, then wisdom has done a good job in that person's life. Did the wisdom really mean something to them and prompt change or did the person go right back to the brainwashing of their past?

What good is wisdom if, after you gain it, you go right back to the same stuff you had before? The old way made you feel good about yourself? Then wisdom was a useless message for you. It was a waste of your time and maybe money on your part, not ours. Truth will always be truth. Either you listen to truth and absorb it or you listen to truth and let it fall away from you because it doesn't fit what you believe or the brainwashing of your religion, denomination, or lifestyle.

Is there a difference between truth and wisdom? Yes. A person may have wisdom to write a book, preach a sermon, to teach people what they believe, or make a million on a business deal. But does the fact that it can be found in a book make it the truth? If you hear a message in a sermon, does that message become your truth? If a teacher points out something, is that always a true concept? A person making a million on a business deal doesn't point to the truth. They may get a cash reward, but that alone doesn't make it truth.

A person may pray for truth and wisdom, but what happens when your wisdom interferes with your truth? Does your truth get altered to fit your wisdom? Most people would say no, but we have found out that people like to twist truth to fit their lifestyle. Then, after time, they can always find a preacher who will align themselves with them. In some way or other, the preacher will make the person feel like he understands them and will work in their favor.

This may not be a very nice thing to say, but we are not here to powder-puff the message. Most people are like pigs! If you clean a pig and the pig sees a mud hole that he has always enjoyed, he goes right back to roll in the same mud hole he knew before he was cleaned up because he likes the feel of the mud. He is just like he was before the cleaning, maybe even worse!

Whether they admit it or not, most people will go right back to their favorite mud hole after hearing the truth. Why? Because they are comfortable with the brainwashing of a certain religion, denomination, or the message of some preacher even if it doesn't line up with the truth. What matters most to them is that they feel good while alive on this place we call earth. You might say they feel good until they find out that the truth was not where their pastor led them. It's sad to say, but it's then too late for them because this life is over after the new one starts. We have to ask ourselves if this new one is the place the real truth takes you or the spot where you don't hear the truth at all?

Now we are by no means saying that since we wrote this book your eyes should be open to the truth or that we are smarter than you. NEVER take our word for it. Study so the unaltered truth will set you free from the everlasting torment that will start when our Savior returns.

Most people point to a large number of scriptures to prove a point. We do believe that the scripture is the real unaltered truth. Be careful not to let the brainwashing alter what, how, and why it was written. Here is an example of what we mean - We have heard preachers say they were so smart on the topics in scripture that they can use it to argue both sides to any of the topics and make either seem logical to the listener.

Maybe that's why banks and certain financial places of business only give good money to the people who work there to study, so when they handle a large amount of cash, they notice the counterfeit bills when they come along. That's what we have been told. We feel an individual doesn't need to hear or see the counterfeit to know the real truth. Why would a preacher who has all knowledge need to know both sides of every topic? And if he does, why does he feel the need to announce it from the pulpit? Does that make him feel smarter? Maybe, in his mind, that makes him look smart to the congregation. Why do so many preachers have an "I" syndrome when they talk to a group or preach to a church? Most people should look past the "better than thou" attitude of their preacher and be like the people at the banks who only look for the real stuff and truth.

We know that there are some who are thinking, "I believe what my church says is the truth," or "If I don't know both sides then how do I know the truth?" Good thought, but our answer to that is what we said before - Study, Study, Study! Never take our word for it. You need to study so you find the truth. This writing may give you something on which to lean, but you need to not hold on to leaning. You need to stand straight and tall for the unaltered, unmistakable truth of the Word. Please avoid watered-down denominational viewpoints. Study to find the truth. It Will Surprise You!

People want what we call the "fast food religion." Like these fast food chains, they get you in and out in a matter of minutes. We get the feeling that there are people saying, "What's wrong with that? You learn, you don't have to waste time, and then you're on your way." That may be good if you're ordering an ultra-thin burger. That may taste ok and it may even look good, but when you take that first bite and get all topping and bun, you can't find the meat. You're receiving just the bun and the condiments of the advertisement. That seems how most religions are - a lot of false advertisement. When you take that first bite, there is just bun and condiments with no meat. That burger may taste good, look good, and feel good in your hand, but there's no meat with that bite. There is no meaty nourishment whatsoever in that bite. Oh, if you keep eating you eventually get a small taste of meat, but it's the idea of the meat that they want you to have and it's nothing like their advertising.

We remember, when fast food chains started up, you could actually see the burger. Now it seems you have to send out a search party to find it. The prices have gone higher while the size of the meat is about 90% imagination!

That's the way it is with a lot of religions today. The Father may have been the focus at first, but now it seems you have to take a few bites before you get past the bun and condiments of each religion. When you finally get past the bun and condiments, you may get a very small idea of The Father, if you get to Him at all!

This part is about Wisdom, not hamburgers. So let us say that it is amazing how the people of today want the same fast lane for both!

In Proverbs, it states a number of things God hates. Yet, we have heard preachers preach that God doesn't hate anything or anyone. Well then, maybe their preacher just skipped the book of Proverbs. Oh, they have some interesting, influential explanation. We are sure of that!

Your wisdom of The Father should come on everyone because wisdom through studying is what we should all desire!

> Proverbs 3:35 (CJB) - *The wise win honor, but fools win shame.*

Every version we have all points to the same interpretation, maybe not using the same exact words, but the meaning is that the way of wisdom leads to honor and the way of fools leads to shame.

This may not be the smartest thing we are ever going to write, but here goes - We're not that Bright! We really don't know how or why The Father gives understanding to some and not to everyone. Maybe it's because He has put the desire to study for the truth in the people He knows will follow through with it.

We have to study topics, sermons, teachings, and denominational doctrine over and over before The Father allows us to get past our old church doctrine and the denominational brainwashing to get to what the truth in scripture really points to. Most people give up on finding truth way before they should. It's easier to just go along with what their denomination says. It makes you feel good and it's easy. It's the fast food chain all over again!

We can hear the argument now. "My church has always believed this way and our denomination is right! Why? Because that's how they taught me and all of my family." Here is another good one, "Our denomination only preaches and believes in teaching the whole truth because we only go by what the Bible says!"

We are not saying your church, denomination, pastor, teacher or even your children's teacher is saying anything wrong, but we can't say they are leading people down the right path either.

In our opinion, all pastors and all teachers, no matter what their religion or their denomination is, should be pushing individuals to study the word without the wall of what they have heard in class or in church. If you study with an open mind to the truth and clear your mind of the denominational brainwashing, you just may find out that what you've been told for many years doesn't line up with what the scriptures really say. You just might find out your belief lines up with the Word on certain topics, but you have to come up with that by the Word, not by what you've been taught in a certain religion or by a denominational teaching of your past.

All preachers say they go by the Word. All teachers say they only teach the true Word of God. If either one of those is true, then why do we have so many different kinds of doctrine in the same religion? If you stop and think about that one, it's saying, "I believe a certain way because of the teacher I had or the preacher said so." Is it really the truth of the Word or is there some kind of brainwashing along the way? Of course everyone knows that if you feel good afterward that's all that counts… right up until you breathe your last breath. Then it's too late to change, but you did feel good while you were here. Maybe people think, "Who cares?" after that!

It doesn't matter to us if you agree with us or not. This isn't about what we believe is right or wrong, it's about studying and finding truth.

It's not our job to get anyone into Heaven. That is between the individual and God! Most people, whether they're a believer in the God of the Universe or not, think they are good enough! Good enough for what? Good enough to get to their heaven. Good enough to live the life they want. Good enough because, according to them, they're living a nice life without trusting in God, the Father of everything!

After all, that's all that counts, isn't it? If you are buried in the ground, a pile of bones, lost in water at sea, cremated, or some other form of total deterioration to this body, does it really matter if someone else can find your physical remains? Does it matter that The Father has an account of you because of your true following of Him or was it that you were chasing anything because it made you feel good even though it had very little real truth whatsoever!

Do we follow and believe because of what some teacher or preacher talks about? Do we follow a denominational teaching on any topic? Do we read the word without an in-depth study of what the Word says? The answer to all those is NO and that should be every believers answer also. If it isn't, then you're brainwashed as much as any person. A dictator leads the people of his country with the same hope that the people will follow him because he said so. Most likely, you follow without any amount of study. In all reality, you trust someone else with your Eternity. A dictator wants to prove that he is the only one who can give you truth or get you what you desire. Don't believe the bible anymore. Believe what the dictator wrote and line up with what he believes. After all, if everything lines up, then God sees to it that you get those warm fuzzy feelings, doesn't he? There is more on that in another topic!

Is there more to the truth than what people see in their church? Is the denomination making sure you see and believe only what they want you to? There are a lot of denominational beliefs that say that they want you to study with an open mind to the truth. When you do, here is what it says and guess what! Somehow it lines up with their doctrine, one way or another!

STUDY

Wisdom isn't learned by reading this book. Wisdom isn't learned by listening to a preacher. Wisdom isn't learned by studying with a teacher. When you do any of those learning steps, you have a tendency to learn what they want you to learn and that isn't always the real truth. Wisdom isn't a magical event that happens when The Father snaps his fingers and poof! you get wisdom. Wisdom is learned by studying the truth with open eyes to what the bible is really saying. It is not learned through a preacher or teacher and certainly not by finding out what your denominational doctrine says.

When you read James 1:5, you find that if you lack wisdom you should ask God for it, who gives it generously to all without finding fault. But when you ask, you must believe and not doubt. The Father gives you wisdom. You may be swayed by your denominational upbringing, a church, a preacher, a teacher or even by your success. What The Father gives you is truth. You may have to sift all that other stuff like sand through a screen to get what's left. Hopefully, that would be the wisdom from God!

Wisdom isn't an easy topic to write about. When we talk about wisdom, it seems to step on people's toes. Everyone who thinks they understand the message from God believes what their denominational teaching has guided them to. That seems to be the logical way of looking at scripture until you really study with your eyes open to find truth!

Wisdom is such a small word with so much impact on every individual concerning the life here and the hereafter!

Study with The Father's leading, not by some denominational doctrine, preacher's sermon, your church philosophy, teacher's lesson, or even any leading you may get from this book!

You will see this next writing a number of times through this book.

Don't believe anything because you read it in this book. STUDY to find your truth with The Father! He will open your eyes and James 1:5 will mean so much more to you than ever before!

THE EYE

Matthew 6:19-24 (NIV) - *Do not store up for yourselves treasures on earth, where moths and vermin destroy, and where thieves break in and steal. But store up for yourselves treasures in heaven, where moths and vermin do not destroy, and where thieves do not break in and steal. For where your treasure is, there your heart will be also. The eye is the lamp of the body. If your eyes are healthy, your whole body will be full of light. But if your eyes are unhealthy, your whole body will be full of darkness. If then the light within you is darkness, how great is that darkness! No one can serve two masters. Either you will hate the one and love the other, or you will be devoted to the one and despise the other. You cannot serve both God and Money.*

Those are very interesting parts in scripture. You might say that preachers and teachers hit them lightly unless they want people to tithe more. They may say something like, "A good eye is one that is fixed on God." Can anyone argue that point? Of course not. That is a true statement. But, in reality, that statement has nothing to do with what preachers usually talk about when they use that part of scripture!

Some bible headlines for those verses read, "The Messiah teaches about money" But what they said in verse 22, "the eye is the lamp of the body," doesn't sound like money anymore. Then verse 24's ending is, "you can't serve both God and Money."

If the heading talks about money and the end talks about money, then the middle must also talk about money!

The KJV wording and informational section seem to point to darkness as unhealthy when it says "evil eye." It sounds so spiritual to say that the "evil eye" means something that comes from the dark side. Does the dark side mean money, Satan, and riches, or could there be a very logical explanation that translators seem to miss?

There are a number of things we need to remember. Matthew was a Hebrew, a Jew. As a matter of fact, his name would have been Mattityahu. Being a Hebrew, he would have thought and written like a Hebrew, using the Hebrew language! In our English versions, it seems that verses 19, 20, and 21 talk about money or at least your treasures here on earth.

We have heard preachers and teachers say that this means a man shouldn't look at a pretty girl twice. If you look once and then you look away, it means you're not lusting. If you look the second time, it means you crossed over to the evil eye, you're lusting, and you've sinned because your eye was unhealthy.

If you believe that, that's your choice, yet that is not what verses 22-23 are referring to at all! We fail to see the connection there. The Lord, The Messiah, The Son of God, He is the one who threw the statement about unhealthy eyes right in the middle of talking about money, and your treasures. There has to be a connection with verses 19 all the way through verse 24. The Lord didn't have a moment of daydreaming about the unhealthy or lustful eye, in the middle of stating his point about money and whom people serve. He kept to the point all the way through His speech. To figure out how and why He did this, a person has to go back to the Hebrew meaning of the words used. The Hebrew wording sets everything in place and on the right track!

We need to go over this part first. Is your wealth based on the money you have, your checking account, savings account, the car you drive, the size of your house, how many houses you own, where you live, the size of your investments, your job title, or your job itself? They all may point to your success here on earth to your friends or the people you meet. Well, that's fine and dandy while you're alive and maybe after death you will leave some family member very happy. With that theory, it benefits you while you're alive and others after you die. But what about you? The after death part is where it gets interesting. After death, have you stored up your treasures just for your earthly life or do you have your treasures in Heaven? Most people will answer that with: "I have my treasure in Heaven! You don't know the good work I've done in my life. The people who invested with me were blessed. The people we employed were blessed by having a job. Consider the contractor I paid to build my factory and the ones who built my three houses. Look at all the people I've blessed with my money!" You may have blessed a lot of people, but rust could destroy and those thieves could break in and steal. We are not saying those things aren't good in themselves. You have been blessed for your hard work and knowledge. Great job!

One version once said that "the eye is the lamp of your body, if your eye is good, your whole body will be full of light." Spiritual vision is our capacity to see clearly what God wants us to do and to see the world from his point of view. But this spiritual insight can be easily clouded. Self-serving desires, interests, and goals may block that vision. Serving God is the best way to restore it. A "good" eye is one that is fixed on God. That sounds fantastic doesn't it! It sounds so spiritual! It makes one feel as if that has to be what the eye, the lamp, the body, the good eye, and the light must pertain to.

We know there were many, many smart people, even some you would have to call scholars in the field of scripture working on this, but they missed the point of most of this section! We can hear the loyal fans of their versions saying: "How dare you say that scholars in the field of scripture were wrong? Who do you think you are?" All we can say is, if they are wrong, they're wrong!

Let's go over this one more time, Matthew was a Hebrew, a Jew. The Lord who is doing the speaking was a Hebrew, a Jew. The meaning would pertain to and align with The Hebrew language, since they would have been using the terminology of the Hebrew culture. They both would have used the words "Ayin Tovah" meaning "having an eye that's good." With a lot more studying we find that having an eye that is good really means "being generous!"

Here is verse 23 in the KJV - *But if thine eye be evil, thy whole body shall be full of darkness. If therefore the light that is in thee be darkness, how great is that darkness.* We need to go back to the Hebrew, to find the meaning. The Lord and Matthew would have said and written "Ayin Roah" when referring to having an eye that's bad. Those two words mean being stingy!

So let's put those into the terminology of the writer, as it is in scripture, verse by verse. Again, we'll use the NIV.

> Matthew 6:19 - *Do not store up your treasures on earth, where moths and vermin destroy, and where thieves break in and steal.*
>
> 20 - *But store up for yourselves treasures in heaven, where moths and vermin do not destroy, and where thieves do not break in and steal.*
>
> 21 - *For where your treasure is, there your heart will be also.*
>
> 22 - *The eye is the lamp of the body. If your eyes are healthy* (if you are generous), *your whole body will be full of light.*
>
> 23 - *But if your eyes are unhealthy* (if you are stingy), *your whole body will be full of darkness. If then the light within you is darkness, how great is that darkness!*
>
> 24 - *No one can serve two masters. Either he will hate the one and love the other, or you will be devoted to the one and despise the other. You cannot serve both God and Money.*

If you look at it as a good eye meaning you are generous and a bad eye meaning you are stingy, then verses 19-24 work with one thought and reason. If your money is your God, then you will be stingy. If you are generous, then The Father is your God! One cannot be both generous and stingy. If you are worth billions and you give to the poor, schools, outreach for disasters, and churches only for tax deductions, then your money has you. The poor, schools, disaster help, churches are all worthy causes and thank you for your support. But are people donating with a good eye or bad eye?

We are not naive enough to think that all rich people should give away everything to the poor or any other group. However, we as a society base our ideas about the individuals on their outward appearance or what we read about them. We don't see into their heart. We don't know why a certain individual does what he does. Whether you are rich or have very little, it still boils down to the simple fact that you can't serve both God and Money!

The same goes with people who have little. Who do you put your trust in? Do you tithe? Do you sit back and expect money to flow in because you tithe? Is God your savings account or your Savior?

There are a number of verses that pertain to or seem to point to money. You've probably seen the number of preachers on TV saying God wants you to be rich. "If you send money to my ministry, God will bless you beyond what you can dream of. Here are the names of some of those people who got blessed."

What a way to get people to come into your church! "If you come in our church, God will see to it that you become rich. He doesn't want you poor!"

He may not want you poor, but there will always be poor among us. That's what The Lord said in Matthew 26:11. That's what he told his disciples when a lady put expensive perfume on The Lords head. Do you think he would want you rich if you will make your riches your god?

To be totally honest, we are no different than most people. Does God want us rich? We hope so! We've served God when we had very little and when we've been blessed with enough. If you look around the world, many people consider us to be very well off. We would have to agree with them.

STUDY

According to what third-world countries have, we are totally blessed. The Father is still The Father. He is to be worshiped by us through His Son!

So whether you're Ayin Tovah (generous) or Ayin Roah (stingy), it's all about who you serve, God or Money! Mathew 6:24 says you can't serve both and that's according to what the Messiah said!

Those are not our words. They're The Lord's words to you, us, and our house!

WHO DO WE SERVE?

WHY

That is a very big word, a large question, and a word that leads to a lot of confused answers when most people look at the scriptures!

WHY would Cain say he would be killed when he was sent out of the land where his mom and dad were living? Who was out there?

WHY would The Father choose a bunch of people to call His own while knowing they would fall? He already knew that He would have to send His one and only Son to be tortured, humiliated, spit upon, and hung on a tree while naked and in great pain?

WHY pick those people knowing what was going to happen?

WHY in Matthew 15 would the Messiah say he was sent only to the lost sheep of Israel?

WHY were there only a few real close friends to The Messiah? Would you consider the 12 his friends or simply ministry companions that He or His father picked to follow Christ and make up His ministry?

WHY were some of his ministry companion's uneducated, smelly fishermen?

WHY would a well-educated, intelligent man, who was a Pharisee himself and part of the group who wanted to do away with everything that even pointed to that Yeshua, be picked to help out the cause?

WHY would people accept fast-talking individuals as their spiritual leaders?

WHY would a Hebrew continue to be of the Jewish Faith knowing that the treatment before the end will be devastating to say the least?

WHY would people believe they are saved because some preacher points out that if they read scripture a certain way and call on a name that has no definitive meaning whatsoever, then they are on their way to heaven?

WHY, when someone says The Messiah's real name, do people look at you like you don't know what you are talking about. Are we wrong to even say his real name? You may know this type of person, he is right even though he might as well call on Fred to be saved.

WHY is that Path to that small gate getting narrower? If you walk there, you will be able feel the grass that has been growing. Due to the lack of traffic, it will not be worn down. It will not be a dirt path. You will be able to feel the grass under your feet, if you walk down it at all!

WHY has the path that leads to destruction become so large? You might say it has become an eight lane interstate with a beautiful gate standing wide open so it won't hinder the huge amount of people entering it?

WHY would The Messiah say, "Not everyone who says to me Lord, Lord, will enter the kingdom of heaven, but only the one who does the will of my Father who is in heaven," and then say "I NEVER KNEW YOU"?

WHY is there only one way to Heaven? Why did our Lord say, "I am the way and the truth and the life"? People study to find out what Our Messiah said, yet there are only a few that are really listening!

WHY- has it taken so long to figure out what The Messiah was referring to with Matthew 7:21-23?

WHY are there times when good people are poor and then you find that the bad people become rich?

WHY doesn't God, The Father of the Universe, just start all over again with everyone? If you read the end you find out he does!

STUDY

WHY is there a time and place for everything? We know that there will be a different time and different place for you?

That word WHY is such a little word in our English language. After you really study that word, It seems to bring more questions,. The Messiah isn't that complex. He stated a lot of things that people run wild with, because they believe without any real study. Just because the preacher or teacher say so doesn't make it truth! Never stop asking WHY.

GOD'S METHOD

It may not always start out the same way!

There are a number of methods for The Father to interact with humans. We in no way know them all and we don't pretend to. With this study we are trying to show you just a number of ways He has used in the past. They may be to get people's attention or for the true meaning from God to come to His chosen people! Quotes from scripture are from the NIV unless otherwise noted.

Genesis 32:24-29 – So *Jacob was left alone, and a man wrestled with him till daybreak. When the man saw that he could not overpower him, He touched the socket of Jacob's hip, so that his hip was wrenched as he wrestled with the man. Then the man said, "Let me go, for it is daybreak." But Jacob replied, "I will not let you go unless you bless me." The man asked him, "What is your name?" "Jacob" he answered. Then the man said, "Your name will no longer be Jacob, but Israel, because you have struggled with God and with humans and have overcome." Jacob said, "Please tell me your name." But he replied, "Why do you ask my name?" Then he blessed him there.*

Genesis 32:30 (CJB) Ya'akov called the place P'ni-EL (face of God), "Because I have seen God face to face, yet my life is spared." (The method was God himself)

> Luke 1:11 - *Then an angel of the Lord appeared to him standing at the right side of the altar of incense.*

Luke 1:30 - *But the angel said to her, "Do not be afraid, Mary, you have found favor with God."* Luke 2:10 - *But the angel said to them, "Do not be afraid, I bring you good news that will cause great joy for all the people.* (The method was an Angel)

Genesis 28:13 - *There above it stood the Lord, and he said: "I am the Lord, the God of your father Abraham and the God of Isaac. I will give you and your descendants the land on which you are lying."*

Genesis 37:7 - *"We were binding sheaves of grain out in the field when suddenly my sheaf rose and stood upright, while your sheaves gathered around mine and bowed down to it."*

Genesis 37:9b - the sun and moon and stars were bowing down to Joseph.

Genesis 41:16 - *"I cannot do it," Joseph replied to Pharaoh, "but God will give Pharaoh the answer he desires."*

Matthew 1:20 - *But after he had considered this, an angel of the Lord appeared to him in a dream and said, "Joseph son of David, do not be afraid to take Mary home as your wife, because what is conceived in her is from the Holy Spirit."*

Matthew 2:13 - *When they had gone, an angel of the Lord appeared to Joseph in a dream. "Get up," he said, "take the child and his mother and escape to Egypt. Stay there until I tell you, for Herod is going to search for the child to kill him."*

(The method for the last five was by the way of a Dream)

Daniel 5:8 - *Then all the king's wise men came in, but they could not read the writing or tell the king what it meant.* (The method was, a finger writing on the wall)

Numbers 22:30 - *The donkey said to Balaam, "Am I not your own donkey, which you have always ridden, to this day? Have I been in the habit of doing this to you?" "No" he said.*
(The method was a talking donkey)

Exodus 13:21 (The method was, a pillar of cloud and a pillar of fire)

Jonah 2:10 (The method was a fish)

Genesis 12:1-4, Exodus 7:8, Matthew 3:17, and Acts 18:9. (When a person looks all those up you will see that, in each passage, the method was a verbal conversation with the Lord God.)

Exodus 3:2 - There the angel of the Lord appeared to him in flames of fire within bush.
(The method was fire)

Our point is that The Lord God has and can use any method He wishes. We as humans may not understand or recognize the method, but that doesn't take away from or add to the method He wants to use. If you remember nothing else, remember this - we are not the ones in control of everything. There seem to be times where we think we are but boy, are we wrong!

WRONG INTERPRETATIONS
OF THE TORAH

We know that some of the Jews perverted The Torah into legalism. Because of this, you have two different Torah followers in the Jewish faith. Number one - you have the Jewish believer of the Torah that is looking for the Messiah and keeping the God-given Torah as a way to live. Number two - you have the legalistic Torah. In other words, they make it their Law!

Some of the people who call themselves Christians have perverted all the Torah to mean the Law of legalism. Christ, who was a Jew, broke no Torah while here on earth. They teach he actually did away with all Torah with his death. In our opinion, The Jewish Messiah was not a Christian and will never be one! He may have done away with the legalistic misrepresentation of the Torah that some of the Jews were trying to make people follow. The Christian Faith has been misinterpreting the Torah for a long time. To see this, all we have to do is point to the anti-Semitic feelings toward God's chosen people!

Matthew 5:17 does not contradict itself. Let's look at it in NIV English - *Do not think that I have come to abolish the Law or the Prophets; I did not come to abolish but to fulfill them."* Here is the same verse from the Complete Jewish Bible - *Don't think that I have come to abolish the Torah or the Prophets. I have come not to abolish but to complete.* If you look at both translations, you may come away with mixed feelings. If a person reads that The Messiah came and did away with the Law or the Prophets, then we guess he fulfilled it? But if one reads it "to complete" (in other words, He was the aim the Torah and the Prophets were shooting for), then that statement is true in both cases. As it states, He has not come to abolish, but HE IS THE GOAL the whole Old Testament points to and that was achieved through The Messiah!

Translations differ from one generation to the next, so saying that there is a best translation may really mean that you simply like one over the other. You may say that the easiness of the wording of a certain version ministers to you. Cultures differ, sentence structure differs, and even the individuals differ drastically on their likes and dislikes. There are a number of reasons why some believe one or another is best! We do agree that some translations are better than others and we guess you could say that there is a worst translation among all translations.

We know that for a long time the King James Version was looked at as the perfect translation. We do not agree. Even though the KJV may be an excellent translation, a number of misleading "Old English" connotations have been found within it. There are other versions that seem to help individuals who may not understand "Old English."

What we have come to believe is that each translation seems to serve a purpose. That may be to show people who God is, to elevate spiritually, help the relationship between the individual and the Maker, or to assist people, one way or another, in what life is. One would have to say that each translation might give some individual a new meaning with life while they walk this earth.

We know that what we read and classify as The Old Testament was originally penned in Hebrew. But in the 3rd Century BC, the Greeks translated it into the Greek language by the work of some 70 scholars. They rewrote what was originally called The TANAKH in the Jewish Faith. Moses wrote in Hebrew, as did every writer of the Old Testament (TANAKH)!

English translations have far too often misled readers and so-called scholars in the Torah of God. The word Torah doesn't mean "law" as some translations such as the KJV have it. That is the start of the misleading of the Greeks who wanted the Jewish background taken out of the scripture. The word Torah doesn't always mean law! There were laws that Moses and others were given for the Jews to live by but in most cases the word Torah literally means "teachings." So when you have the Torah of Moses, what you really have are the teachings of God given to Moses for the Jewish people! Over the years, people and countries have futilely tried to force their ways on the Jewish nation. As a matter of fact, in more times than not, it backfires!

Moses didn't tell everyone how to live. He was teaching his people, the Hebrews, how God Their Father wanted them to live!

There is an Old Covenant and now there is a New Covenant. Both point to the same person. The difference is that, during the Old, the people looked *for* The Savior and during the New, we look *at* The Savior. Now that's a BIG DIFFERENCE!

When you look around the world, you see people, churches, denominations, and even most religions run wild with a dislike or contempt for The Jewish Faith. Most religions preach that if everyone believed the way they believe and did what they do then everything would be right with God. They just *know* that The Father of the Universe had His hand on the founders of their faith, denomination or church. We are not here to tell you He doesn't or that he does!

Most religions, denominations, or churches differ in only minute ways, but they do differ and the difference seems to be blown out of proportion. They have erected huge dividing walls between themselves that are built of passages taken out of context. Are they really looking for truth or are they just being divided for the sake of someone's ego?

The sad fact is that the translations help with the divide-and-conquer concept.

We personally don't care which translation you start with. Just get started. Now, if you are a speed- reader, then by all means get a translation you find difficult to do that with. It may help you to slow down and really grasp the whole meaning of the written word. Most speed-readers we've talked to say that the KJV is a very hard translation to use that talent with. We say that's good! Not everyone likes the "Old English" type of writing, yet some say they like the beauty it brings.

Our philosophy is to get started. Find a translation you enjoy and dig your whole being into it. After a while, you may find yourselves drawn to another translation. If that happens, then start over and let your knowledge of both translations lead you in a direction of study! Just get started. After all, you will never finish a race if you never start. Far too often people try to start at the finish line when the long race is the real joy of life... to finally reach the goal line... to enjoy the journey... to receive the crown. Don't try to steal the crown without running the race. Don't let Satan or anyone else rob you of the pleasure you receive on the journey. Teachers and preachers should guide, direct, and maybe lead you in a direction for you to find the truth but it seems most push what we would call "their truth." With personal study, everyone should come away with the truth!

Get started, get motivated, get real and get what Adonai (THE LORD) has for each and every one of you!

Isn't the bible's main purpose to tell people about GOD and show them how to live! Doesn't it teach about the real meaning of life and how to and how not to react towards the Maker of the universe? If those are true, then why does mankind not want to follow His directions?

If any translation does that, isn't it the Spirit leading that individual into the direction they should take? Right or wrong, you still are being led. We are not saying that you shouldn't believe your teachers or your pastor, but you must study and make sure you walk down the right path. Don't be lead by some fast-talking person you may respect or sit under. Remember - you're the one being lead astray or swayed in a direction. It's up to you to make sure what is preached and taught is correct!

If people agree with us or they don't, if they follow that example or not, if they pick up a bible that they like or one someone else said they had to purchase because that's the only true word, all we say is get one. If you find yourself not being filled by that translation, get a different one.

We personally use six different translations for our study. We use the King James Version, the New International Version, the New American Standard Version, the Good News Bible, the American Standard Bible, and the Complete Jewish Bible.

In our opinion, the brainwashing translators, preachers and teachers who tell people that their version is the only true word of God should be ashamed of themselves! In a way, they try to paint the picture of correctness by using a misguided concept for God's chosen people. They may be doing it out of ignorance or to fill their building, but what do you think that God The Father is thinking about when He sees how those who lead the people are going against His chosen?

Truth be told, we haven't found a handful of people who even know what the Messiah's real name was! If it wasn't for this book, WOULD YOU?

Here are some interesting facts about some of the translations.

The Complete Jewish Bible was translated around 1989. We believe that it was just the New Testament. We're not sure of the date, but it's about as close as we could find.

The Good News Bible was published somewhere between 1966 and 1976.

The American Standard Version was published in 1901. The New American Standard Version was published between 1963 and 1971.

The King James Version was translated in 1611 from what was known as The Bishop Bible. We believe the date for that bible was 1568.

There are more but we use most of these for our study. Not the Bishop Bible, we have never seen a copy of that one!

Our point isn't which one is more correct. It's more like we believe you should get one and start your study! After you get totally convinced that the one you like is correct, purchase another and have the smarts to start all over again in order to find for yourself which one you believe is correct!

You may be surprised with what you come up with! There will be people (usually preachers) who say the one they use is the only correct Bible and they may try to convince you to buy that kind. If that happens, so be it. Just get started with one and grow in your knowledge of and belief in God The Father!

PRAYER

What is prayer?

(1) A wish list?

(2) An Avenue for healing?

(3) Our Wants?

(4) Our Desires?

(5) Fulfilling of a Command?

(6) Just something The Son told us to do?

Read Matthew (Mattityahu) 6:9-13. Why pray like this? Is this just an example The Messiah dreamt up or is it a great example to follow?

1. Do we really need to state that He is The Father or should we state, out loud, that He is Our Father not just a Father?

2. Some skeptics ask if we really need to tell him that His name is holy. Shouldn't he already know that? Here is a shocker, in a way we believe they are right... sort of. Yes, He knows who He is, but here is where we and the skeptics disagree: saying "hallowed be your name" lets The Father of the Universe know that we acknowledge His name is to be kept holy above all names!

3. What kind of Prayer is it? Have you ever really thought about the Lord's Prayer? When you have said the prayer, have you ever noticed that it's for a group of people or a society? It's not a prayer for individuals at all.

4. The wording says it all. (1) Give *us*. (2) Forgive *us* what *we*. (3) As *we*. (4) Wronged *us* (lead *us*) (5) Keep *us* (Deliver *us*).

5. If The Messiah uses the plural wording in what we call The Lord's Prayer, what should that tell us how our prayers should

be? The Christian believes he can go to the forgiveness table as an individual. The Hebrew, even in the time when The Messiah walked on the earth, believed you come to The Father as a group of people. It wasn't and still isn't an individual act.

6.   Your Kingdom, Power, Glory Forever Amen! In the oldest manuscript, that ending is not found! It was added to the writings many, many years later. Revelation 22 warns us not to add or take away from "this book." We know there are people who say that only refers to The Book of The Revelation but however you want to believe is up to you!

Some Bibles have the writing in red lettering, which indicates that The Lord was talking then. Our point here would be, if it was added many years later, maybe, just maybe it should not be in red print, unless you believe The Lord came back and added that ending himself.

Perhaps The Lord's Prayer is something you were expected to learn as a kid. Maybe someone told you to memorize and repeat it for a class. Whatever the reason is, that too is your business. In all reality, these are just a few facts that you may accept without question because your parent or teacher told you to. We just want you to study to find truth.

We know that there is someone who just said, "God knows what I mean or what I said has my feeling and he understands when I just repeat words." If that's your philosophy, you do not need to repeat what The Messiah said. After all, he knows what's in your heart even if you don't know what you're saying, right?

Why praise The Father or acknowledge how great He is? Do we really need to tell him how holy He is? Do we need to even say His Name? Doesn't He already know that? Of course he does. But we are instructed to so we believe we should. Whatever you want to believe is your business.

There are people who look at it this way - you told your husband or wife you loved them one time and that's enough. If anything changes you'll let them know. We hope that is not the same concept you have for The God of the Universe, The one we refer to as The Great "I AM"!

GREEKS

The Greeks rewrote or translated The Old Testament (Tanakh in Hebrew) some 200 years before the Messiah was born. In our English translations, the Old Testament ends with Malachi but the Hebrew Tanakh ends with 2 Chronicles. Our Complete Jewish Bible goes right into Matthew (Mattityahu) after 2 Chronicles without showing a separation between the Old and New Testaments. The Messianic Jew believes that what we English-speaking people call the New Testament is really a continuation of one book, "The Bible"!

That is so interesting. God's one book is divided by man! Some say we need to separate what we call the bible into the old and the new. Why do we accept the concept that The Father wanted one thing for The Chosen People (The Hebrews) and another for the Gentiles? We have heard preachers and teachers say that the Christians are the new chosen people. BIG MISTAKE! They will be held accountable for leading people in the wrong direction! It's too bad that people really believe that God has a NEW chosen people now that The Messiah has been here and now He is back home again. To us it's just another way of Satan doing his job to separate the true followers from the feel-good religions of today!

First of all, the term "Greek" in scripture doesn't always mean Gentile! John 12:20 (CJB) - *Among those who went to worship at the festival were some Greek speaking Jews.* In the KJV it states, *and there were certain Greeks among them that came up to worship at the feast.* Some of the translations we've read make it sound like these were Gentiles who were believers in The Jewish Messiah.

Now we must look back to John 7:35 (NIV) - *The Jews said to one another, "where does this man intend to go that we cannot find him? Will he go where our people live scattered among the Greeks, and teach the Greeks?"*

Everybody who studies those verses needs to understand that the ones who came from Greece were not Gentiles. We know that some translations seem to hint that they were Greek. At times, Paul used the term "Greek" to represent Gentiles, but this is not one of those times!

The true meaning should state that they were the Jews who were dispersed at various times in history. They were sent to the Greek country. John 7:35 explains who the Greek-speaking people were. They were Greek speaking Jews who came to the festival. They weren't nosey Gentiles, but faithful Jewish believers who happen to be living in Greece because of a forced movement by a Greek invasion of Israel!

This is a good example of why we need to study and find truth!

It has nothing bad to say about the Greeks. They were part of history. We just need to study and find the truth in scripture!

ROMANS 10:4

We want to write what Romans 10:4 says in a number of bibles just to show you how the best of intentions and even a meaningful attempt to address a verse may come to a total different meaning than what is written.

(New International Version) *Christ is the culmination of the law so that there may be righteousness for everyone who believes*

(King James Version) *For Christ is the end of the law for righteousness to everyone that believeth.*

(New American Bible) "For Christ is the end of the law for the justification of everyone who has faith."

(Good News Bible) - *For Christ has brought the law to an end, so that everyone who believes is put right with God.*

(New American Standard Bible) *For Christ is the end of the law for righteousness to everyone who believes.*

(Complete Jewish Bible) *For the goal at which the Torah aims is the Messiah, who offers righteousness to everyone who trusts.*

We gave you 6 different Bible versions on one verse, Romans 10:4. They are all different and seemingly pointing in one direction. But if you study each one, you find a number of differences with the wording. We will not say they are wrong, just different.

Interpretations have made the teaching of God to His chosen people a direction of contradictions in scripture. We have The Father telling His chosen children what they need to do and how to act in order to receive what their Father wants for them and from them.

The interpreters have made the whole Old Testament take a back seat to the brainwashing of society!

We believe the New Testament has to continue the Old Testament. The old isn't out of date with the society of our day. There seems to be a number of people and interpretations that slant the message from the teachers and preachers that God is through with the Old Testament beliefs and guidelines in order to influence congregations and denominations

One of the misinterpretations is that the Old Testament is done away with and now it is time for the New Testament to jump to the front. That sentiment runs through Christianity like a fire in an old dry house. By the time the fire fighters arrive, the whole house has been consumed. People mean well in most cases, but when you mess up the intent you are really working for the destruction of the Word itself. God's Word doesn't start with Matthew and end with the Revelation. It starts with Genesis and ends with the Revelation! The Word of God is the *whole* Word of God, not just the parts you like.

The Messiah even stated that He was the Savior of the Jewish Nation. He was here for the lost sheep of Israel! The Jews rebelled against God many times throughout history. Denominations must think that this disqualified them from being God's chosen people any more. After all, we know that the Christian communities have always followed what Christ would have wanted and told those people how to live with what God would want from them, RIGHT?

By the looks of our society, politicians, and religious leaders of today, we can see where the Jews went wrong. We must have learned how not to treat the God of the universe because we know that Christians stand together and back each other in times of need. We never condemn the other church, any other people, or organization. We never point fingers or gossip. We are always acting in a Godly manner, RIGHT?

Since we are so good and upright at all times why can't the Jews see we're right and what God told them long ago in the past has become obsolete. The new great people that God really loves are in control and are showing everyone how to live in harmony between churches and countries! We must show them that God changed His mind with His chosen people. After all, we know that The Father did send His only son to us Christians, no matter what Christ said in Matthew 15:24. We guess preachers and teachers must think our Messiah had a weak moment that day. They must preach and teach to God saying stuff like, "Good god, man! Get things right! After all, you are one of the three bosses of the universe. Why would you make a mistake with that statement, when we know you really were referring to Christians all along?" (We are being facetious)

God is still in control of the Universe. God really doesn't need our help, but we do need His! If He can help a man who was born blind to see, make leprosy go away from people, heal a cripple, and even walk on water, then maybe He should be the example for us!

Do all English versions mean to be anti-Semitic? Do all commentators, of scripture, mean to lead people in a direction that misses the point all together? No, but if you study you will see that most people go no further than what a preacher or teacher has instructed them about any subject!

Here are a few statements that we read: The Torah is eternal. Yeshua upheld his Father's Torah. Our Messiah didn't do away with the law and He did not terminate the law that leads to The Father! The word Torah isn't referring to a Law, but to a teaching from God. The English versions have blinded every individual into believing a mistranslation of that Word! The righteousness that is grounded in trust is really the Torah itself! It was through Yeshua, Our Messiah. Through the Torah, righteousness comes! He kept The Torah. He didn't do away with The Torah. He filtered the legalism that had infiltrated some of the Jewish leaders of that day, but never did he do away with The Torah!

People, believe Romans 11:29 (CJB) - *For God's free gifts and his calling are irrevocable.* The Hebrews are God's chosen people. The free gifts and their calling as His chosen people is still theirs. They are the called of God. They don't give that up every time they sin. Their calling is irrevocable. IRREVOCABLE!

If one talks about some of the untruths that people believe about scripture it would have to include the notion that Christ took all the Torah and did away with it! Some of the Jews have taken legalism and infiltrated their wants into their beliefs. Because some of the Jews have done such a thing doesn't change the fact that they are still God's chosen because that calling is irrevocable. We know that some of their leaders have not followed the Torah totally. But if we are honest, has there ever been a denomination that followed the scriptures totally?

We believe that the anti-Semitic feelings of most Christians are really just following their preacher, teacher, church and their denomination! They don't sit back and think about what is preached or what is said in a classroom or a bible study. Let's face it - most people are lazy! They take what sounds good and run with it. It doesn't have to be scriptural at all. They just like the wording or it makes them feel better about themselves.

Like we have stated from the start - stop being so lazy and start to study what is said and what you hear. Believe what the scriptures say. Do not believe because of blind faith. Remember the blind leading the blind will fall into that hole!

WHAT CONSTITUTES A
GOOD CHURCH?

Is it how many times they open the doors? Is it how often they have communion? Is it how many times they say The Messiah's name? Do they even know what The Messiah's real name was, or will they make up one for their future use? How prejudiced is the church, and the people who attend there? Is the head of the denomination your brains of the organization? How about the pastor? Is he the dictator of your beliefs?

What really is Church? Do you even think about such a question or do you happen to like someone who goes there and just go with the flow? Does their organization do so many good things that it has to be called a good church? Maybe the preacher gets a blessing now and then so that means he is the one God sent to you and your people!

Some people do the work of the church because it's there or maybe then they get a feeling of belonging. There are certain people who need to be needed. To some individuals, that is what keeps them feeling useful. There are some individuals who feel that if they don't do the work then no one will. Are others even qualified to do the work for God like they are? For the preacher and the leaders of your church, has it become more of an "I" syndrome organization? That way you know who is in charge!

Does the board exist by name only, or do they have the final say? When it comes to belonging, do the members belong to the church or to the pastor of the church? Do your language and your philosophy change when you exit the doors? Do they even think that the people should act different while in the building but it's all right to be different when away from the doors of the church? Do the people pray?

Let's face it, most churches wouldn't notice the Messiah if He was sitting in their church even if He was in the front row! They seem to notice and even want to hear the drug addict or the drunkard who changed his life around, but not the goody-two-shoes who has followed the Lord all his life. The homeless guy with nowhere to turn get's a lot of notice, yet the individuals who do the right stuff behind the scenes get no attention whatsoever. They are taken advantage of by the board, pastor, teachers and the church as a whole! They may not want to admit it, but everybody who ever worked behind the scenes knows and has felt what was just stated!

It amazes us that if an individual who did horrible things in their life preaches, people hang onto every word. What we wonder is this - if The Messiah, like the goody two shoes who hasn't broken any law, tells you anything, would you even listen to Him at all? We know that everyone's answer is, "Well of course we would listen to The Messiah!" Remember, He may not come announcing "I'm The Messiah" and, if He did say that, how many would even look twice when He talked! Admit it. If someone said that, wouldn't you think that guy is using The Lord just to get attention?

Is God in control of the Church or is the church in control of God? Way too often it is more of a social club than a collection of God's people!

NOT HOT OR COLD!

Revelation 3:14-16 (NIV) - *To the angel of the church in Laodicea write: these are the words of the Amen, the faithful and true witness, the ruler of God's creation. I know your deeds, that you are neither cold nor hot. I wish you were either one or the other! So, because you are lukewarm, neither hot nor cold, I am about to spit you out of my mouth.*

There is so much to that statement and to the rest of the book of the Revelation. We need to look at and study because there is so much meaning and intent to grasp! We know that you think that your denomination has already explained what we will be saying here, but we feel we need to address it.

As you study, you will find that the letter to the Laodicean people has been lost. That just may be a sign of how little this letter really accomplished! Here in the book of The Revelation, our Messiah finds the Laodicean people only worthy of blame without any praise whatsoever.

Now there are a number of things that should have jumped off the page at you!

This Revelation is a Revelation given to Yeshua, Our Messiah, by God so he could show his servants what must soon take place!

Some believe it was sent by Yeshua, then by communication through his angel, it was sent to his servant John!

Revelation 1:1 has a part where it says, "It would happen very soon." We looked that up in our 6 different bibles and they all say something like, "it will happen soon." What does that mean to us? We all know that in Matthew, Mark, 1 Thessalonians and 2 Peter we read that, when He comes, it will be "like a thief in the night." Yet 2 Peter also says that the Lord is slow to anger. When will the time come? No one knows and it may seem like no one cares. It says in 2 Peter 3:3 (NAS) *Know this first of all, that in the last days mockers will come with their mocking, following after their own lusts.* What do we have today if a person stands on the street corner and proclaims the truth? People avoid that person at all costs like they have something you may catch! Yet, if you have enough people standing and protesting about the police or the fair treatment of a law-breaker, it seems that people come out of the woodwork just to protest! Why do most people avoid the one who is trying to lead them to the Savior and jump in for the person who broke the law and got caught?

We believe the time is short, but the shortness is based on The Father's timing, not ours and not yours! Thank God for that! We may not like to admit it, but most people believe scoffers will come following their own desires. Then you have people whose question is, "When is this day he promised coming?" Well, the last time we checked, The God of the Universe doesn't answer to me or you about when or how He is going to achieve HIS goal! We may pray. We may believe that because we pray He will do this or that. You are free to believe anything you want and it will not change the time or date the Father has set in place! Oh, there may be people who think they can. If that is how you believe, then continue to believe that. As far as we are concerned, it will not harm you unless you go too far by telling people that the Lord's return will be next week! The reason we say that is because no one knows the day or hour of Christ's return. If people keep predicting that The Lord will return next week, sooner or later someone will be right.

Most of us are lukewarm, yet most of us will not admit that. The reason may be that we want to look good to our family or friends. How about the people you go to church with? They all are hot for God right? People will not be honest about this because then they would have to admit they may not be as good as others see or they believe themselves to be! We are not just pointing fingers at others. We need to point them at us also. So don't go away thinking we are preaching to you because we think we are perfect or even good enough to preach what you should do. That is between you and The Father.

Like we have been saying from the beginning, STUDY! Never take our word for it and if you take the word of your pastor, Sunday school teacher, or your bible study teacher, it had better line up with what is right and not based on their denominational brainwashing!

People have told us that they believe that the book of the Revelation is full of a lot of good writings! However, they have a hard time understanding some of it. When they have found what they are looking for, even if somebody comes along and tells them something new, it may make more sense for them. That shouldn't cause anyone of us to stop looking! It should give you the incentive to dig deeper into the wording and keep digging until you find the true meaning! That will not be easy, but then, does anything come easy when you really want the truth?

Remember what Our Lord said to Laodicea. He didn't want them to be lukewarm He would rather have them hot or cold!

From what Christ told them, we also had better be either hot or cold!

LIFE BECOMES DIFFICULT

People complain when life becomes difficult, but that should be the time when they turn toward God The Father, not away from Him to complain that He did this or that to them!

But just like Shadrach, Meshach and Abednego, we see the furnace and decide what we want to do and what side do we want to be on. Do we crumble in our faith to stay out of the fire or do we put our trust in the one who, if he chooses, will walk us through? We believe that the meaning of their story isn't about protection, faith, or obedience. You see all three in their decision! But if you really look at their stand in Daniel 3:16-18, the words "if" and "but" stand out in their statement to King Nebuchadnezzar. They wouldn't compromise. How many of us would say, "If I say this God knows I don't believe what I said so it would be alright in His sight and He surely wouldn't hold that against me"? In other words, we are doing what would have to be called compromising! It's easy for us to say "don't compromise" because we are not going through any testing by fire. But do we compromise in the way we talk or the way we act. Little lies come from our lips and we use the cover of "we don't want to hurt their feelings!"

Do we rob from God of our tithes and try to explain it away with some excuse? What about our taxes? Do we cheat the government by lying and say God would understand that, if we don't cheat or steal from the government, we wouldn't be able to give God what He deserves. As we look at each of these thoughts from Shadrach, Meshach and Abednego to us, it really points to compromising our stand with God or not compromising and actually trusting God, Our Father!

Isaiah 48:10-11 (NIV) - *See, I have refined you, though not
as silver; I have tested you in the furnace of affliction. For my
own sake, for my own sake, I do this. How can I let myself be
defamed? I will not yield my glory to another.*

We have a problem with the teachers, preachers and denominations that
say, "the devil made me do it." We have a choice and we are the ones held
accountable for our actions, not the devil!

Romans 13:7 (NIV) - *Give to everyone what you owe them:
If you owe taxes, pay taxes; if revenue, then revenue; if respect,
then respect; if honor, then honor.*

To us this says to submit to the ones who have been given the authority
including the ones in control of the government and even your jobs. A lot
of people complain about what goes on but want nothing to do with the
aspect of trying to make it better with some of their ideas. But they sure
like to complain.

In reality, this statement from Paul is amazing in itself. We are instructed
to do this by Paul and it was during Nero's time of rule that he wrote this.
Does this mean to you that we should obey the wicked laws of an evil
government? We believe NO! You have to go back to Act 5:29 (CJB) -
We must obey God, not men! That is when the will of the state and the
will of God conflict with each other. The authorities such as the Nazis,
the Communists, or other totalitarian regimes have no place in Gods
realm! They may be in control, but when they make rules and carry out
evil against The Father's rules, they are the ones out of control! We are
reminded of what it says in 1 Peter 2: 13-25. Submit to authority that
punishes those who do wrong and commends those who do right.

There are a lot of people who take only what they like out of scripture and
make that their religion and denomination.

If you rob the government with the thought that, by paying taxes, you are
robbing God, then you are paying out of your checking account, not out
of love for The Father! Oh, we can hear the Christians now, "If I pay the

taxes then God will get less." How about this one, "We give to God and if we have to cheat the government to do that, then that would be alright with God." Are we saying you should not take the legal deductions that the government allows you to take? Heavens NO. But don't cheat to do the evil that Satan wants you to be involved in either!

This statement is from us. We try to give people respect until they show they don't deserve it! People do not get our respect for what they do or who they pretend to be i.e. sports figures or actors. If they show they are the kind of person that children may want to look up to yet their actions are like a spoiled brat then they surely don't have the kind of stuff our youth should be like! The youth of today and any time in history try to be like the people who get their names in the paper, win the Super Bowl, win the World Series, or are in a hit movie. Now those are great things in themselves, but if you are not a good enough person without those then you are not any better with them!

Respect is something people earn! You may see it by the fruits of their labor, how they carry themselves, or how the children and adults try to imitate them.

The same goes with Honor! If a Preacher or someone of authority is doing or preaching something wrong, be on your guard! Don't fall into the same pit as that blind man. Use common sense and watch your step! Do not ever take someone's word for it. Go home and study what you have just heard them say, otherwise be prepared for that landing when you have that sudden stop at the bottom of that hole you just entered! The Children of Israel would follow pagan gods because that is what the people in authority said to follow. When you read about them, were they praised for doing that? NO! Should we? NO! That is unless you want the same type of fate that the Children of Israel got!

To us, the big word is *if*! *If* taxes, *if* fear, *if* honor, *if* respect, etc. In other words, it's not an automatic thing. *If* we take the wrong road, then, when the wrath of God comes, there will be a lot of complaining, just like when the wrath of God came to Israel!

When we pray for the people in authority, should we really pray for their well-being or should we say "keep your hands off of us when you do the evil you do!" Would you really call it a prayer for the government or would we have to say that it really is for us as individuals? Some people say they pray for the ones in control because of their leadership for the believers. Then the question is - believers in what? Could you be praying for the unholy condition of your country or the laws that some politicians want to push through to get votes? It doesn't matter what is right. Their aim is for votes. It seems that they could care less about what's right or wrong. Their concern is only for their party and who gets their votes! Now, if you don't believe that, then just keep on thinking that your party is the right one, even if they pass laws that are contrary to the writings from the Father! Denominations may twist the words, or bend the words to fit their religions. Some believe that the government can do what they want, just as long as they keep their hands off their church. Remember who will be held more accountable when the end comes!

WHAT ABOUT THE KILLING
IN SCRIPTURE?

Have you ever read the bible? Have you ever really read the bible? There is more killing in scripture than one wants to remember or admit!

The Flood killed all but eight people. The ones that died were men, women, children, and even infants. Have you ever stopped to think that the men may have been totally without worth and that the women must have followed their men? But what about the man who was a decent fellow, treated people right, helped the less fortunate, and maybe took care of the child who may have lost his parents? Surely God would spare that type of man from drowning in the flood. After all, God is the God of love. How about the woman who looks after the infant when the mother died in childbirth right before the flood? Surely God would see the heart of that woman and at least send her a small boat. After all, she showed real compassion by taking in the infant. What about in Exodus 32:27 when, because of the people and their immorality, Moses had people killed because they where worshipping a golden calf? Deuteronomy 20:13 - *When the Lord your God delivers it into your hand, put to the sword all the men in it.*

How about when the children of Israel came out of Egypt going toward the Promised Land? When the men explored the land, they had a bad report. (Numbers 13) Moses wanted a report on how to take the land, but they gave a scary report of how fearful the people should be. These spies, the leaders of the Israelites, were struck down and died of a plague because of their unbelief. Everyone 20 years old and older died because of their rebellious lack of faith.

STUDY

Killing isn't something new, but we look at it totally different today than what we read about in the scriptures. We are not saying that killing is right, only that there was a lot of killing in scripture. People of today seem to overlook that. That was what the people in the Old Testament went through.

Our point isn't death! Death comes to almost everyone. We say almost because, according to scripture, Enoch and Elijah didn't see death.

Is death going to be your end or your start? We really don't know that much about death and neither do we pretend to. There is the stopping of the heart with no more breaths to take. We need no more food or water. Our glasses will be useless to us. All those things seem to be handy while we walk this earth, don't they?

Is your philosophy "take what you can, because you won't get anything later"? Maybe it is "take, take, take because somehow you deserve everything". There are people who give and give, thinking that will somehow help them after they die.

People can look good on the outside and maybe even convince themselves and others what they do is for the betterment of others. When they get rich with their scams or angles, are they really doing it for God, for the people, or for themselves? We are not down on rich people or high on the poor. We see areas where some talk like they have everything while others take because of their lack.

Death comes to both and they both have eternity. Almost everyone will be in the crowd going to that huge gate with that eight lane interstate leading to destruction. Then, you have that very small gate with that narrow path that leads to life and only a very small few find it!

If your religion, denomination, church, pastor, rabbi, or teachers say you're going to Heaven, then that means one thing to us: you have to study more than ever before to find truth!

Most people look no further than whatever makes them feel good about themselves and maybe their family. It doesn't have to be truth! It just might give you goose bumps now and then. That is enough to make most feel edified to the point of putting on blinders to the real truth as long as what they believe brings a smile and a warm fuzzy feeling now and then!

Why do you think Enoch and Elijah didn't die? They didn't follow the norm! Why was Noah and his family saved from the flood? They didn't follow others or listen to their leaders! In all three cases, they didn't do or practice what others preached. They just wanted truth in life and death!

The Father isn't against death. In fact, He allows it. In reality, it isn't even a bad ending unless, after death, one finds that huge road and the wide gate to destruction. Those are not our words. They came from the Messiah himself in Matthew 7:13-14!

GOD DOES NOT CHANGE AND SATAN GETS TOO MUCH CREDIT!

Malachi 3:6 (NIV) - *I the Lord do not change. So you, descendants of Jacob, are not destroyed.*

Hebrews 13:8 (CJB)- *Yeshua the Messiah is the same yesterday, today and forever.*

We would have to say that The Father doesn't send good things to one person and evil things to a different person.

James 1: 13-14 (CJB) - *No one being tempted should say, "I am being tempted by God." For God cannot be tempted by evil, and God himself tempts no one. Rather, each person is being tempted whenever he is being dragged off and enticed by the bait of his own desire.*

If it's by our own desires, why do we pass the buck? Is it so we don't take the blame?

Examples:

1. Satan didn't want me to get that assistant manager job.

No. Maybe it's that you are trying to sell yourself to people when you dress or act like you are applying for a janitor's opening instead of the manager's. You are the billboard of their company and maybe you need to look like you want to represent their finished product! Now, there is nothing wrong with the janitor's job, but one should dress and act the part when he or she goes after any position.

2. I had a wreck. Satan didn't want me to get to church today. There must be a reason or special blessing I will miss out on.

Maybe the person texting and not paying attention while driving might have had something to do with it!

In most cases, Satan get's too much credit and he doesn't have to do one darn thing. The person texting was his desire, and that is what caused the wreck! It was your desire to dress and act the way you do and that might not be the way the person doing the hiring wanted his assistant manager to dress. Before someone gets their nose bent out of shape, we are not down on janitors. George was a janitor for a while and he really liked that position.

Because of our actions, Satan can just sit back in his patted armchair and relax. Most of the time, he doesn't have to do one darn thing! Even if he didn't want the credit, he would still get it in a lot of situations.

We have heard all of our lives: GOD, GOOD – SATAN, BAD. If you get something that seems good, it's from God. If you get something bad or bad things happen, it's from Satan. It's no wonder that now, here in the United States, we have a society of "pass the buck."

James 1:17 (NIV) - *Every good and perfect gift is from above, coming down from the Father of the heavenly lights, who do not change like shifting shadows.* (What do you think of that writing?)

(1) Good giving - by us and if someone gives us good! One version says every act of good giving comes down from above.

(2) Then it says every perfect gift is from above. What's the only perfect gift you can receive? Our salvation.

(3) *Heavenly lights who do not change like shifting shadows.* Why state it that way? Because it doesn't change! It isn't altered by change. It doesn't show any shadow on anything because of change! It

will always be what The Father said in the beginning. That goes from the book of Genesis all the way through the book of the Revelation.

Every Perfect Gift is from above. What is a perfect gift? Can you give us a perfect gift? Can we give the perfect gift? Can we share a perfect gift with anyone? If it comes from you or us, is it perfect anymore? It may be good, it may fit just right, and it might be just what you wanted in the first place, but do we ever give a Perfect Gift: the gift that never breaks, never wears out, never bends, and is always perfect for all time? We believe NO!

Now, we know some of you are thinking, "How about Christ? Do you give me Christ?" Do we give you Christ? Have you ever given Christ? The Father gave Christ, not me or you! That is the only Perfect Gift! Neither you nor we gave anyone a son for someone else's soul. Even if that happened, it wouldn't be a perfect Gift and it would be a sacrifice to an unknown god. The Father gave His Son as the only perfect gift from Him, not us or you!

God's desire was to give birth on the earth. How? By speaking it into existence! We, in our own interpretation, may speak by the Word of Truth (which we would say is correct in content) but the vision or insight may be clouded from the original Word of Truth from the beginning of time because of the person's desire or his denominational feel-good philosophy. There seem to be a lot of so-called Christians who say that God's Word, in the New Testament really doesn't relate to the Jews any longer. When a person studies, they should notice that there is so much anti-Jewish brainwashing going on that it should alarm everyone.

We have heard preachers in the pulpit say that Christians are now the new children of Israel. We are the chosen people, not the Jews any longer! God's chosen are the believers in Christ, not the Jews who persecuted Him! If you can convert the Jews, you save their society! The bible, especially the New Testament, only pertains to Christians. We need not pay too much attention to the Old Testament any longer. Those are just a few, but all the preachers and teachers who say those type of misleading things need to read what Paul wrote in the book of Romans!

> Romans 3:31(CJB) - *Do we, then, nullify the Torah by this faith? Not at all! Rather, we uphold the Torah.*

We used the word "Torah" because the word "law" is the wrong interpretation. Unfortunately, it is the only word that preachers and teachers use to get their point across, even though it is the wrong translation of a very important message from Paul.

> Matthew 5:17 (KJV) - *Think not that I am come to destroy the law, or the prophets: I am not come to destroy, but to fulfill.*

Way too many preachers and teachers lead people wrongly by their interpretation. When they lead people in the wrong direction, people get the wrong understanding! The KJV and NIV, with the help of preachers, teachers, and most of the rest of the interpretations, lead people to believe that Christ did away with the law when the scriptures say He fulfilled them.

> Romans 3:31 (NIV) - *Do we then nullify the law by this faith? Not at all! Rather, we uphold the law.*

See how, when you put "law" in the phrase instead of "Torah", it seems to have a negative connotation to it. In reality, Paul was stating that the Torah is not abolished (Heaven forbid) but the Torah is confirmed, upheld, established and placed on a firm foundation!

Here are three versions of Matthew 5:17-18:

> KJV - *Think not that I am come to destroy the law, or the prophets: I am not come to destroy, but to fulfill. For verily I say unto you, Till heaven and earth pass, one jot or one tittle shall in no wise pass from the law, till all be fulfilled.*

NIV - Do not think that I have come to abolish the Law or the Prophets; I have not come to abolish them but to fulfill them. For truly I tell you, until heaven and earth disappear, not the smallest letter, not the least stroke of a pen, will by any means disappear from the Law until everything is accomplished.

CJB - Don't think that I have come to abolish the Torah or the Prophets. I have come not to abolish but to complete. Yes indeed! I tell you that until heaven and earth pass away, not so much as a yud or a stroke will pass from the Torah - not until everything that must happen has happened!

After reading all three, one should see how the KJV and NIV seem to put a negative spin on the phrase. The true meaning is about the fact that not one stroke will by any means pass from the teachings of the Torah until everything is accomplished! That is everything, not some things, but everything!

Our point is that too many preachers and teachers say, "Christ did away with the Law when he fulfilled them. We aren't under the law anymore."

We guess that, when Christ was speaking right after the Beatitudes, He must have had a weak moment, when he said, Do not think that I came to abolish the Law (Torah) or The Prophets.

If you believe Christ abolished or did away with the law (Torah) and that the prophets aren't for all time, then we guess our Messiah lied to his closest followers, the disciples. Maybe the anti-Jewish movement has brainwashed us to believe Christ turned His back on the law and the prophets.

We have stated this before and we will state it again, but here goes: The Messiah was from the chosen people of Israel (the Hebrews, the Jews). He was born a Jew, He lived as a Jew, He kept all the Jewish rules, and He even died as a Jew! We believe when Christ comes back He will come back as a Jew not as a gentile!

He will come back the same way He went. That is from Acts 1:11, when two men dressed in white stood beside the men of Galilee! Our question is this: how many Gentiles will recognize him? We know all are saying, "Of course we will". But when he comes back as a Jew... what? He can't come back as a Jew. Isn't he coming back for us Christians who believe in this Jew? Wait a minute. Isn't that what it says? He will come back the same as he went!

> Matthew 10:5-6 (NIV) *These twelve Jesus(Yeshua)sent out with the following instructions: "Do not go among the Gentiles or enter any town of the Samaritans. Go rather to the lost sheep of Israel!"*

Matthew 15:24 (CJB) – He said, *"I was sent only to the lost sheep of the house of Isra'el."*

THE CALLING OF MATTITYAHU (MATTHEW)

Here are a few topics for individuals to think about while you get ready to study the calling of Matthew:

The events in scripture before the calling of Matthew.

Healing of the paralyzed man. (Mark 2, Luke 5, Matthew 8)

Miraculous catch of fish. (Luke 5)

Healing of Peter's mother-in-law. (Luke 4, Mark 1, Matthew 8)

Evil spirit comes out of a man, testifying that he is The Holy One of God. (Luke 4, Mark 1)

Preached in Galilee with power. (Mathew 4, Mark 1, Luke 1)

Rejected in Nazareth. (Luke 4)

The Roman centurion demonstrates Faith. (Matthew 8)

John in prison. (Luke 3)

John prepares the way for the Messiah. (Matthew 3, Mark 1, Luke 3)

The Messiah gives the Beatitudes. (Matthew 5)

Teaches about salt and light, the Torah (law), anger, lust, divorce, vows, retaliation, and loving your enemies. (Matthew 5)

Teaches about giving to the needy, prayer, fasting, money, and worry. (Matthew 6)

Teaches about criticizing others, ask-seek-knock, the way to Heaven, building house on rock not sand. (Matthew 7)

Calms the storm. (Matthew 8)

Demons into the herd of pigs. (Matthew 8)

Calling of Matthew. (Matthew 9)

Think about this: After all of these events, Matthew was called to follow The Lord! That means, according to scripture, Matthew wasn't there to hear the beatitudes or Our Messiah teaching about salt, light, lust, etc. Our point is Matthew wasn't around during all those happenings from God. Yet he wrote about it.

We know that some people will be saying the herd of pigs wrote Mark 5 and Luke 8. Well, you might be right. According to Mark and Luke, that came after their rendition of the calling of Matthew. They have it written after the calling so we could not put it in the same writing!

Then we guess there still might be hope for us!

We weren't around either, but we still have to hear and study truth, not the brainwashing of some denomination or some make-believe idea of some group that wants to rewrite scripture. No brainwashing for anyone. People just need to grasp what the true scriptures say, not what man wants to make believe is true. DO NOT believe because your preacher or teacher says it's true. You need to STUDY to find THE TRUTH. Don't believe them or us alone. You need to grasp the truth of the Word through your study. No brainwashing of your past and no denominational pointing by anyone!

DATING THE BIRTH OF CHRIST

This topic has taken a lot more time and study than any of the rest because there are scholars who have good points of view in all their ideas and directions. That will be explained later, but we have to say that whatever a person believes or wants to accept is totally up to the individual.

The question is should we even talk about this? Most so-called believers know that the Messiah was born on Christmas Day, right? That is another misleading brainwashing of denominations that try to get people to come in on December 25 to celebrate our Savior's birth. That date is not correct!

We know that the child was born. We know that the date for Christ birth was not year 0. A monk named Dionysius Exiguus miscalculated the AD (Anno Domini, which means "in the year of our Lord"). Many Bible footnotes or commentaries say the date of the Lord's birth was 6 B.C. Because of certain events that happened around the birth, we can honestly say that we believe that date is wrong.

While teaching a class a few years back, we heard some people comment, "Oh! How boring to try to figure out the date, let's just go with December 25th. Let's just believe the way we've always been taught, what difference does it make?" There are people who wouldn't believe the truth if it poked them in one of their eyes!

A lady (we will call her Carol) says in class, "There are so many more interesting things about the birth of Christ. We should look into them." The noise of unhappiness and complaining small talk that came from the class was disrespectful, not only to her but to Christ also. All I said was, "You should be ashamed of yourself!" The annoyed twenty or so people must have already known everything about Christ. They all knew everything or maybe they liked the tainted leadership of their church and their denominational teachings. We agreed with Carol.

Back to the birth - It would have taken the Magi a long time to walk the 1000 to 1600 miles. A man going from point A to point B at 2 miles an hour for 10 hours would travel 20 or so miles a day. We have no idea how fast a camel could walk the 1000 to 1600 miles. Considering the load the camels must have had to carry and the distance they would have covered, it would have taken them at least five months to reach their destination.

In Luke, the shepherds came and they found the Lord in a fat'-nay. This would have been a feeding troth or manger for fodder, not the little wooden manger that is seen on TV or the manger we see in people's yards.

Scripture says that the Magi followed the Star of the King of the Jews. Some people say that it was a bright light and that it was only a one-time occurrence. That may sound logical, but that is not scriptural according to the Greek wording.

The Lord was to be born in the city of David, Bethlehem of Judea. According to Matthew 2:2 they followed the Star to find the King of the Jews. They came to Jerusalem and asked, *"Where is the newborn King of the Jews?"* (CJB) Herod secretly met with them to find out the exact time the star had appeared to them. He then sent them to Bethlehem. They followed the star to the house. Every bible we studied states that they came to the house. This means that the family was no longer in the barn when the Magi first met The Child.

If the one-time bright light went out when they came to Jerusalem, it must have come back on when they left Herod the Great.

We are not saying it wasn't a bright light. As a matter of fact, it sounds more logical than to say they followed a star. It sounds so supernatural to say it was a one-time bright light for the King of The Jews, but there is nowhere in Matthew that even hints at the one-time theory.

The scripture does state the star stopped over the place where the child was. Matthew 2:10 says that they were overjoyed when they saw the star.

The Magi (some call them astrologers, wise men, or kings) must have been very intelligent individuals who knew enough about the Jewish culture to know that a Savior would be born to the Jewish nation.

The year is still confusing to most people. In our KJV (and most of our other versions), the footnotes estimate that it would have been 5-6 BC. We believe that takes a stretch to come up with that date! According to scripture, Christ was between 30 and 31 when He started His Ministry. John started his preaching and baptizing a little time before.

Elizabeth was in her 6th month of pregnancy when Mary became pregnant. Mary went to visit Elizabeth a short time later. So John would have been 6 months older than the Lord.

Here is where we get to the information that you need to digest for yourself and make up your own mind! According to history records, we know that Herod the Great died in 4BC. He ruled from 37BC to 4BC. He was a Jew by birth. He enlarged and reconstructed the Second Temple. He was also a very paranoid man who had many people exterminated, including some of his own children and at least one of his wives. Augustus was Emperor of Rome until his death in 14 AD. Tiberius Caesar then became Emperor until 37AD. We know by Luke 3:1-2 that John started his Ministry in the 15th year of the reign of Tiberius Caesar, that would make that date 29 AD. If John stated in the year 29 AD, then Christ would have started just a short time later, if he was 30 or 31 years old. Then we believe that Christ would have been born 1 or 2 BC.

Some scholars have written that Herod the Great's sons took over in 4 BC. Other scholars say that Herod's sons really took over in 1 BC but lied about the date so they would not have certain problems counted against them. Still other scholars state that activity of the eclipse proves that he was born around 4 BC. Through a lot more studying, we found that there were eclipses in the years of 1 and 2 BC. We were not there, so we could only go with what someone wrote about those things. Did his sons lie to protect themselves? Did the scholars misjudge the eclipse of the day? Was there proof as to when Herod died?

Truth be told, we have not and cannot tell you without a doubt what year or the exact day of the year Christ was born. With certain festivals that were going on, you may come up with a time period, but to be correct we would have to say sometime in September, not December. Christ would have been referred to as the King of the Judeans, because he was the King after King David and David was King of all the Jewish Nation - all the Judeans. We do not have all the answers and don't pretend to, but it did make an interesting long study to try to find the truth. Like before, make up your own mind and celebrate Christ's birth on whatever day you want. Truth be told, we should celebrate His birth every day in our prayers and in our life. Everything we do should be done with the thought that Christ is the only one we need to lift up as our Savior, Lord, and King!

It was said to us a long time ago that Satan can't read your mind. That may sound great. It was also said that Satan didn't known when the Lord was going to be born and he didn't know where. Those statements must have been untrue because the place was Bethlehem in Judea, and it was foretold some 700 years earlier. In the book of Daniel, scripture states that he would be born 483 years after the decree to rebuild the temple in Jerusalem. Let's look at why that is such an important statement. If Satan can't read your mind or know what the future holds, does he know what was done and foretold in the past? For example, did he know what the Old Testament said about the timing and location of the birth of Messiah? We don't think Satan has to do that much work. It seems that Christians and Jews alike have the problem with understanding the who, what, and where concerning our Messiah's birth. How did it happen and why did it happen to mankind?

Have you ever told your Messiah that you love Him? Have you ever asked Him to have His way and just kept quiet and listened to what He has for you? Most people say yes to those questions but then go right back to their denomination and say their religion is the only one that tells the truth from the whole bible. Yet they want you to pick just part of the Old Testament to believe in. After all, that was for the Jews, right? That would mean you are more anti-Semitic and anti-Christ than what you want to believe! Like we have stated a number of times, Our Messiah was and will always be a Jew. Our Savior died a Jew. Most Churches may say this but will never really stress it because that would mean that Christ, our Messiah, wasn't and will never be classified a Christian! If that makes you feel uncomfortable, that is OK with us. Maybe, just maybe, you will study to prove us wrong or maybe you will do what most people do - go to your teacher or preacher to find out if your denominational leaders believe this way or if they want you to follow them to wherever they are going. Will it be on the small path or that eight lane interstate that most religions are on?

Are we always right? NO! But don't take our word for that either.

You should try to prove us wrong with your own study and maybe you will find we are right! Like the book says, Study! For your sake, know what you want and keep looking for the right answer. You just might be surprised!

WHERE ARE YOU WITH THE FATHER?

That should be such an easy question to answer, but is it?

Some say that God is the center of their lives. Others say that Christ is the head of their all because He is their leader in times of trouble and the one who leads their steps. The Father is the one who sent His Son to earth to die for our sins.

May we ask just a few questions? If God is your Father and Christ is the center of your life, how often do you go to Him in prayer? How often do you just go to Him for a conversation with your Father? Do you talk to Him as your Father or treat Him as a crutch or lucky charm to have around when you need Him? You talk and pray to Him in time of trouble, but no real quality time is spent with Him. Maybe you're so busy that He takes a back seat until you have some trouble. That's when you need Him most, isn't it?

In most cases, God the Father seems to be a forgotten part of our everyday life! We may say His title when we pray, but why do people even bring Him up except maybe because He is our Savior's Father and mentioning Him goes right along with the flow in our prayers. But what high esteem do we really pay Him? Do you exalt God with your prayers? Would He have to look at the prayer as an insult or an afterthought? How many people really realize what they are saying with the words, "our Father"? Maybe we are wrong and everyone thinks about who The Father really is when they use those words. Maybe we are just not around the right people and if we stopped hanging around those church people we would get different vibes!

Jeremiah 2:27 (NIV) - *They say to wood, you are my father, and to stone, you gave me birth. They have turned their backs to me and not their faces; yet when they are in trouble, they say, Come and save us!*

When you read those verses, doesn't it sound like the time before 9-11? Right after the planes hit the towers, churches were filled but the memory faded with time. When you look around now, it seems to be worse than before!

Most of the people who wanted protection from the God of the universe have turned to the wood or stone for their help. People have turned their backs to the Father for various reasons such as science, society, peer pressure, having abundance, not getting what they desire, or politicians. Maybe the threat of death has subsided or maybe the satanic realm is getting stronger and people are buying into it.

How long will the Father put up with us? How much junk do we pile up before it's enough? How many empty prayers will our Father hear before He states what He did in Jeremiah 11:14? *Do not pray for this people or offer any plea or petition for them, because I will not listen when they call to me in the time of their distress.* (NIV)

The God of the Universe told Jeremiah not to pray for the Jewish nation at that time because of the distance between them and the Father. The Hebrews had become so distant from Him and His desires for them that He let them get what they deserved! What do the people of the world deserve today, right now, in this society? Do we deserve The Father listening to our prayers because of who we are or what we've become? Maybe He has to hear us because we follow the Messiah to the letter. Yeah right, like that would ever happen! Yes, we know we try to be good. That's all we need to do, right? If we try, that's all that counts. He surely wouldn't turn His back on us true part-time believers and part-time followers. After all, He knows we follow as long as it fits our schedule. He knows how busy we are doing whatever we want. He even knows our hearts are in the right spot even if what we do isn't! We guess that old saying goes here too - a husband would say, "I don't need to tell my wife I love her. I told her once and if it changes I'll let her know!" That may sound strange but if you think about how people say they came to The Lord and that seems to be their only claim. Those people have the same philosophy.

Think about who you are following. Think about The Father and the Glory He should possess! When our Messiah prayed, He went to The Father. When answers came, they were from The Father! There is only one way to The Father. Hebrews 13:8 stated what it was and it will always be the same yesterday, today and forever. That doesn't and hasn't changed with time! If you believe, you need to keep looking or you haven't found Him in the first place!

Where can people look and for how long do we have to look? Will it be hard to find or will it just fall into place the way most preachers tell us?

Here is the best and smartest advice we can and will ever give you: When you look, look hard, look long, and look with the intent of finding the truth, no matter what the true answer may be! We always pray that your answer leads you to that narrow path with that small door. If you get to your spot after you die and there is a large group of people and you have this huge door for your group, you will wish you had studied harder and smarter!

THE KEY

Matthew 23:37-39 (NIV) - *Jerusalem, Jerusalem, you who kill the prophets and stone those sent to you, how often I have longed to gather your children together, as a hen gathers her chicks under her wings, and you were not willing. Look, your house is left to you desolate. For I tell you, you will not see me again until you say, "Blessed is he who comes in the name of the Lord."*

After studying these verses in seven different Bibles, it is clear that The Messiah was telling The Jews they would not see him the second time until their leaders call on the name of Yeshua! We believe that Christ spoke to Jerusalem as a city because the Hebrew faith is one of community rather than individuality in worship. He was using the Old Testament tradition of what could be called corporate salvation.

The Hebrews believed in a group setting instead of an individual salvation. According to Matthew 23:37-39, it will be when Israel *as a nation* says, "blessed is he who comes in the name of the Lord" that Christ will return. Now open your Bible and look up Matthew 21:6-9. After you read those verses, you will see that The Messiah was referring to Himself!

Here are a few statements that should catch your eye. (1) He was here only for the lost sheep of Israel (the Jews). See Matthew 15:24. (2) He is the way and the truth and the life. No one comes to the Father, except through Him. See John 14:6. (3) Matthew 7:21-23 (NIV) - *Not everyone who says to me Lord, Lord, will enter the Kingdom of Heaven, but only the one does the will of my Father who is in Heaven. Many will say to me on that day, Lord, Lord, did we not prophesy in your name, and in your name drive out demons and in your name perform many miracles? Then I will tell them plainly, I never knew you. Away from me, you evildoers!* (4) This same Messiah will come back the same way you saw him leave. (Acts 1:11)

With that in mind, when Christ comes back, it will be in the same way and at the same place when The Hebrews accept him as Their Messiah as a nation, not before! If one studies the scripture without the denominational brainwashing of your past, you will be able to see the real KEY to seeing Our Lord when the time is right. It can and will only be after the Jews as a nation collectively believe and accept their Jewish Messiah!

We as Gentiles may pretend, twist, and imagine that we are the reason for the season or that it matters to the Messiah where the non-Jews stand on any topic. Here is a shocker - we don't hinder, help, or put Christ on the fast track for His return! According to Our Messiah and his words, it's The Hebrew Nation, Jerusalem, which seems to be the trigger for Him!

For that reason, some state that we should evangelize the Jewish people. Well if that's your stand, so be it. You may try, but you also need to remember that the Hebrews have been taken captive, murdered, and dispersed by people who claim to be Christians and now they may be a little hesitant toward your advances.

There is a time for The Lord's return. Before that happens, we need to remember that we are not in control of Him. He has the controls. Christ gave the people and the city of Jerusalem His command and one would have to say now that it's up to The Hebrews!

In our opinion, that's the KEY!

DOES GOD ANSWER PRAYER?

Are there special words we need to say? Is there a holy way to ask? Do we need to believe a certain way? Does The Father only listen if you are a believer? If you say you are a Christian, does that give you a direct line to His throne? If you claim to be a Jew, are your prayers heard more than others?

Our answer to all these is NO! Scripture gives us a guide. We read about a woman whose daughter was sick in Mathew 15:22-28. The point isn't that she is a Gentile who is bothering the disciples. We look at it this way - she has great faith and her request is granted. Remember verse 24. Yeshua said He was sent only to the lost sheep of the house of Isra'el. Then why was her daughter healed?

There is more than one thing to grasp from that wording.

Do we need to belong to a certain religion, denomination, or culture or worship in a certain way to get our prayers answered? With what happened, the answer would have to be NO. The Messiah said he didn't come to earth for anyone except the Jews, the lost sheep of Israel. Those are not our words. They are His. But this and other places tell us of people who God answers prayers for and they were non-Jews.

There may be a number of people saying, "No, you have to believe in the Messiah to get your prayers answered." In the Old Testament (Tanakh in Hebrew) there were a lot of prayers answered. That was before The Messiah was here. Before the time of Abraham, there seems to be religious people who were Gentiles. One of these was Noah and he found favor with God so much that he and his family were saved during the flood. How about

Genesis 5:24? *Enoch walked faithfully with God, then he was no more, because God took him away.* (NIV) Another Gentile? What is going on here?

Does this mean that, from the beginning, Gentiles were shown favor from God? Of course! All the prayers and requests that the Father granted before Abraham were from Gentiles. Abraham wasn't even born until somewhere around 2160 BC. That means we Gentiles were here first! Gentiles were the ones who ate the fruit from the tree of knowledge of good and evil. The Gentiles are to blame for the curse of mankind. The fall came because of what the Gentiles did, not the Jews. Jews were still a long way off when the two ate of the fruit.

Adam and Eve were formed by God. You might say they were his chosen two. That means the first chosen that we know of were actually Gentiles!

When your eyes are opened, you see that sin entered the world through a Gentile and was paid for by a Jew for the Jewish nation, the children of Israel. What we call Church came about because the Roman's kicked the Hebrews out of Jerusalem after the second Jewish revolt in 117-138 AD. Some say it was the second Jewish war. The first revolt came around 70 AD. That left only Gentiles to preach the Word. That was accomplished by the exit of all Jews, and spread the Word of God throughout the regions of Judea and Samaria and into the rest of the world.

That's why Acts 8:1 says persecution broke out against the believers. Let's take a close look at that! The believers in what? The same person who we read about in Matthew 15:24 who came only for the lost sheep of Israel! If you study Acts 8:1, then you just might realize that the ones who were persecuted and scattered were really Jews who believed in the Jewish Messiah, Messianic Jews. What we don't understand or maybe have never been taught is that the first fifteen bishops of what we call Church in Jerusalem were Jewish men who believed in the Jewish Messiah, Messianic Jews! Yet a lot of us Gentiles look at the Jews as second-class believers. They were the first to grasp the concept of a Messiah! They were a group of Jews who took the truth to the areas around them and then to the rest of the world! If those few Jews hadn't been Messianic in the first place, then the word may have died off for another time in history. No one really knows.

We are not saying that everyone should be a Messianic Jew, but we all should believe in the Jew who came only for the lost sheep of Israel. If one believes in the Jew and accepts that He came for and died for the Jews, then you should acknowledge that the Jews are the root of the tree and we Gentiles may at best be grafted into the tree as a branch or a twig of the tree. People who call themselves Christians have to stop acting like they are the tree! When they listen to some sermons or talk scripture, they act like they are the tree and get pious about their talk. That may give you the idea that they think they are more than a twig. A lot of them, down deep, must feel like the tree, and the root of all religion. Why, they are the foundation, the ones the Messiah was here for. They are number 1.

Doesn't that sound like what some of the Pharisees started to act like? Are people who call themselves Christians starting to act more like some of the Pharisees as time goes by? They say things like, "We're saved and you're not. Christ died for us Christians." Some start believing they are the tree and some must be thinking that now they are the true believers and they must be the root! We are not here to put words in their mouths, but just look at the attitude of most Christians. Their sermons say you can be rich. God wants you and all Christians to be wealthy. God wants all his people to prosper, so just believe. There are now preachers who teach their congregations to think positively in order to get the God of the Universe to bless them with what they want.

There are some who preach that the end is right at the door. There have been sermons on that since we all were small children and sooner or later someone will be right about that one. One year or fifty thousand years from now, someone will be right. No one knows. Neither The Son nor we know when that will take place. We know there are some people who are saying that The Son is with The Father and now Christ knows when it will take place. That may sound good but we haven't found that in scripture. But it sure sounds religious, doesn't it? Those may be the same people who believe that the whale evolved from a minnow, you know, through evolution.

Don't take one verse and make a religion out of it! Don't pick and choose. It is one book from Genesis to the book of the Revelation. We need to study what the Word says without the flowering of some teacher or preacher who may try to give you feel-good goose bumps mentality. We believe that's how some denominations try to draw individuals into their fold. If the words they use make you feel connected and happy at the same time, then it must be truth, Right?

When Our Messiah was teaching His friends (usually the Jewish people) by his way of life and preaching, He was relaying His truths to the children of Israel. He didn't pick Gentiles. He picked Jews. We as Gentiles should realize that and accept that we are only blessed because of the Jews. Then and only then will we start to grasp what Our Messiah really did and how all of us are better because of that Jew!

We go to the Father in the Son's name. The Father answers our prayer. He may also answer the prayers of the non-believer in his Son or else, from Adam to Abraham, he didn't hear people's requests. He wouldn't have heard Noah or Enoch when they prayed. Does God answer prayers? YES! Is there a special formula? NO! There doesn't seem to be a special religion that seems to get their prayers heard more than the others. They may be able to give you a warm fuzzy feeling now and then, but warm fuzzy feelings mean that whatever your request is or sermon you've heard makes you think, desire, or feel good about something you've just heard or helps you remember a special event.

Can the God of the universe answer prayer? YES! Do you need a special person to pray for you? NO! Do you need to be in a certain religion or denomination? NO!

Does God always hear and answer your prayers? Read Jeremiah 11:14! That tells us He doesn't have to! As you read all of Jeremiah 11, you will see a nation who turned their back on God and didn't obey God's rules. Look what happened to the Hebrews. Now look at our nation? It's a question of when, not if, the Father will say verse 14 to us. They heard, "Do not pray for this people, because I will not listen when they call to me!"

Who are we as a people or nation to tell the God of our universe what He has to do! He's the boss and our leader. He is God!

We like to believe that He hears our prayers and answers them. But that is just our request, our hope, and our desire. It's still up to Him if He listens or cuts us off because of what we as individuals or we as a nation have become.

You may still get that warm fuzzy feeling and you may still think that means you're right. Well, keep believing that and don't change. It just might be the only thing that you have to look forward to!

THE LAW

English speaking teachers and preachers talk about the law like it was an evil legalistic set of laws that people were put under during the Old Testament times in history. That interpretation has been preached and taught since I was a small boy in Potosi, Wisconsin. But remember - if you tell a lie long enough, people will start to believe it's the truth. We have stated that many times and it is truer about scripture and life today than at any time in history!

With all that brainwashing set aside and all the prejudice stopped or at least brought out in the open, one needs to study to find TRUTH. We have stated that many times in this book because it's the most important aspect of this writing. The Truth will last the test of time, but the misleading, the misinterpretations, and the misguided brainwashing of religions, denominations, and churches told over and over for an extended period of time will sway all societies in the direction of that large door at the end of that huge path!

Now back to what we call the law in our English writings of scripture. If you do a little study without the brainwashing of your denomination, you should find out that "The Torah" is what translators changed to the word "Law" in every instance. When you put some effort into your study, you can see that they substituted a negative sounding word in the place of Torah. By doing that, they made a separation from the true meaning to one that people will look down at - Law! That word just makes it sound harsh. It's not the loving way that most preachers and teachers like to portray scripture so that you feel good about yourself. That word seems to bring out an instant dislike to the concept of whatever they were talking about!

But the meaning of the word "Torah" is literally "Teaching Doctrine"! Our Messiah said, *"Do not think that I have come to do away with the Law of Moses and the teachings of the prophets. I have not come to do away with them, but to make their teachings come true."* (Matthew 5:17, GNB) Now if you say that He did not come to abolish the teachings of Moses or what the Prophets said, then He didn't abolish. He really made their statements complete by being Our Messiah!

That puts a whole different outlook on what Our Lord said. He did come to obey the teachings of Moses (The Torah) and, by doing so, He didn't do away with the teachings. While Christ was here, He lived by the Torah and we should also! Whether you want to call it "Torah", "biblical teachings", or "the teachings of Moses", no one did away with God's rules in the Old Testament or in the New Testament when Christ was walking on this earth!

There are some who preach and teach that what the English translation says in Matthew 5:17 means that the Church has replaced the Hebrews as God's chosen people. That statement alone leads a whole lot of good people down that large road to the huge door. There must be a lot of preachers who feel they have to go along with what their denomination dictates to them or maybe they will be out of a job. They should remember that the ones who preach and lead people down the wrong path will be judged more harshly than the ones who follow their false teachings, although they both end up at that huge door. The problem is that neither ends up on that small path that leads to that small door. Remember that only a few will find!

Now, if the Messiah didn't come to do away with the Torah or the Prophets but came to complete them, then that refers to what they wrote in scripture about Him. That's why we say that we are now complete in Him. The one they wrote about long ago was standing right there in front of them. He was the one they wrote about. I AM, the Way, Truth, and Life is standing right here! He completed what they have written because He was the one they wrote about. He never changed to be a Christian. He didn't lead His religion down the wrong path. He never gave up on the Jews. He was one, is one, and will always be a Hebrew, a Jew, and a part of the people known as God's Chosen People! He came as one of God's Chosen People as well as THE Chosen One from Heaven!

Christ not only obeyed it, He was "The Torah". He was the one every Jew was looking for, at one time or another!

You have heard this for years, but the time is coming for Christ return. It may not be today or tomorrow. It may be not for thousands of years, but He will return! When Christ does, know what road you are on. You will always have people saying that Christ can return anytime He wants. Then you have people who say He can't come back today because of this or that. Someday they will be wrong. If you are wrong on that day then you are wrong for ETERNITY!

2 CHRONICLES 7:1-14

The Glory of The Lord filled the temple. In the Hebrew Bible it says, The Glory of the *Adonai* filled the house.

The People do not look for the glory of the Lord to fill their houses, be it a temple, church, or any house where people worship Adonai himself. We read that, when Solomon finished praying, God's Glory came. God's proclamation was for the temple in Jerusalem, in Israel. Chapter 5 ends with the cloud being so thick the priests couldn't perform their duties for the service.

Do people today want God's Glory to fill their house? The natural answer would be yes, but do people really, really want that?

Far too many people believe and too many preachers and teachers say this one little verse, "We all fall short of the glory of God, so ask and then do what you want, then ask again!" Our question is this - will the glory fall on you with that attitude? How many people that you know, if the glory came into their house and the cloud filled the room, would open the doors and windows to get the house clear so they could see again. How many would understand the cloud and the glory at all?

If the cloud filled any house, would we even notice it came from God?

GOD

We find it difficult for success to be gauged by the amount of toys a person has! When a person is so concerned about gray hair, any hair at all, the color of hair, or the amount of it, it is a good indication of how worldly or superficial a person has become!

Becoming older may mean you have been here longer or that you may deserve respect, but it's not any gauge of how smart you may be. If you want an example look at our government officials!

Being in God's will doesn't mean you have or obtain a huge church, own a business, drive a semi, or even preach to individuals who ride motorcycles.

We look at Jeremiah. He didn't have people who wanted to listen to his preaching or hear his warnings. He was never given a large supply of food so he could make people believe that he was the reason for the season by handing out some food. People didn't like what he said. He was poor, put in prison, and taken like a slave to another country. He would be cataloged as having no success whatsoever!

We would have to guess, for his time in history, he would have been called a failure. Would he be gauged any better today? Why do we think that to be in God's will you need a new home, bigger motor home, new car or truck, reach hundreds or thousands of people, have a food ministry, dress real nice, and be able to spend any amount of time away from the ministry and still convince your congregation you're doing what God wants you to do!

Being rich is not a form of godliness. It can be a tool some preachers use to draw certain people or convince others to believe that he is in the will of God. "Just look at all that God has blessed him with because he is a preacher." Success isn't measured by how many things you have. Success should mean you don't have to advertise what you do or convince others your intentions are what God has for you!

Help us to understand, Father. We are wondering why people don't jump on your band wagon. Why do they run to every deadbeat denomination or religion there is, but try to hide from the one and only when there is no hiding place you can't see?

To us, it doesn't make sense… but that's just might be us. Why would anyone follow a world that was just a chance beginning with some bang in space? There must be some monkeys or apes that are really mad that they weren't good enough for the evolution of the apes to man. They had to stay at the ape level or maybe, just maybe, they've seen *Planet of the Apes* movies and they are waiting their time to ride horses, conquer mankind, and be the leaders of the world. Even so, they still look like apes, don't they? It must be one of those evolution things again!

Don't laugh. That makes as much common sense as some of the scientists' theories about how life started. Was it by chance? Did everything happen by chance in the past but now it's all working out?

With all that we do, The Father still loves us. With all we say, He still forgives us. He is waiting for the appointed time to send His Son back, He is waiting for people to worship His Son. Do people even know His Son's name? His name was and is YESHUA!

We can only talk. We can only point to truth. We can only try to help the message get out. If anyone listens, that is not up to us. That is up to them!

All we can say is, "Father God, help their ears to hear, their heart to accept, their eyes to see, and their desire to be for your Son, YESHUA, and YOU!"

ARE YOU JUDGED AFTER EARTH?

Daniel 12:1-2 (NIV) - *At that time Michael, the great prince who protects your people, will arise. There will be a time of distress such as has not happened from the beginning of nations until then. But at that time your people - everyone whose name is found written in the book-will be delivered. Multitudes who sleep in the dust of the earth will awake: some to everlasting life, others to shame and everlasting contempt.*

Daniel 12:1-2 (CJB) - *When that time comes, Mikha'el, the great prince who champions your people, will stand up; and there will be a time of distress unparalleled between the time they became a nation and that moment. At that time, your people will be delivered, everyone whose name is found written in the book. Many of those sleeping in the dust of the earth will awaken, some to everlasting life and some to everlasting shame and abhorrence.*

Daniel 12:1-2 (KJV) - *And at that time shall Michael stand up, the great prince which standeth for the children of thy people: and there shall be a time of trouble, such as never was since there was a nation even to that same time: and at that time thy people shall be delivered, every one that shall be found written in the book. And many of them that sleep in the dust of the earth shall awake, some to everlasting life, and some to shame and everlasting contempt.*

Here are three interpretations of the same verse: NIV, CJB, and the KJV. Preachers and teachers have taught from those verses many years. They may be wrong or they may be right. Let's look at what those verses really say and why!

There are two ways of looking at these verses. Verse 1b (NIV) - *But at that time your people-everyone whose name is found written in the book-will be delivered.* The angel was referring to "your people". Who were "your people" to Daniel? They were the Jews who will be delivered because their names are found written in the book! But some people have been taught that "your people" refers to all believers who will have their name in the book. At that time, everyone will be awakend from the dust of the earth.

Would the angel who was talking to Daniel be talking about the Jews when he says "your people"? When he talks about multitudes that are dead (or asleep) in the ground awakening to either everlasting life or shame and everlasting contempt, do you think he was talking about the Jews one time and then, in the same sentence, he would talk about the Gentiles?

Michael was telling Daniel about the Hebrews: His people in the earth who are written in the book. The distress, everlasting life, and the everlasting contempt that Michael talks about were for the Hebrews, not Gentiles in the least!

Now if you study Matthew 24 1-25, you see that it refers you back to the prophet Daniel. In verse 4, the Messiah warned to watch out that no one deceives you. He also talks about things that will and must happen but says the end is still to come. All of this has taken place for many centuries and will keep on happening until Christ returns. Our point isn't whether he was referring to Gentiles or Jews. It is to remind you that when your preachers or teachers say that you are saved and tell you how you need to believe, you had better make sure it lines you with scripture and not them! Remember, many false preachers and teachers will come and lead many away from the Truth. We believe this has been happening for a very long time and will continue for a much longer period of time!

Do we claim to have all the answers? NO! One thing we will say is that, in Daniel, the angel Michael was talking to Daniel about the Hebrews.

Jeremiah 30 talks about the trouble the Hebrews will have. Eventually, a king will rise up for them and they will no longer be enslaved.

In Jeremiah, Matthew, and Daniel, the writings were to the Jews. Our Messiah was talking to His closest friends and followers who were Christ's Hebrew disciples.

We know that every preacher and teacher will be saying that they were referring to Gentiles as well. We are not bold enough to state that the wrath of God spoken of through the prophet Daniel does not give us a free pass as long as we follow some preacher or take their denominational stand.

Like we have always said to you, STUDY with an open mind to truth, not a denominational brainwashing or a leading from someone who has been taught how to brainwash you and your congregation! Do not read this and believe what we write because we wrote it. Do your own study with an open mind for finding the truth! Remember what we have said before - no preacher or teacher will agree with our writing because that would mean that they have been leading people in a direction that is unhealthy for their congregation. They will be held more accountable for their stand and they will have to answer for all the people who may have been lead astray by them. With all that placed on their heads, they will have a real hard time with eternity!

ROMANS 8:1-8

Therefore, there is no longer any condemnation for those who are in union with the Messiah. Why? Because the teachings of the Spirit, which produces this life in union with Our Messiah, has set us free from the teachings that lead us to sin and death. For teachings by itself, has or lacks the power to make the old nature cooperate. But God the Father sent his sinless Son to deal with sin, and in doing this he executed the punishment against sin in the human nature of things. So that the requirement of the just teachings might be fulfilled in us and we will not be running our lives by the old nature. People who want to live by their old nature have their minds set on old nature activity. But, people who try to live by the Spirit have their minds set on the things and the teachings of the spirit. The problem comes when you are taught with a denominational overtone, instead of what the word really says. It may sound right, you understand it, and therefore it lines up with what you want to believe, that or we should say, none of those mean it's the truth! Even when people, feel good about it, that doesn't make it, the truth. The man who desires the old nature is death, but the person who follows the teachings of the spirit is life and peace. Controlled by your old nature means you're hostile to God, Because you do not submit to God's teachings. Those controlled by the sinful nature cannot please God.

When you are brainwashed by a denominational philosophy, you follow the denominational teachings. In most cases where your denomination and God differ, you are taught what your denomination dictates. That person with all the good intentions in mind does not submit to God's teachings at all. It is impossible for you to go against God and still be in His will! So our advice is to study more and grasp what The God of our universe has for you in His Word.

What is leading so many individuals wrong today is that the Mosaic teachings are improperly understood and are perverted by those who make it into a legalistic system. In our opinion, the religious leaders of today are acting just like the Pharisees did during the time of Christ!

Think about what your Preachers preach and your Teachers teach you. If it sounds good or bad to you, you should take time to study more, not to prove them wrong, but to make sure you are doing as much as you can the right way! We are not concerned about the preacher or teacher. They have made their own bed and have to lie in it, so to speak. But you have a chance to make sure what you hear, say, believe, and pass on to your children is right with The God you want to worship!

A miracle doesn't make what you hear right, neither does a philosophy, fasting for weeks at a time, listening to scholars, nor repeating something you read here. None of those make you right with The Father, His Son, or anyone who you look up to! You need to put your time in and find that God has everything lying in front of you. You just have to look hard enough and find it.

We will never stop saying this, but you need to STUDY more than ever before! Put aside what we say and whatever you hear from a classroom or the pulpit in your church. Find that God has all the answers and they are right in front of you. Most of us never take the time to set aside the brainwashing of our past and start working on our future!

This book and all this studying aren't just for you! This book is as much for our family as it is for anyone else!

A GREAT POINT TO THINK ABOUT!

Where before the birth, life, death, and Resurrection of our Messiah did people go when they died? Was it, If good, Heaven? If bad, Hell? If that is so, then why did the Lord have to come and die? Was it Hebrews - Heaven, Gentiles - Hell? We hope that's not true!

After studying some of the Hebrew culture, we believe it gives us a hint to the answer.

We are going to try to put it in a way that everyone should see. We know that there are Jews who could explain it in a better way, but this is as good as we have found.

In Hebrew, the place of the Dead is called, Sh'ol. It is not a place you can pray your loved ones out of like purgatory. According to the Old Hebrew, when any person died they went to Sh'ol. There were two sections of Sh'ol: Ades (a place of torment) and Abraham's Bosom / Abraham's side / Paradise (a safe place).

When you study about the rich man and poor Lazarus in Luke 16, you read that the rich man lived in luxury while there was a beggar at his gate named Lazarus. The poor man had dogs licking his sores. They both died. In Sh'ol, the rich guy was in torment. He looked up and saw Abraham with Lazarus at his side. You know the story. The rich guy asked for a finger tip of water to cool his tongue. Then in verse 26, Abraham said that between them was a great chasm and that no one can cross over between there and here. Then he asked if he could go to his father's house and warn his 5 brothers. Abraham said they have Moses and the Prophets. Then the rich guy said if someone from the dead goes to them, they would repent. We put a lot of that in our own language, but we hope you understood a very important point which most, if not all, religions overlook.

That story fits the Hebrew beliefs and points to where the dead went before the birth, life, death, and the resurrection or our Lord, The Messiah!

> John 14:6 (NIV) – *Jesus(Yeshua) answered, "I am the way the truth and the Life. No one comes to the Father except through me!"*

Luke 23:39-42 states that the Lord was cursed by one of the criminals, yet the other one asked the Lord to remember him when He came into His Kingdom. Verse 43 b - *"Today you will be with me in Paradise."*

Everyone who died, from the beginning of time until the Second Coming of Our Messiah, just may be in Sh'ol!

Some Hebrew's may say Gey-Hinnom. We believe that is part of the old city Jerusalem where they burned rubbish. Some of them say that represents what Hell, or Ades, will be like.

Remember, neither Elijah nor Enoch died, so they didn't need Sh'ol!

WHAT

What do you want from scripture? Is it a warm fuzzy feeling? Is it peace in your soul? Is it direction for your life? Is it a direction for you to point your children to? Maybe it's a cushion to fall back on or a goal to live by.

What most people want is a book that tells them they are living right according to their lifestyle or, at the very least, forgiven no matter what they do, want, or have become. Their God is the God of Love, right?

This might be a good spot to take another drink of that tea or coffee because you will have a lot of thinking to do with what we are about to say. Guess what, you have heard this all before, but you had better sit back and get ready to absorb some information, nothing new. It's just not powder-puffed like most, if not all, preachers do!

God is Love. He is a Just God, a kind God, forgiving, understanding, faithful, sweet, nurturing, and patient… that is until you stop putting Him first. When that happens, we find out He is a jealous God. He isn't blown away by some dumb reason we are not faithful to Him. After all, He is all we have. Even His chosen people went too far and He told Jeremiah in 11:14 -*"Do not pray for this people or offer any plea or petition for them, because I will not listen when they call to me in the time of distress."* (NIV) That was for His people who were lifted up many times. The Father is a just God, but you can push Him too far! You can walk the wrong path, but that is your choice! We all have a job to do. Some like it and do it. Some like it but ignore it. Some never look for the job. Some think they search but never find. In reality, they want other people to do the work while they reap the blessings. Still others want pastors or others to do the looking so they can claim what some other person found! After all, they are much too busy to do the legwork for the answer. Either they are too busy with their job or they are too busy with church to have time with the Father.

We have heard some say that others are called to teach. They don't understand or grasp the meanings, so they want the more religious people to tell them what the bible says. Isn't that being lazy? That is saying to The Father, "What I'm doing is more important than what You are telling me!"

We have a lot of people who try to explain the Word and guide people either to the right path or down *their* path - right or wrong, to the left or right, long or short, wide or narrow.

The bible is such an easy lesson that most people can't or don't want to follow. Let's put it a little more simply. The Old points to the Messiah, the New is about the Messiah, and the hereafter is the Messiah. Isn't that simple? Now go and be blessed!

We don't believe it has to be more or less. Just do what it says. We have a hard time with people that teach and preach while they have no idea what our Messiah's true name is! We were talking to a pastor at a funeral one day and he made the comment that at least we know the New Testament was written by Christians and not by some Jews somewhere! My little alarm went off and I asked him to tell me the names of the Christians who wrote the New Testament? He stated all of them. I asked, "Could you name a couple?" He started with Matthew. My question to him was, "Wasn't he a Jewish person who collected taxes from his own people, and that was one of the reasons people didn't like him? At least that's what our bible says." Then he said John was a close follower of Christ. My comment was, "That's true, but wasn't he a Jewish fisherman along with James his brother?" Then the pastor mentioned Paul. I said "Didn't Paul himself say he was a Pharisee, the son of a Pharisee, and doesn't that say he was trained and a leader in the Jewish Faith?"

The preacher told me he had been a pastor for forty years, been to the finest Christian schools in the country, given speeches in the best seminaries in the world, and, without a doubt, they were all Christians. We smiled at him and said, "Not according to scripture. Maybe in your doctrine, your interpretation or maybe the brainwashing of some teacher, but according to the true word, they were all Jews except one and that would be Luke, the doctor, and most experts believe he was a proselyte." When we started to explain what a proselyte was, he turned and walked away.

In reality, we didn't feel good about the conversation because we started to think of all the individuals he has influenced over those forty years… the sermons, the speeches, the misinterpretation of the Word by a man of God that didn't know and wouldn't accept the truth.

We believe that most people believe because of what some other person said rather than personal study to find the Truth. The one word that is either left out or taken the wrong way from your studies is the word "IF". In the English translation, it is said over 1500 times. "If" is such a large word, when it's put to the right context. When you find the word "if", you should study what the meaning around it and find out what the 'if" stands for.

Most people really don't study enough. After all, isn't that the pastor's job? Isn't he the one who knows all the "ifs"? Isn't he the true director of what we should study or are we the ones who need to open the word and find out what the "ifs" are all about! We have known a lot of people in our travels. Very few study to show themselves approved and even fewer examine what preachers say in their sermons or what they mean. Even fewer take time to grasp what the word really says. That statement in itself is a shame. People are too lazy or too busy in the world to spend time making sure what was said was correct. "Let others be concerned. After all, it doesn't concern me! Right?" No. That should bring out a flashing red light because it's wrong!

Let's get the "ifs" back in our Word. Let's study to find why we are here. After all, we only have one chance to help and to lead. Lend a helping hand to your own salvation and STUDY!!

JEREMIAH

These are a few writings from the book of Jeremiah that we thought were interesting and deserved more study from us and you! All passages are quoted from the NIV.

7:8 - *But look, you are trusting in deceptive words that are worthless.*

7:16 - *So do not pray for this people nor offer any plea or petition for them; do not plead with me, for I will not listen to you.*

9:25 - *"The days are coming" declares the Lord, "when I will punish all who are circumcised only in the flesh."*

11:14 - *Do not pray for this people or offer any plea or petition for them, because I will not listen when they call to me in the time of their distress.*

14:11 - *Then the Lord said to me, "Do not pray for the well-being of this people."*

Jeremiah was told in 15:19b *"If you repent, I will restore you that you may serve me; if you utter worthy, not worthless words, you will be my spokesman. Let this people turn to you, but you must not turn to them."*

31:31 – *"The days are coming," declares the Lord, "when I will make a new covenant with the people of Israel and the people of Judah."*

23:5-6 – *"The days are coming" declares the Lord, "when I will raise up for David a righteous Branch, a King who will reign wisely and do what is just and right in the land. In his days Judah will be saved and Israel will live in safety. This is the name by which he will be called: The Lord our Righteousness Savior."* (In Hebrew it would be *Adonai Tzidenu* or *Adonai our Righteousness*)

Those are just a few writings where God told one of His followers not to pray or ask for favor because He would not listen. The Father can and does get to the point when He has had enough!

THE MARK

This is an interesting topic. Is the Mark a sign on our head or right hand? Maybe it is a computer chip under your skin, so no one will know if you're a follower or a believer. Will society make it mandatory to have a chip put in babies when they're born? If so, all babies could be identified in case of a kidnapping, rape, or if they were lost or murdered and found in the woods. It makes sense, with the chip and the computer systems they are coming up with. As soon as the baby or person was abducted, the authorities would be able to follow their moves until they are rescued by the police.

If the right computer had the right information and numbers, it should be able to find the lost person in minutes. It would no longer take months or years. That sounds so right, how could you go against a device like that? The ones in favor of this process could advertise by having parents who have had young girls and boys abducted and later found dead say, "I wish I would have had this opportunity when my child was a baby, then I believe my child would be alive today." It sounds like a child protection agency advertisement.

If *we* can come up with something that makes the Mark sound like a great thing, then those who are a lot smarter than us can and will come up with an even better ploy. They will have a more convincing angle to draw people into their fold.

We also believe it will not be called the Mark!

It wasn't that long ago, if people would have even talked about something like this, it would have been a futuristic type of venture you'd only see in the movies. Now, it's within our grasp. At the very least, it's right around the corner. It's kind of scary to think that with this angle, people would actually invite the Mark into society with open arms.

If the Bible thumper complains, then they will be branded as not caring about people. The religious people will be the individuals who have no feelings toward the babies or young people being molested by perverts or the cold hearted killer.

The people against this "child care protection program" would be made to look like they didn't care about that fifteen year old who was raped. It could have been prevented with the Mark! How dare you call yourself a Christian? How dare you say your God is the God of love, when you won't even stand up to fight the wrong in society today?

People need to understand that the Mark will get into our lives. There will be a huge push for it. Most people will not even see it coming because of the blinders on them and the lack of desire to really find truth by studying.

Don't blame God or accuse Him. When the Mark is used in our society, it will be because of our laziness. We can't say we haven't been warned!

JAMES (YA'AKOV)

In English-speaking countries, when a Messianic Jew refers to the Messiah, they usually say Yeshua. When they refer to his brother, they say James. Why don't they refer to His brother as Ya'akov, his real name? When Ya'akov wrote his letter, it must have been one of the first letters written in the New Testament. Some say that Galatians was the first letter. We believe both were written around the same time. It makes sense that both were around or before 50 AD.

Mark and Luke were written before Matthew (Mattityahu) or John (Yochanon). The last two actually walked with Christ. They are considered true Faithful Followers. They knew Him personally and were part of Christ's inner circle.

The letter from Luke was a personal communication between a doctor by the name of Luke and his friend Theophilus. He wanted Theophilus to have an account of what he came up with after his investigating was complete.

> Luke 1:2 (NIV) - *Just as they were handed down to us by those who from the first were eyewitnesses and servants of the word.*

It seems he had writings—or at least heard speeches—from some who must have been eyewitnesses and servants of the Lord. He may have heard Matthew, John, Peter, James, Andrew or one of the other disciples talk. He may have also read something they had written.

Luke was a companion of Paul. It is believed that he traveled with Paul on at least one of his journeys. He was a doctor and most likely a friend of Paul. His writings couldn't have *only* come from Paul's teachings. This is evidenced by what we read in Luke 1:2. We know Paul came onto the scene after Christ death.

Back to James (Ya'Akov), a brother of the Lord. Some denominations believe Ya'Akov was a distant relative of Yeshua. Some say he was a brother in the religion Yeshua was setting up, not a blood brother at all. Others believe that he grew up with the Messiah as a playmate, perhaps he was a follower of his older brother. (Most younger brothers look up to their older brothers as role models in their growing up period of life, although some brothers would never admit that.)

Imagine if Ya'Akov—as a true blood brother of the Lord—followed Yeshua around, looked up to him for guidance, mimicked him as younger brothers do, and then one day heard Him say He was the Son of God. We believe it would have been quite a shock for someone who knew Him from birth to hear a brother make that kind of statement. He most likely would have been thinking, "I played with Him, we talked at night, we ran, we even told each other secrets, and my brother never once told me he was God!" How hard would it be for you if your brother made a statement like he was the Son of God? Would you automatically think that you had played with the King of the Universe? Would you think He must be God, because you never saw Him do anything wrong?

Or would it be more like, "My brother always was a dreamer. He never once baptized me when we were playing in the lake. If my brother really is the Son of God, He would have at least tried to dip me in water so I would have a chance of being saved myself."

Our point is, in all likelihood, a brother—or any family member—would have trouble automatically accepting such big news. If your father and mother sat you down when you were old enough to understand, and told you about how your older brother was conceived and was born, then you most likely would have thought your parents had gone off the deep end. It would have been hard not to think, "He always was Mom's favorite!"

Stop! We know there are people saying, "Of course we would believe Mom and Dad." But in reality, who would believe a story like the one told by Joseph (Yosef) and Mary (Miryam) would have told their sons and daughters? We can look back and question why they would not have believed, but as late radio commentator Paul Harvey would say, it's because we know the rest of the story. They didn't know the rest of the story and it would be harder for them to accept.

I am the seventh son of our family, and finding out something like that would have been a big, big shock. It's not that I don't love them, but that kind of statement from Mom and Dad would have seemed kind of strange, to say the least.

We believe James (Ya'Akov) was the Lord's younger brother, son of Joseph and Mary. That's how we feel. How you feel or believe is your belief. Will it, or should it, change the way you read or look at James? That's still up to you! It doesn't and won't make a bit of difference to us how you look at it or how you believe. That's the beauty of it. It won't add one day to your life or make it one day shorter. According to what we read, we all have eternity. It will either be in a blessed area or one of torment.

When both of us die, do we think we will get a special place for trying to get people to believe in Yeshua? NO. We believe He will first scold us for not doing enough. Then, if He forgives us, we just might be able to go to the lowest spot in God's Kingdom. That is far better than anything we can think of. What we do or have done isn't enough. What is said isn't stated strongly enough to get people to turn from names that have no meanings, or idols who lead people away from Yeshua.

As we look at churches, preachers, and teachers, we see lessons that are flowery but only relate to outside activities. The pews are collecting more dust than butts! The focus on outside activities is taking over for the inside activity of God. It may look good for the people going by, in the church, and even to the people who participate… but when God becomes a side show, then it's just that: a side show!

We personally don't believe that the Lord needs our help. The people we talk to will have no excuse when they stand before Yeshua and state, "Did we not prophesy in your name? We drove out demons in your name. Why we even performed many miracles in your name. We gave food to the homeless in your name. We even went to the old folk's home to make the elderly feel better. We preached in your name. We taught others to believe in that name."

Then they will come to find out when they stand before the Lord that they didn't use, don't know, and never heard of the name Yeshua! They worshipped a made up name that has no real connection to salvation whatsoever. They worshiped a different person, in a different culture, a different religion, and a different name than the true name of our Messiah!

Will The Father say well done, George and Bonnie? NO! He will say we didn't do enough! We didn't perform the task He gave us. We should've done more, so more people would go down that narrow road to that small gate. People wouldn't listen. They plugged their ears, they turned their backs to us, they may believe that following a made up name is good enough. That's just what Satan wants them to believe and follow; an empty name so more people hear, "I never knew you. Away from me, you evildoers!"

You may help a million people. You may make millions smile. You may preach to tens of thousands at a time, or just twenty at a service. You can feed countless homeless people. You may teach a few women or men. You may pray every day and fast every week. You may have the most beautiful voice on earth. But if you are worshiping any other name but the real name of Yeshua, you're heading to that wide gate and down that broad road. Why would our Savior accept any made up name, in any other religion than HIS?

Satan loves it when you use a made up name. He just sits back and lets your words go out! He doesn't need to do any work at all. He doesn't need to work whatsoever. You do his work!

His brother James (Ya'Akov) called him Yeshua. His parents called him Yeshua. The people who truly followed him called him Yeshua. His true friends called him Yeshua!

So do we. In our opinion, so should you!

ADONAI

In many places in our English versions of the Bible, the word "Lord" is used in a place where Jews wrote "Adonai." We got the idea that somehow Yeshua was connected with the verse when we would read the word Lord. It seemed like a logical connection, even in the Old Testament. (The Hebrews called it The TANAKH.)

We believe that is one of the deceptions of our English writings. Not only do the denominational brainwashers want you to connect the word Lord with Yeshua, but they also want the word Yeshua connected with Adonai. That way when you start to believe their brainwashing, you believe that when a Jew wrote or said Adonai, they were really referring to Yeshua. We believe through study you will see that is totally wrong.

First, Adonai is not the other name of the Son.

Second, linking Yeshua as Adonai in the Old Testament is like putting the cart before the horse. He wasn't born yet! Consider Isaiah 53:2.

> Isaiah 53:2 (NIV) - *He grew up before him like a tender shoot, and like a root out of dry ground. He had no beauty or majesty to attract us to him, nothing in his appearance that we should desire him.*

Christ grew up. He did not come to this earth well-formed like the movie people portray him. He wasn't handsome. His pure beauty didn't attract people. Isaiah 53:3 tells us a lot of people despised and avoided Him. He was a man of pains, well acquainted with illness. He was someone from whom people turn their faces. He was given no value.

After reading this, you should realize that it was written around 700 years before the Messiah was here. Isaiah saw exactly what was going to take place, down to Christ's personal features.

As we searched for the answer to a number of questions, the book of Daniel jumped out to us. After he was taken as a captive from Jerusalem to Babylon, Daniel wound up in the Babylonian government. You can read what he wrote about the furnace, the banquet, and the lion's den. The last chapter of his writing, chapter 12, tells us about the end times.

Daniel is told that at the right time, Michael, the great prince who protects his people, will arise. Did you catch that? Daniel is told that his people (who are the Jews) are the ones that Michael will protect. At that time, his people will be delivered; everyone whose name is found written in the Book. Many of those sleeping in the dust of the earth will awaken. Some will awaken to everlasting life and some to everlasting shame.

It seems that we need more studying on this one. On one hand, all you have to do is get your name in this book then you have it made! Yet it says, many who sleep in the dust of the earth will awaken; some to everlasting life and others to everlasting shame and contempt. Think about this: first you have to get your name in this book, and that doesn't seem to guarantee you heaven. When you come out of the ground you will go to the place prepared for you.

> Daniel 12:3 (NIV) - *Those who are wise will shine like the brightness of the heavens, and those who lead many to righteousness, like the stars forever and ever.*

First, remember the Messiah died for our sins. This is in accordance with what the Old Testament says.

Second, know that Christ was buried and raised from the dead. This is also in accordance with what the Old Testament says.

When you study the Old Testament in our English versions, and find the word Lord, go to the Hebrew version and find out if the Jews would have said Adonai. If they did, the word Lord is not referring to the Messiah Yeshua. It refers to "The Lord God." The Messiah wasn't here yet.

Is this statement true and perfect? NO. We can only study and try to get more people involved in their own study. We just hope that it comes from a clear study and not the brainwashing of some denomination.

GALATIANS

All of Galatians 3 talks to the Galatians about what they are doing wrong.

Paul starts out by telling them how foolish it is to allow themselves to be lead astray. He says they just might be under a spell.

The main topic isn't trying to be Jewish, but to follow the Jewish Messiah.

Paul (Sha'ul would have been his Hebrew name) says he would like to learn one thing from the Galatians. He asks if those who received the Holy Spirit received it by trusting in the Messiah or from following the legalistic rules set up by the Torah. Essentially, did you receive the Spirit by human acceptance or by faith?

The Torah gives instructions. You're not saved by instructions. You're saved through faith in Yeshua, The Messiah!

> Galatians 3:6-9 (NIV) - *So also Abraham "believed God, and it was credited to him as righteousness." Understand, then, that those who have faith are children of Abraham. Scripture foresaw that God would justify the Gentiles by faith, and announced the gospel in advance to Abraham. "All nations will be blessed through you. So those who rely on faith are blessed along with Abraham, the man of faith."*

Our main concern in verses 6-9 is that most writers of today's interpretations say that Jews taught that you had to become a Jew in order to become a Christian. Some scholars believe that the letter to the Galatians was written around the year 49 AD. What Paul was teaching makes us believe that we would have to call them Messianic Jews. There were Jews and Gentiles, and some of the Jews were zealous about their faith. In other words, they wanted everyone of believe like them. Does that sound like the Christian tone of today?

Paul (Sha'ul) was saying, "You do not need to be converted or live as a Jew! You're Gentiles, live as Gentiles. You do not need to be a Jew to follow the Torah. You do not make it to heaven by the Torah."

We believe it's good to follow the teachings in the Torah, but it won't give you heaven! It's by faith in the Jewish Messiah that you're saved, not by legalistic means. It's by faith in Him!

We personally believe that the Law is necessary. They are written to keep the law-breakers corrected. Most people who call themselves Christians are brainwashed to believe that the Torah in the Old Testament is the Law of Moses. If you spend time studying, you will find out that it's really the teachings of Moses. There is a legalistic part of the Torah, instructing Jews how to live and what the Jews should do. The problem with certain religions is that they like to lump it all into one negative word: "LAW."

Every Nation must have laws to live by. Israel was no different. Any country without laws to be governed by will soon fall. A lack of laws will result in chaos within their government, states, cities, and people. The United States is a good example of this. Look at what has happened and is happening in America. We have chaos, disrespect, and a destruction of our society. We have rules, but now we have lawlessness revolving around confusion.

The confusion isn't about what law to follow. The confusion is about what a mess an individual can cause to make a law look like it is bad. Then they can see what laws they can get away with. It seems that our society has turned into a society of, "Let's break the laws that our fathers said we are to follow."

There are people who have influence over large groups. Many times, they convince the group that because they don't like a certain law or rule, then no one in their group has to obey that law.

STUDY

Here is one thing we have observed: the young people of today need to be raised to show respect to their parents, the police, firemen, and the military.

The worst thing to happen to our society was when the government stepped in and began trying to govern families. Parents have to be allowed to be parents. When a parent can't control himself, then he should be held accountable. We—as a society—have to think before we act.

There can't be one law for this group and a different law for that group. If it's good for the big name person in Hollywood, then it's good enough for the man from Potosi, Wisconsin, or the man from Mobile, Alabama. The laws have to be the same, no matter to whom they apply.

Raise up a child to respect you and your authority. If you do that, then you will raise a productive adult for society. Your race won't matter. Where you come from won't matter.

Our final statement on this is: we have to get to the point of respecting the laws on the books. If one needs to be changed, then go about it the proper way. We should not reward any people who break the laws.

WE DO NOT MAKE REQUESTS
TO YOU BECAUSE WE
ARE SO RIGHTEOUS!

When the church of the second and third centuries began to drift away from its Jewish roots, misconception developed concerning God's Torah. This was due largely to the influence of Greek philosophy and Pagan ideas.

> Daniel 9:18 (NIV) - *Give ear, our God, and hear; open your eyes and see the desolation of the city that bears your Name. We do not make request of you because we are righteousness, but because of your great mercy.*

This should teach us that the Torah, or "law" in English, is about God's Mercy. It's not a negative word at all.

Here is another big misconception: in Hebrews, it states "a better covenant." That is only referring to Christ's sacrifice. It means His sacrifice was a better one than that of the sheep. Consider what Paul wrote in Romans 3:31.

> Romans 3:31 (NIV) - *Do we, then, nullify the Law by this faith? Not at all! Rather, we uphold the Law.*

In reality, both places where the English translator wrote "Law," it should have been Torah. The misconception here is the Law is a negative concept. It should not be and it isn't. In our English, we think of Law and Lawbreakers, rules and rule breakers, police and crooks. To think like that misjudges scripture.

STUDY

Matthew 5:18 (NIV) - *For truly I tell you, until heaven and earth disappear, not the smallest letter, not the least stroke of a pen, will by ANY means disappear from the Law until everything is accomplished.*

Again, we believe it would be more correct to use "Torah" where they have used "Law." Perhaps then people would not look at it as a negative.

Christ stated, "I came not to destroy, but to fulfill." In other words, to fulfill means to complete. Christ came to bring perfection! Far too often people (who call themselves Christians) interpret it to mean that Christ renders the Torah obsolete. What He does is fulfill it in such a way as to perfect a foundation on which to build further. That is how it is written and that is how we need to interpret the word.

We personally believe Jews and Christians are somewhat alike. Both are hard headed and brainwashed to believe that their religion knows all the answers and that's all there is. Our philosophy is that we need a blending of the two. Sounds like a cop out, doesn't it? But let us explain.

The Jews want more proof while they trust in their leaders for direction. The Christians don't want truth because they have faith while following their leaders. The Jews need to justify the actions of their leaders. The Christians like to point to the injustice the Jewish leaders once committed, while overlooking their own leaders actions and injustices.

The Jews look at the Torah and pick out what they want. The Christians look at the New Testament and pick out what they want.

After looking at each of those, we would have to say both are not only acting somewhat alike, but in some instances treating scripture in the same way.

The Jewish leaders discredit much of the New Testament. The Christian discredits a lot of the Old Testament. The Jews use the New to justify the Old. The Christian uses the Old to justify the New. You might say they both use both only when it pleases them.

The real wrench in the cog is the Messianic Jews. How dare they use both. How dare they use what was foretold with what was fulfilled. How dare they use the best of both worlds to see what happens if they work together. What a strange concept. Are they really trying to make both The Old and The New work together? How dare they look at God's Word like that! Is this a new concept, or just an old one that is being brought back to life?

People of today have been taught that Paul was called a Christian. Yet, He stated, "I am a Pharisee, the son of a Pharisee!" You notice he didn't say *"I was"* a Pharisee, but that *"I am"* a Pharisee. He never gave up that title, nor did he start a new religion.

Paul read and pointed out to his fellow Jews that the true Messiah was already here, and that He was a Jew. The new concept was an old concept. But this time, instead of looking ahead for the Messiah, Paul was writing his letters to prove the Messiah was already here. He used the Tanakh (Old Testament) to do it.

In John 14:6, Yeshua answered, "I am the way, and the truth and the life." We believe, because of that, the name the Messianic Jews were given was "The Way." Yes, we know Antioch was the first place to call them something besides, "The Way." Of course, the interpreters have changed it to "Christian."

People say that the law has been replaced by grace. When you get brainwashed enough, and use the law as a negative, that sounds great. There is one little problem: the Torah of Moses is really the Teachings of Moses. Those teachings came from the Father. Consider the Ten Commandments. God wrote them, Moses taught them, and they are part of the teachings of the Torah!

It's not enough to give lip service. We need a complete service of soul, mind, and body. We should be asking The Father for His will be done on earth as it is in Heaven. That is what and how we should pray, according to the Messiah we follow. He said it and we should do it!

There are some Christians who think you have to distance yourself from the Jews (Orthodox or Messianic) because they are wrong. This concept doesn't make any sense. Think about this: our Messiah was a Jew. That alone should make every so-called Christian stop and think twice.

We have seen some individuals claim that there is room to work together. What they want is their truth. One will always want to be in control, and have the final say so. They feel like if there is a disagreement, their way is the only way.

We need to realize that working together and looking for truth is not going to bring a happy go lucky feeling all the time. You might find that the way you learned, what you follow, and what you truly believe is wrong, misleading, and may lead you to Biblical disaster.

That may be too strong or too hard of a statement for most people to grasp. Everybody believes the other side is wrong. Maybe if we patronize them they will come around to our way of thinking. You know the real truth!

Here is a statement that is the truth: even though most people believe like this, they will not admit it! They think, "We are right, you're wrong, no matter what the Bible says!"

That statement will make a lot of believers twist in their chairs.

They might even think, "How dare they make a statement like that. Why, we always go by what our pastor says. We believe what our teachers instruct us to believe, and we fully follow what our denomination dictates about scripture. When I read scripture, I see everything exactly the way our leaders do. They interpret and follow the way God wants us all to."

Have you grasped the point yet? No one should listen to a sermon and believe it that way just because your pastor, Rabbi, or teacher presents it. You need to study what was said with an open mind. The teacher wants you to follow their way of believing. But how do you know the teacher is always right?

STUDY

The Bible is looked at in many different ways. Everyone thinks that their religion, church, denomination, and their leaders are always right.

The Bible will stand the test of time. It already has. There have been attacks against it throughout history, but it still stands tall.

IN THE BOOK OF THE REVELATION

Revelation 20:12 (NIV) - And I saw the dead, great and small, standing before the throne, and books were opened. Another book was opened, which is the book of life. The dead were judged according to what they had done as recorded in the books.

John, in the book of The Revelation, wrote what he saw. In his vision, he saw the great judgment of the dead. There seems to be a number of books including the book of life. At that time, the dead are judged according to what they have done in their life. The sea gave up the dead that were in it. The ground gave up its dead. Death and Hades gave up their dead and each person was judged according to what he had done. In other words, we are all judged at that time!

Now some denominations teach that, until you reach the age of accountability, you are going to Heaven, no matter what you do. Our Messiah said in John 14:6 – *"I am the way, and the truth and the life. No one comes to the Father except through me."* (NIV) That states there is only one way to Heaven. By that writing, it seems that no one gets there by how old or young they may be.

There are people who believe that each individual's name is written in the book of life and it stays there unless you do the unpardonable sin. That way they give each baby an automatic entrance to the place called heaven when death comes. They feel the baby has not yet committed any act that would be considered unpardonable.

Religions have every right, within the framework of our laws, to stress their points of view, to draw people, to look for more converts, hold to each of their teachings, and minister to their people. You might say we have to tolerate them. But tolerance does not and cannot mean we are agreeing with the other religions or claiming that their beliefs are true!

We are to make request in Yeshua's name, if you are a follower, because of Christ, His authority, and what He did. God does not obligate Himself to hear the prayers of sinners. As a matter of fact, He told one of His best, Jeremiah, not to pray because He would not listen. If The Father would not listen to Jeremiah, then why would any Christian or Jew believe He has to listen to you?

Moses wrote in Deuteronomy 6:25 that we are to be careful to obey all the commands before the Lord our God, as he has commanded us and that will be our righteousness. In other words, they were to keep the rules God had given them. That would be their righteousness until The Messiah came, died, and was raised from the dead.

The Father must not see Jew or Gentile. He may see believers in something and He has every right to accept them or not. The real question is, believers in *who* will be saved? There is no magic word, no super phrase, and no name-it-and-claim-it-and-grab-it!

When you pray, it should be in The Messiah's name. If you are a follower of The Messiah, then you are addressing God. Yeshua is no less God than the Father. They are one in the trinity. Our Messiah states that you are to ask in His Name. No other name will do! If you petition Yeshua then you are petitioning The Father! Every person should see that Yeshua is the divine Son! He is God our Savior!

THE BIGGEST AND MOST DANGEROUS MISCONCEPTION

The biggest and most dangerous misconception in life and in the Word is using a made-up name with no definitive meaning, whatsoever.

The second is worshiping a kind of book because, by you doing so, you are making it your god just like rich people who worship money that has become their god. There are also poor people who worship money because they don't have any. The outcome would be the same for all three!

Some worship the Corvette they bought or the deal they made.

This may be an unhappy statement for some preachers. Most preachers correlate scripture based on what they have or their lifestyle, but very few Preachers have their lifestyle based on scripture!

There are preachers who worship the collection plate, the size of their congregation, or how large of a building they are preaching in.

There are preachers who focus on mission work. People who may have been on a trip or two seem to zero in on that church. After all, we are to go and make disciples of all nations. The missionaries themselves hunt for and, in most cases, find a spot that leans more toward missions to stay.

But most people who go on a mission trip feel what they are doing is the right thing to do. When they get back home they can tell a lot of stories. They point to the fact that they went, what they saw, what they did, maybe even how their life has been changed. All that is great except, after a few years, the only things left are their memories of the past with little or no lasting power in support of a calling.

We all have to be careful whom we worship and what leads us to that point. Do we believe because of some preacher or what he points to in his sermon? Do you study to show yourself approved and, when you do study, has anyone influenced your reading and beliefs? Are you swayed toward a certain direction in your studies? Are you scared people will know you're different if you tell them? Who would want to confess anything that would lead people to sit back and think about what and how to study? Are we supposed to just sit there and believe everything that person says while he or she is standing in front of the congregation? After all isn't that what they get paid to do? Aren't they the most knowledgeable people? They are the ones who can really talk to and talk about God. People must think that those preachers are the only ones who know the real way to God.

If Satan really knows scripture better than we do, then what would be his best weapon against each individual? Let us give you a hint: B-I-B-L-E. We know that right now there are some who disagree. That's OK. Some believe that Satan can't use the words of the Holy Bible to sway people. They are as wrong as wrong can be!

Let's take a quick look.

(a) How many people argue over the kind of Bible you use?
(b) After all, there is only one true bible.
(c) You must read it in a certain way to get the truest, best, and most from it.
(d) Some must believe that you only need to believe certain parts while the rest is just filler.
(e) There are major and minor parts.
(f) Here is a good one: The Old Testament doesn't pertain to us any longer, that is unless it helps to prove a point or a direction for living, then it's alright to use!

(g) Do people only use it when it helps them or leads to their way of thinking?

(h) People follow the Word as long as it doesn't interfere with what they want to do.

Those are just a few, but we hope you get the point.

We must fit the scriptures, not twist the scriptures, to fit the lifestyle, we want to live.

TIME TABLE FROM ADAM TO NOAH

MAN	Age at son's birth	Birth	Lifespan	Death
Adam	130	0	930	930
Seth	105	130	912	1042
Enosh	90	235	905	1140
Kenan	70	325	910	1235
Mahalel	65	395	895	1290
Jared	162	460	962	1422
Enoch	65	622	365	987
Methuselah	187	687	969	1656
Lamech	182	874	777	1651
Noah		1056		

The above table lists the Genealogy from Adam to Noah, how old the father would have been, the year from day 1, how long they lived and the year they died. The information was obtained from Genesis 5, the written account of Adam's line. (NIV)

So many people have counted these years and made statements like, "they don't add up" or "if those are the years then how old were the individuals they wrote about?" This section may help you understand how it works with the time frame of scripture.

How little do we really understand and how little time do we put into trying to understand the Word?

At first, Genesis 5:1-32 sounds like a bunch of people and ages running together in an overlapping and confusing mess. It will help you to open your Bible to Genesis 5 before we start looking at this. We really don't care which Bible you want to use, but it might help you if you open it to Genesis 5! That way you're not just taking our word for it. You will be reading or at least following along in your Bible. We have said before and we'll keep saying it: Don't believe us! Study for yourselves to prove Scripture to you and yours.

According to Verse 3, Adam had a son and named him Seth. He was actually his third son. Remember, in Genesis 4:1, it says Adam and Eve's first son was Cain. Then, in Verse 2, she gave birth to Abel. By verse 8, we see that Cain kills Abel. So Seth would have been their third son. This may sound like grade school teaching but remember, not everyone who reads this is a biblical scholar like you. To get to the truth, we need to start with the basics. You may be surprised on how much all of us can learn from the basics! This just may help at times to break through the biblical brainwashing of denominational teachings!

We've heard preachers say there were 2000 years from Adam to the flood, 2000 years from the flood to Christ, and now there will be 2000 years until the end of time. That makes the earth 6000 years old. Scholars can say anything they want but, according to scripture, that doesn't add up! If you want to just add the years, then let's do just that. Let's call The first year, year 0, from the beginning. From Adam to the flood, according to scripture, was 1656 years. That didn't come from us or any scholar. It came from Genesis 5. That is the number of years that were recorded.

We've noticed that, according to scripture, Noah was born in the year of 1056. That would mean that Adam, Seth, and Enoch would have been the only ones not alive when Noah was born.

By the chart, you see that Lamech was 182 when he fathered Noah and lived to age 777. There are so many interesting dates in history that preachers and teachers never talk about. We feel it would be wrong if we didn't list some of them and let you figure out how much your denomination has left out of your studies!

(1) Adam was alive through all their births except Noah.

(2) 1656 years passed between God creating Adam and sending the flood.

(3) According to Genesis 6:6-8, the Lord had enough with the wickedness of man, yet Noah was a man who found favor with God.

(4) Since the flood came in the year of 1656, look back on the chart and see how many of Noah's listed relatives were still alive when Noah was born. It goes all the way up to Enosh, Seth's son, with the exception of Enoch. God had already taken him because he walked with God.

(5) Noah's father was still alive when God told Noah to build the Ark. Methuselah, Noah's grandfather, the one who lived the longest, was also alive when God told Noah what to do. Yet, The Lord found favor only with Noah and his family. Genesis 6:9 says *Noah was a righteous man, blameless among the people of his time, and he walked with God.*

(6) It took Noah 100 years to get all the work done. Genesis 5:32 says that Noah was 500 and then it says who his sons were. Genesis 7:6 says that Noah was 600 when the flood waters came.

(7) These next two were the most interesting to us. Genesis 6:12 states *God saw how corrupt the earth had become, for all the people on earth had corrupted their ways.* Noah's father died only five years before the flood, so he and the rest of his family were part of the great wickedness of mankind.

(8) Noah's grandfather, Methuselah, was alive when God talked to Noah. If you look at the chart, you will see that Methuselah died the year of the flood! Nowhere in scripture does it say how he died. Did he happen to die naturally in the same year God sent the flood or was he caught up in the floodwaters and drowned with all the other wicked people? The flood was 1656 years after Adam. Methuselah died in 1656!

From the start of the flood to the family coming out of the ark was 1 year and 10 days - Genesis 7:11 going in and Genesis 8:14 coming out. If you study these you will get a clear picture of the timetable for the days in the ark. You will have to study for some time to grasp the amount of days and picture for yourself how it was and how long it took.

But that study is one of the most interesting and rewarding bits of research you will ever accomplish in your life!

MATTHEW 23:39

For I tell you, you will not see me again until you say, blessed is he who comes in the name of the Lord. (NIV)

Yeshua was telling the leaders in Jerusalem and the city itself that they would not see Him again until they say, "Blessed is he who comes in the name of The Lord!"

To us, that seems simple. The Lord was telling the leaders in Jerusalem that he will not come back until the leaders of the Jewish faith accept and ask for Yeshua to do just that!

The temple could be built for 200 years with all the other requirements fallen into place but Yeshua won't come back until the Sanhedrin (the Jewish Leaders) ask him to!

When the Sanhedrin accepts the fact that Yeshua was and still is The Only Son of God, then and only then will The Messiah be seen again in the Human form. We believe The Sanhedrin must become the leaders of Israel again, before the Messiah will return!

WHAT SHOULD BE ON YOUR MIND WHEN YOU PRAY FOR PEOPLE

Be thankful for their Faith and possibly their changed lives.

Ask God to let People know what He wants them to do.

Ask God to allow the people to get deep spiritual understanding.

Ask God to show them how to live for Him.

Ask God to give them more knowledge of themselves.

Ask God to give them strength for endurance.

Ask God to fill them with joy, strength, and thankfulness.

LEADERS IN SCRIPTURE?

When you read about some people in scripture it seems that as soon as you hear their name you think of a leader. That is not always the truth. When you read about some individual and skim over them you think nothing about a leader, yet they had great leadership and took absolutely no credit for it!

In this section, let's look at a few leaders and a few so-called leaders.

Adam was the leader God made with his own hands. He should have been a great leader, but when you look at him in Genesis 3:12 he falls short - *The man said, the woman you put here with me, she gave me some fruit from the tree, and I ate it.* (NIV) Now would you call that being the leader of the woman or the follower? The man showed his lack of leadership when he was tempted. Don't try to tell us that he ate because the woman asked him to avoid an argument. Our Messiah was tempted when he was hungry in the desert. By Matthew 4:3, we see Satan saying, "If you are the Son of God, turn these stones into bread." Unlike the first Adam, He didn't fall for Satan's trick. Now that was dedication and leadership!

Noah was a farmer first, but he was also a man who believed what he was taught and followed his belief to the tee. He became the second father to the human race. He had to have a lot of faith in God to take on a project like building a huge ship on dry ground. This man had patience and obedience. He led his family in the direction they had to go. He may have embarrassed himself when he got drunk, but the man was a follower of God and a leader to his family. You might say this man was the leader of all mankind!

Ishmael, Abram and Hagar's son, was raised for thirteen years as the son of Abram. When Sarah became pregnant and had Isaac, Ishmael became second in Abrahams eye. Ishmael went from being number one to not being even in the line any longer. Ishmael and his mother Hagar were sent away because Sarah recognized that her son would have to put up with the teasing of his older brother. Yet Ishmael became the father of twelve tribes. That is found in Genesis 25:13-16. Now here is a topic that we have never heard a preacher or teacher address:

> Genesis 25:9 (NIV) - *His sons Isaac and Ishmael buried him in the cave of Machpelah near Mamre, in the field of Ephron son of Zohar the Hittite.*

The interesting thing is that scripture states both of his sons, Isaac and Ishmael, were recognized, when they buried their father, Abraham. Ishmael must have been a leader because he is credited as being the founder of the Arab nations, who were and still are enemies to the Hebrew nation of Israel.

Isaac was part of Gods plan, but he seemed to compromise or lie to avoid confrontations. He received a lot from his father, Abraham, but he didn't seem to be a leader so much as a back seat driver. We know that there are people who will say that he was the leader of the Jewish faith and therefore deserves to be recognized as a great leader. You may say that if you want, but to us he would not get credit as a great leader.

We would say that Abraham, Isaac, and Jacob were among the most significant people of the Old Testament but this significance would not be based on their personal behavior or their character. It was because of God!

Jacob, the father of the 12 tribes of Israel, had 12 sons with Leah, Rachel, Zipah, and Bilhah. Zilpah was Leah's maidservant and Bilhah was Rachel's maidservant. Jacob may be called a good businessman, but when he was faced with a conflict, he fell back to his own way of doing things instead of listening to what God would have wanted him to do. Some scriptures state that he did wrestle with God. Others say he wrestled with an angel. However you want to believe is up to you. We don't believe you will lose your salvation because you believe Jacob wrestled with an angel or God. But we do believe you must follow Yeshua! According to, Genesis 32:22-30, Jacob did wrestle with God. Yet you still have people who say that no one has seen God face-to-face and lived. Make up your own mind, but just remember what Genesis 32 states!

Joseph was a very interesting person to say the least! His whole life seems to be one conflict after another. There seemed to be a trust and a belief that everything would turn out the way God had planned. Here was a boy who saw a vision about himself and those around him. He was deserted by his brothers, punished for doing what is right, imprisoned, and overlooked by two people he had helped. If anyone in scripture ever had a reason to doubt, it would have been Joseph! However, he was a person who seemed to overlook the hard times, the setbacks, the lies, and trouble from his youth all the way into his old age. God had given him leadership ability from the start! Most of us would have given up long before things turned around. We know we would have!

As you read the writings of Matthew the tax collector, you want to look at him as one of the disciples' great leaders, yet we find that difficult. Oh, it took a lot of faith to walk away from a great job that gave him wealth and friends. The calling from Yeshua had to have a whole lot of spiritual power behind it. Plus, our Lord knew what Matthew could do and become. Although we find very little that pointed to him being a great leader, he was one of the chosen called by the Lord.

Peter was one of the three in the core group of disciples. Even though he showed his human side and disowned The Messiah, he turned and became a bold man for his Lord and one of the Messianic Jewish leaders in Jerusalem!

James was a very short-tempered and ambitious man. He was the one who wanted to call fire down to destroy a Samaritan village. He was one of the three that Yeshua took with Him when He went up the mountain and was transformed before their very eyes. Those three were Peter, James, and John, James' brother. We believe that James was the first disciple who was martyred.

John, the one our Lord loved, was ambitious. Like his brother, he became one of the leaders in the Jerusalem area.

With the rest of the disciples, you have Simon the Zealot. He had been a fierce patriot, so you can imagine that he was a very forceful type of person and, some would say, a leader. Bartholomew was the one who called the Messiah the Son of God and King of Israel. He was honest and a true Israelite!

Among the Disciples, there were five fishermen and one tax collector. We haven't discovered what the other six did as a profession before being called by Christ.

We couldn't leave out the next two!

It could be said that Moses was the greatest Jewish leader. He was the man who led the Hebrews out of Egypt, even though God had to convince Moses that he was the man for the job. God even told him to use his brother Aaron. Moses, a true leader, had to handle Pharaoh, the Hebrews, and even his brother and sister. Moses had to ask for God's favor for his people because they kept messing up. He had to be a good listener as well as a great leader. If you look at what was presented to him from all sides, one would have to say that it's no wonder he made a mistake. Yet God is the final authority and what he says goes. We believe Moses was a great leader and carried himself very well through a lot of terrible times for the Hebrew nation!

Joshua was the man God instructed Moses to choose to take his place of authority when God took him. Joshua was one of only two men who spied on Canaan and came back with a favorable report to go in and take the land flowing with milk and honey. Caleb was, the other one who wanted to go in right then. The scriptures state in Numbers 14:4 (NIV) - *And they said to each other, we should choose a leader and go back to Egypt.* Verse 6 states - *Joshua son of Nun and Caleb son of Jephunneh, who were among those who had explored the land, tore their clothes.* This would have been done to show that they believed the assembly was wrong in what they were trying to do. Joshua, like Moses, was submissive to God. Joshua was the Hebrew military leader. When God spoke he listened and obeyed. With all his spiritual influence and God's direction, Joshua would have to be considered one of the great leaders in scripture. The Hebrews conquered the land and kept the spirit all of Joshua's life. He seemed to lead by example.

Joshua 24:15 (NIV) - *But if serving the Lord seems undesirable to you, then choose for yourselves this day whom you will serve, whether the gods your ancestors served beyond the Euphrates, or the gods of the Amorites, in whose land you are living. But as for me and my household, we will serve the Lord.*

This verse is a statement that is printed more than most, but we would also have to admit that it is broken more than most. This is done because people either do not know the truth or because we just live in a weak society. People will follow a good speaker or listen to ungodly people when they are hunting for something. We hope that they and you find The Father and turn away from all misleading individuals! Joshua would be classified a great leader. We on the other hand would not! Not that we are down on ourselves, but don't follow us anywhere. We have said and will always say STUDY to find truth. Don't listen to us or believe because someone else believes. You need to follow God and his leading, not man!

In our opinion, those are a few of the leaders and followers. Make your own list and believe the way God wants you to. Get instructions and get direction. You can listen to as many people as you want, but get to the point where God, The Father of the Universe, would be happy that you studied and found what He wants for you and yours!

SOME SIGNS OF FALSE PROPHETS

A lot of the time, preachers water down God's message in order to make it more comfortable for their people. They tend to be arrogant and self-serving, appealing to the desires of their audience instead of being true to God's Word. They may even encourage their listeners to disobey God while making their way and their speech sound and feel better. Almost every misleading, untold sin starts with a little untruth until it has become a denominational doctrine.

They appear to speak God's Word and give His message, but they are often not living what they preach and that leads to not obeying God's direction or his Word. Therefore, people who listen and heed to their message do not live by God's principles. That goes for the teacher, preacher, or the people they influence.

False prophets entice you to follow them by using God's Word. The only way you can break the falseness of this deception is by studying in order to find truth. Neither a man and his denominational doctrine, nor his ability to make you think you will have an easier life will help you. You have to study with the purpose of finding Truth! It doesn't matter if it lines up with your way of life, your church, religion, denominational doctrine, or what you like or dislike. You need staying power for life's purpose. You need to determine if you really understand the Word or just going with a flow someone else points you to.

There are preachers who want what's best for the people in their church, but that's only when it pertains to them and when it benefits them. The denomination in reality has very little say-so or leading with that kind of thing and who the people hear or believe in. No one crosses him or her and stays very long!

Did you catch the trend? In God's church, some preachers must want and believe that *they* are the reason for the season and their season must go from January 1ˢᵗ to December 31ˢᵗ every year!

When you hear a preacher stating facts and he seems to be the center point, you just might as well say he is! The Holy Spirit takes the back seat in his church, that is if the Spirit is there at all.

There are Pastors who jump in and help when there is physical labor and then there are some who jump out of the way. They may organize something in order to make it seem as if they did their job, but they would rather sit back and watch some 65 to 85-year-old who can hardly walk without a cane do all the physical labor. We have often asked ourselves, "How could any person just sit there and feel good when the work gets completed?" We're sure he would say something like, "That way the older person and everybody who worked felt useful and connected with the project and the work for the Lord." That preacher didn't have to do any physical labor at all. He just watched that 75 year old do the work, yet he gets all or at least most of the credit. He may throw a bone out and say something like "I couldn't have done it without you!" That way he might have them the next time he wants something done.

Are all preachers like that? NO! But we have seen some who must believe that their calling is for the preaching and organizational part of church while the other work should be left up to ordinary people of their congregation. A false prophet doesn't have to be a visitor to your Church. He may be there right now!

144,000

Romans 11:16 (NIV) - *"If the part of the dough offered as firstfruits is holy, then the whole batch is holy; if the root is holy, so are the branches.*

What Paul wrote in Romans 11:16 and what the apostle John wrote in the book of The Revelation 7 and 14 about the 144,000 may both be saying that 12,000 from the each tribe of Israel are sealed. This indicates that they are holy and believing in Yeshua. Then the whole loaf, in other words, All Israel is Holy!

A person once asked, "What is the phrase 'All Israel will be saved' really pointing to?" If one looks at this with the information that was just stated as an example of how God wanted it, it becomes obvious how it will come to pass.

Revelation 14:4a talks again about the 144,000 and it states, *These are they which were not defiled with women; for they are virgins.* (KJV) Most commentaries state that these are not celibates even though it mentions women. However, when you have misdirected worship in the scriptures in both the Old and New Testaments, it is called whoring! This is not because of a sexual encounter, but because of the misrepresentation of worship to the Father and the Son!

Here is one more scripture to think about. Revelation 14:13 (NIV) - *Then I heard a voice from heaven say, "Write this: Blessed are the dead who die in the Lord from now on." "Yes" says the Spirit, "they will rest from their labor, for their deeds will follow them."*

When you read Revelation 7:5-8, you may see that the names of the Twelve Tribes differ from the twelve tribes listed in Genesis 29-30. You will see the tribe of Dan is missing. Joseph's son Manasseh is listed in Revelation but not in Genesis. As you know, Joseph's sons were not yet born in Genesis 29-30. We also noticed that Genesis 46 states that Reuben was the first-born son of Jacob yet, in the book of the Revelation, Judah is listed first. We know that most preachers and teachers will say that this is because the Messiah came from the line of Judah. While we realize that our Lord came from the tribe of Judah, we find no evidence to prove that that was the reason he was listed first, except those explanations from the ones who want to influence people to believe in their way and their religion. In all reality, the first-born would have gotten a double portion of the inheritance. However, the only one who received a double portion was Joseph because he and his son are mentioned. So the double portion really went to the second youngest son of the family. That was just something to think about.

When the number is stated 12,000 from each of the twelve tribes (making the 144,000) that does not mean Gentiles! Some people who have taught forever seem to put their own slant on this. They state that it is really saying the 144,000 are the Christians who believe. Being that we are Christians, we believe that is a good idea! IT IS TOTALLY WRONG, but it sure makes the Christians of the world feel superior to those Jews doesn't it? What a shame that the people who are supposed to lead the Christians feel they need to twist the truth to fit their religion. We can't change the real meaning so it fits our denomination, church, or religion! The 12,000 from the twelve tribes were and always will be Jews!

A NUMBER OF WRITINGS WE FOUND INTERESTING

After the exit from Egypt, the Israelite Nation was at the foot of Mount Sinai for two years while they listened to God and heard what he had to say to them. Some say that for those two years, from Exodus 19 to Numbers 10, they were at the foot of Mount Sinai waiting for God's instructions and rules to live by.

Leviticus 19:28 (NIV) *Do not cut your bodies for the dead or put tattoo marks on yourselves. I am the Lord.* Now does that mean if you want a tattoo it is wrong? This only says tattoo or cut your body for the dead, is wrong. We have no real desire to do either!

Leviticus 10:8-9 (NIV) *Then the Lord said to Aaron, "You and your sons are not to drink wine or other fermented drink, whenever you go into the Tent of Meeting, or you will die. This is a lasting ordinance for the generations to come."* Does this tell us, that people should not drink at all? Our opinion is NO, it does not tell people not to drink wine or other fermented drink, unless you are a Jew and you are going into the Tent of Meeting, because then it says you will die if you don't listen to what God said!

Leviticus 4:13 (CJB) *If the entire community of* Isra'el(Israel) *inadvertently makes a mistake, with the assembly being unaware of the matter, and they do something against any of the mitzvoth(commands) of* Adonai(the Lord) *concerning things which should not be done, they are guilty.*

Deuteronomy 5:9-10 (NIV) - *you shall not bow down to them or worship them; for I, the Lord your God, am a jealous God, punishing the children for the sin of the parents to the third and fourth generation of those who hate me, but showing love to a thousand generations of those who love me and keep my commandments.*

We really don't believe that Yeshua replaced any Law. He was the one promised to the Hebrews in the Old Testament. Therefore, he didn't do away with the Law for us but, as he stated in Matthew 15:24, "I was sent only to the lost sheep of Israel." Those are not our words but that is what the Lord said! The Lord fulfilled a promise that was made to the Hebrew Nation!

What amazes us is that we Gentiles follow some of the laws as long as they fit what we like or want. In reality, do we obey laws? Do we? Are we a lawful society? Are our laws that we follow based on what is good and actually biblical? When we as a nation don't follow the rules God set up or we change them to ungodly laws, is that or has it ever been to our benefit?

Luke 7:33-34 (NIV) - *For John the Baptist came neither eating bread nor drinking wine, and you say, he has a demon. The Son of Man came eating and drinking and you say, Here is a glutton and a drunkard, a friend of tax collectors and sinners!*

Here, our Lord states that he drank. This shows that it is not a sin to drink. Since the Lord said that and since He did drink, it must not be a sin as long as the drinking doesn't consume you and become a necessity for your existence!

Deuteronomy 24:1-4 (CJB) - *Suppose a man marries a woman and consummates the marriage but later find her displeasing, because he has found her offensive in some respect. He writes her a divorce document, gives it to her and sends her away from his house. She leaves his house, goes and becomes another man's wife; but the second husband dislikes her and writes her a get(divorce document), gives it to her and sends her away from his house; or the second husband whom she married dies. In such a case, her first husband, who sent her away, may not take her again as his wife, because she is now defiled. It would be detestable to Adonai, and you are not to bring about sin in the land Adonai your God is giving you as your inheritance.*

Jeremiah 3:1 (NIV) - *If a man divorces his wife and she leaves him and marries another man, should he return to her again? Would not the land be completely defiled? But you have lived as a prostitute with many lovers-would you now return to me? declares the Lord.*

According to Hebrew Law, the two who get a divorce and marry another can't remarry each other. The Husband and wife are like God's promised land to each other. Once the land has been defiled, it is no longer good for the man or the woman! Most explanations (usually at the bottom of the page of your bible) say this doesn't mean God said it is all right to get a divorce or that this writing was to prevent casual divorces. We even read one that said Judah divorced God and married other gods. There seem to be explanations for almost everything that some denominations, religions, and churches want to point out. They seem to want to push their point and they say that it is all right because God is Love.

Do people who call themselves Christians really know that the Hebrews are still God's Chosen people? Believers may be grafted into the Root of Israel, but they need to stop trying to dig deep enough to find that Gentile root of The Messiah. He was born, lived and died a Jew, not a Gentile! He didn't convert at the cross like we have heard some churches preach. Most people have no real concept of who The Messiah really was or why he was here!

Gentiles should not think of their union with Israel as a matter of rights and privileges. Rather, it implies an obligation to observe a godly way of life that has its origin in God's relationship with the Jewish people, tribes, and nation! That seems to be the most overlooked aspect of our Christian religion! We are not the center of the universe and we are not the chosen people. At the very best, we may be grafted in. We have seen how most Christian denominations have changed or, at the very least, taken apart the scriptures to make themselves look good enough to have bigger congregations while they are leading people astray.

WE HOPE THEY KNOW THAT THEY WILL BE HELD ACCOUNTABLE FOR EVERY ONE OF THOSE PEOPLE WHEN THEY DIE OR THE END COMES!

BLASPHEMING THE HOLY SPIRIT

What believers need to understand is that a nonbeliever who says something against the Son of God may not receive God's wrath because they may be unaware of what they are doing.

If a person knows that Yeshua is the way, the truth, and the life; If a person knows that no one comes to the Father except through Christ; If a person has the knowledge that there is no other name under heaven given to men by whom we must be saved and he who acknowledges the Son has the Father also; and denies that Yeshua is the Messiah, Savior, Lord, and the Son of God, then he is not forgiven in this world or the world to come.

Those verses from John, 1 John, Luke, and Acts, in our opinion, come down to this verse: *Land that drinks in the rain often falling on it and that produces a crop useful to those for whom it is farmed receives the blessing from God. But land that produces thorns and thistles is worthless and is in danger of being cursed. In the end it will be burned.* Hebrews 6:7-8 (NIV)

If the land produces a good crop, the farmer is blessed. If his land starts to become infested with thorns and thistles and becomes useless to any individual except to be burned up, then the farmer is cursed to hell. To the nonbeliever and the new believer those verses are not about the corn or wheat a farmer produces. Yet they do point to the souls that are affected by the believer who plants the idea of our Lord in the minds of individuals. But we need to be very careful when we start to influence people that we do not follow a denominational brainwashing of some individual whose main goal is to fill a church.

Listen to what Luke 12:8-10 says: *"I tell you, whoever publicly acknowledges me before others, the Son of Man will also acknowledge him before the angels of God. But whoever disowns me before others will be disowned before the angels of God. And everyone who speaks a word against the Son of Man will be forgiven, but anyone who blasphemes against the Holy Spirit will not be forgiven."* (NIV)

Doesn't that show you that disowning Yeshua does not consist merely in speaking words against him? You are then fighting against the Holy Spirit while the Spirit is holding the truth about Yeshua right in front of you. The reason is that you are a Christian and, because you acknowledge Yeshua, you feel that you are turning your back on what you have always been taught and believe. Yet most people who believe that are really already rejecting and blaspheming the Holy Spirit!

We will leave you here with one thought:

Matthew 15:13-14 - *He replied, "Every plant that my heavenly Father has not planted will be pulled up by the roots. Leave them; they are blind guides. If the blind lead the blind, both will fall into a pit."* (NIV)

When you think about the religious leaders of today and think about how some twist the Bible to fit their denominational doctrine it's easy to see it as a case of the blind leading the blind!

You may want to look at it like this: only when a person understands the Gospel in his mind, heart, and Spirit while persisting in rejecting it, is he blaspheming the Holy Spirit and risking eternal punishment. But don't take our word for it. Study those verses he wrote and make up your own mind. IT'S YOUR ETERNITY. IT'S YOUR FAITH. IT'S YOUR CHOICE. WE HOPE YOU MAKE THE RIGHT ONE!

PROVERBS 28:4, 9-10

4 - Those who abandon Torah praise the wicked, but those who keep Torah fight them. 9 - If a person will not listen to Torah, even his prayer is an abomination. 10 - Whoever causes the honest to pursue evil ways will himself fall into his own pit, but the pure hearted will inherit good. (CJB)

We looked up those verses in five different Bibles, in every other version it said Law where the word Torah is except in the Complete Jewish Bible. The word "Law" has a negative sound and connotation. "Torah" is literally "a teaching." There are a number of Torahs, such as the Teaching Torah. Then there is an oral Torah, which may be considered authoritative in Judaism. Then you may have a torah (not capitalized) may be understood as "law" or "principle". The title "Torah Teacher" is used for a scribe. However, through study we have found out that the first century scribes were apparently non-ordained teachers of Torah. One example is Matthew 2: 4 where King Herod called his chief priests and his Torah-teachers. In some translations, it says scribes or teachers of the law. Therefore, one could believe that they were not really ordained teachers of the Jewish faith! They were appointed by the king for his purpose and were under his complete control. They were not for the Hebrew Nation whatsoever!

The people who look at the Old Testament as things gone by or something that is outdated are mainly Christians. We have heard them say that the Old Testament doesn't apply to us. Although at times they seem to use it, but only when it helps their cause. Then they say we need to adhere to the point it makes! What about the not subtracting or adding anything to the book? Do we really need the writings of so long ago? Have we added to the deception of human thought with the interpretations of people who tried to put the Bible into our English language? We are very thankful to the people who have tried but, after studying scripture, we have come to the conclusion that their attempts are only good to get people more involved and reading what they have pointed to for centuries even if that person isn't pointing in the right direction at all!

Are we down on the individuals who have tried to lead people down their path? No, because they have at least tried. All we can say is that it may be in the wrong direction, but at least they are not just sitting around waiting for someone else to do all the work. Do we always agree with them? No! But we would guess they don't see eye to eye with us either!

THE ENDING

REVELATION 21:6 (NIV) - *He said to me: "It is done. I am the Alpha and the Omega, the Beginning and the End. To the thirsty I will give water without cost from the spring of the water of life."*

REVELATION 21:8 (NIV) - *"But the cowardly, the unbelieving, the vile, the murderers, the sexually immoral, those who practice magic arts, the idolaters and all liars- they will be consigned to the fiery lake of burning sulfur. This is the second death."*

This book doesn't have all the answers and we would never claim that. We hope that the one thing this book might do is to get people to study to find the truth. Please don't take our word for anything. You have to study to find the truth!

Thank you for the time you put into reading this book. Now it is up to you to do your own thing. We hope that is to STUDY on your own!

Printed in the United States
By Bookmasters